No Small Change

No Small Change

Why Financial Services Needs
A New Kind Of Marketing

LUCIAN CAMP
ANTHONY THOMSON

WILEY

This edition first published 2018
© 2018 Anthony Thomson and Lucian Camp

Registered office
John Wiley & Sons Ltd, The Atrium, Southern Gate, Chichester, West Sussex, PO19 8SQ,
United Kingdom

For details of our global editorial offices, for customer services and for information about
how to apply for permission to reuse the copyright material in this book please see our
website at www.wiley.com.

Wiley publishes in a variety of print and electronic formats and by print-on-demand. Some
material included with standard print versions of this book may not be included in e-books or
in print-on-demand. If this book refers to media such as a CD or DVD that is not included in
the version you purchased, you may download this material at http://booksupport.wiley.com.
For more information about Wiley products, visit www.wiley.com.

Designations used by companies to distinguish their products are often claimed as
trademarks. All brand names and product names used in this book are trade names, service
marks, trademarks or registered trademarks of their respective owners. The publisher is not
associated with any product or vendor mentioned in this book.

Limit of Liability/Disclaimer of Warranty: While the publisher and author have used their best
efforts in preparing this book, they make no representations or warranties with respect to the
accuracy or completeness of the contents of this book and specifically disclaim any implied
warranties of merchantability or fitness for a particular purpose. It is sold on the
understanding that the publisher is not engaged in rendering professional services and neither
the publisher nor the author shall be liable for damages arising herefrom. If professional
advice or other expert assistance is required, the services of a competent professional should
be sought.

Library of Congress Cataloging-in-Publication Data is Available:

ISBN 978-1-119-37803-7 (hardback) ISBN 978-1-119-37801-3 (ePub)
ISBN 978-1-119-37804-4 (ePDF)

Cover Design: Wiley
Cover Images: © RoBeDeRo/iStockphoto; © Rawpixel.com/Shutterstock

Set in 10/12pt, SabonLTStd by SPi Global, Chennai, India.

Printed in Great Britain by TJ International Ltd, Padstow, Cornwall, UK

10 9 8 7 6 5 4 3 2 1

Anthony dedicates this book to Louise, James, Sarah and Felix.

Lucian dedicates this book to Judy, Chloe, and Oliver, without insisting they read it.

Contents

Preface

No-one at all familiar with our CVs will be surprised to find this book calling vigorously – indeed, passionately – for more and better marketing in retail financial services. Between us, after all, we've been focused on financial services marketing for over 60 years. After such a very long time, it would cast a large and dark cloud over both our careers if we concluded there wasn't much to be said for it.

Naturally, we haven't. On the contrary, we're convinced that good marketing is the driving force behind a virtuous circle, in which companies succeed by providing customers with things they want and need. And the reverse, we believe, is also true: if customers aren't getting things they want and need, and/or the companies providing them aren't succeeding, then by definition there must be a lack of good marketing.

But while you might justifiably think that our belief in the benign power of marketing can be more than a little idealistic, we don't want you to think we're naive. This book wouldn't be useful if it was just a plea for peace, love and understanding to enlighten the wicked world of financial services.

In particular, there are two kinds of naivety from which we're determinedly immune. First, while this book certainly doesn't hold back from criticism of the financial services industry, we don't believe that practices in financial services are much worse than in other major sectors of the consumer economy. For reasons we'll consider, we think there has been *more* marketing in most other sectors, but we don't think that much of it has been *better*. It seems to us that in a competitive world where it's increasingly difficult for firms to behave with transparent fairness and still make profits, sustain their share price and hit their bonus targets, a lot of opacity and unfairness are all too common. Whether it's car builders cheating emissions tests, or international corporates creating elaborate structures to duck local taxes, or digital media owners channelling advertisers' money to terrorists and paedophiles, or just supermarkets injecting chicken breasts with water to increase their weight and price, there are a great many more pots than kettles. And these examples, of course, have all broken the golden rule 'Thou shalt not get found out': how many others still remain unknown?

The second species of naivety that we don't entertain is perhaps more fundamental. Our championing of 'good marketing' can, we know, sound a little hippy-dippy. Oversimplified, our message can take on a tree-hugging tone, seeming to propose a world of total transparency, uncompromising quality and rock-bottom pricing, in which consumers' needs are always perfectly identified and met by means of sales and marketing techniques that ooze with fairness, balance and impartiality.

To be clear, we don't think marketing can or should be like that at all. Marketing is by its nature a partisan and persuasive activity, intended to encourage people to do things they otherwise would not have done: buy a firm's products and services in preference either to other firms', or to not buying anything at all; pay more than the lowest price for a product, in the belief that it's worth the extra; pay attention to a communication that they otherwise might have ignored. In all these ways and many others, marketing is manipulative and self-serving. It has to be. But our point is that at the same time, it can and should serve the interests of consumers, too.[1]

This book discusses why we think it's important and urgent that it should do so much better, and much more often, than previously, and then goes on to examine, in some detail, what we think 'better' should look like.

These views are based on a very great deal of experience, but still in the end they are just views. We'd take some persuading that financial services marketing doesn't need to move on, but we're very open to persuasion about exactly how. One of the least controversial themes of the book is that when it comes to communication, what once was a monologue must now be reframed as a dialogue, and what's true of financial services marketing is also true of books on the subject. If you'd like to agree with, disagree with, add to or indeed subtract from anything you read here, we'd love to hear from you.

---

[1]Although its proponents don't quite like to admit it, the fact is that this kind of mutuality of interest is also the basic premise that underlies much of the behavioural-science-based 'nudge' marketing that has developed so rapidly in recent years. Initiatives such as auto-enrolment into workplace pensions involve 'manipulating' consumers by exploiting behavioural biases that make them more likely to participate – in their own long-term interest as well as the country's.

Acknowledgments

Neither of us has ever written a book before. That meant that we needed a lot of help.

We needed help with the content, and we got it from a great many people in the industry who generously shared their thoughts, opinions and insights.

We needed help with the innumerable practicalities, from arranging to record and transcribe all those interviews and focus groups through to maintaining some sort of grip on the head-spinning subject of version control.

We needed a lot more help than most experienced authors with the lengthy, complex and often somewhat mysterious process of making the initial sale, and then producing and promoting the eventual product.

And finally we needed both practical and emotional support from the people around us, both at home and in our day jobs. You can't write a book without imposing a good deal on them.

In return for all this help, the only thing we had to offer was a name-check in the Acknowledgements section, so in the next few paragraphs we'll aim to pay what we owe.

First, we received a lot of input from members of the Financial Services Forum, the membership organisation dedicated to improving standards of financial services marketing and chaired by Anthony. All this help was orchestrated for us by the Forum team, and particularly by the irreplaceable Richard Nolan, ably supported by Kate Taylor and Rachel Shackleton and led by David Cowan.

We're grateful to all the members who completed our quantitative research questionnaire, and even more grateful to those who took part in our focus group discussions: Ian Henderson, Malcolm Oliver, Mark Mullen, David Lundholm, Mark Evans, Nicola Day, Annabel Venner, Ali Crossley, Sue Simpson, Clive Kornitzer, Stephen Gunkel, David Wright, Pete Markey, Ken Hogg, Bradley Gamage, Jonathan Spooner, Nigel Gilbert and Richard Royds. Additional thanks go to Ian Henderson for making the Boardroom at his agency AML available for these sessions, and to Hobie Walker for feeding and watering us during them.

Bradley Gamage also made the facilities of his agency, SapientRazorfish, available for our '30 Under 30' workshop in which we consulted a number (actually rather fewer than 30, and not all of them aged under 30, so not our greatest-ever workshop branding) of the financial marketing world's rising stars. These included Joe Buzzard, Audrey Adjei, Sophie Church, Jessica Cordery, Richa Jaiswal, Pete Knott, Hayden Leith, Charlie Lynch, Jeremy Morat, Victoria O'Callaghan, Jess Over, Phil Rook, Alex Sangster, Daniel Saunders, Charleen Sparks, Laura Steel and Ben Stokes.

And Tony Langham made the Boardroom at his agency, Lansons, available for an exceptionally illuminating session on data, artificial intelligence and machine learning with a group of pointy-headed gurus who somehow managed to share their wisdom with us in remarkably understandable English. This group was recruited by Ian Hitt of Ninety, and included David Francis, Giles Blackburn, Peter Pugh-Jones, Nick Timon, Russel Goldie, Salvatore Pennino and Thom Rodde.

When we weren't picking people's brains in groups, we were picking people's brains individually. Rory Sutherland, who may be the single individual who best understands the overlap between the academic discipline of Behavioural Economics and the extremely unacademic world of direct marketing, was generous with his time. So too was Professor Adrian Furnham, whose academic record in financial services speaks for itself. And both John Smythe and Stewart Bromley (separately) gave great insight into the complex and difficult subject of building internal culture.

Meanwhile, this project wouldn't have advanced very far without the substantial assistance of our agent, Jonathan Hayden, who must often have been startled by the naivety and ignorance of his first-time authors and indeed frustrated by our slow rate of progress, but managed to hide all such negative emotions. And at Wiley, we're grateful for all the efforts of our commissioning editor Gemma Valler, and our tireless project editor Emily Paul.

Many thanks to Sian Rance and Emil Dacanay at D.R.ink for the jacket design and a lot of further design work on our website, social media presence and graphics for other marketing and launch events.

Thanks to our lovely wives Louise and Judy for all their necessary supportiveness and encouragement, even though it's very difficult to see anything much in it for them.

And finally sincere and heartfelt thanks to anyone we've forgotten. We recognise that sincerity and heartfeltness don't count for much when you can't see your name in print, but, honestly, we are very grateful.

About the Authors

Lucian Camp

Lucian's marketing services career stretches back well over 30 years, the large majority spent as a specialist in financial services. Over that time he has played four overlapping roles: he began as an advertising copywriter, then was for many years as an agency creative director, then founded and chaired two agencies of his own, and then after the sale of the second became a one-man brand and marketing consultant. He has also written, blogged and spoken extensively on financial services brand, marketing and communications issues. Lucian is married to Judy, and they have two grown-up children. He lives in north-west London and south-west France.

Anthony Thomson

Anthony is a marketer and entrepreneur. In the 1980s he co-founded what became Europe's biggest financial services marketing agency. Since then he went on to be founder and chairman of Metro Bank, the UK's first new High Street Bank in over 100 years, and then founder and chairman of Atom Bank, Europe's first bank delivered through mobile devices.

From 2014 until 2017 he was chairman of The National Skills Academy for Financial Services. From 2011 to 2014 he served as visiting professor to London Metropolitan University Business School, and is currently the David Goldman Visiting Professor of Business Innovation & Enterprise at Newcastle University Business School.

He is married to Louise and has three grown-up children. He lives in Somerset.

CHAPTER **1**

About This Book

Everything in this book is based around a single central idea: that in a consumer economy like ours, good marketing is good for consumers, companies and society as a whole.

We'll define and describe what we mean by marketing, and specifically good marketing, in much more detail further on in this book. It's important to be clear about this – of all the terms commonly used in business, there can't be many with a broader, less precise and less consistent range of meanings. For the time being, let's just say that at a high level marketing helps with figuring out what consumers want or need, and then finding ways that organisations can successfully provide products or services that satisfy those wants and needs while meeting their own goals.

On this basis, it seems clear to us that good marketing, in financial services as elsewhere, is a good thing. It results in products, services and experiences which please and satisfy consumers, which they perceive to offer them good value (a concept we'll discuss later), which offer a profitable and sustainable future for the companies providing them and which generate economic activities that benefit society as a whole.

All of which makes it particularly regrettable that in financial services, unlike many other parts of the consumer economy, we've seen little good marketing over the years. There has been a growing amount of not-very-good marketing – much of it simply ineffective, but a good deal of it actually bad for consumers and for the companies responsible for it. And a lot of firms have carried on without very much marketing at all, relying on other ways to build and maintain their businesses.

There are exceptions. There are always exceptions. Inevitably, this book will deal largely in generalisations, and may not always emphasise the exceptions that exist, but they always do. The most basic of our many generalisations, of course, is the idea that there is any kind of single, homogeneous thing that can meaningfully be described as 'financial services'. In fact, as we discuss in Chapter 5, the term embraces a huge number and very wide variety of businesses with little in common. In many respects mortgages have little in common with asset management, which has little in common with car insurance, which has little in common with retail banking.

In this large and diverse industry there are a few sectors where we have seen heavier investment in marketing for longer than others, particularly those where firms deal directly with consumers. And within almost every sector there are individual firms that have chosen to do the same thing. But on the whole the retail financial services industry has grown extremely large, and extremely successful, employing some 2.2 million people, over 7.3% of the UK workforce, and contributing almost 11% or £176 billion to the total UK economy, without feeling the need for a great deal of marketing.

This is in sharp contrast to almost every other major sector of the consumer economy. Marketing as a discipline emerged, back in the Victorian era, in the field of packaged goods: it was an essential function enabling firms to make the most of their new ability, as a consequence of the Industrial Revolution, to manufacture consistent products in large volumes. Marketing has been integral to the success of fast-moving consumer goods (FMCG) manufacturers and retailers ever since.

An integral part of this development of marketing was, of course, the development of brands and branding. As soon as you can make every day's production of Pears soap or Bass beer look and perform exactly the same as the previous day's, it becomes important to give consumers a way of recognising the brand from one day to the next. And from there, it's a small step to the realisation that at the same time, it would be helpful to give consumers a clear and distinctive sense of what they could expect from your product. At this point, you've started to create the first true brands – a subject we discuss in much more detail, as far as financial services are concerned, in Chapter 17.

But over the years, the essential role of marketing has spread far and wide from its beginnings among grocery brands like Pears soap and Bass beer. It played the same vital role as industrialisation started to create similar volume manufacturing opportunities in much higher-value sectors, like motor cars and electrical appliances. And for well over a century, marketers have also been establishing an increasingly important role in service sectors, like travel, hospitality and entertainment.

That said, while the distinction between 'products' and 'services' was once fairly clear, there were always grey areas between the two, and over time these have steadily expanded. Today, as we discuss in Chapter 5, the dividing line is very blurred indeed, and we suspect that the distinction is on the way to losing any real meaning. After all, there is a single key requirement that underpins marketing and branding activity in product and service sectors alike: the need for *consistency* of customer experience. True, on the whole consistency is easier to achieve in packaged goods than in services, but a certain core level is essential before any kind of effective marketing can be brought to bear. (We're aware of the odd, rather desperate service brand that claims that this core consistency in fact lies in the organisation's amazing diversity, but we're unconvinced by this attempted sleight of hand.)

In developing volume manufacturing it was essential that the product was 100% consistent, that every can of beans tasted exactly the same. In financial services, the products are not 100% consistent. Your authors could have exactly the same car insurance policy, but our experiences of making a claim are quite likely to be different.

Nevertheless, in every sector, product and service alike, the basic story is always the same: as firms develop the ability to deliver consistently and at scale, it becomes increasingly important to make sure that what is being delivered meets – and is seen to meet – a real requirement of at least a segment of consumers in the marketplace. There's little point in delivering a million bottles of shower gel in a market where no-one showers, or building 1,000 hotel rooms in places where nobody stays.[1]

These days, it's difficult to think of many significant parts of the consumer economy where marketing has not successfully and visibly played this directional or navigational role, aligning what a company delivers with what a consumer segment wants and/or needs. Two main areas come to mind.

One consists of those service sectors that are still highly fragmented and populated by very large numbers of extremely small firms or even single individuals. You won't find many marketers working in the window-cleaning sector, for example, or among child-minders, dog-walkers or landscape gardeners. Small firms or individuals in sectors like these are effectively responsible for their own micromarketing, usually in their own local catchment area – and many, by the way, are extremely good at it.

The other (on the whole, and allowing for a fair few exceptions) is retail financial services. This very large and very diverse sector has relied on other factors for its growth and success, with marketing playing a supporting but generally much more limited role. We'll consider those 'other factors' in a later chapter. But at this stage, we should raise two broader points.

First, we think it's clear that the consequences of this marketing-lite development have been generally bad both for firms and for consumers. Time and again, situations have arisen in which consumers have been presented

---

[1] Actually, of course, this is a little simplistic. It might well be worth building a hotel in a particular location if the reason no-one stays there is a lack of hotels. There's an old joke about two shoe companies which send marketers out to a remote corner of the world to report on the size of the market opportunity. The first reports back that there is no opportunity – no-one wears shoes. The second sends back an excited message, 'Fantastic opportunity, send as many pairs as you can, no-one has any shoes'.

with products and services that haven't properly met their needs, or indeed in some cases haven't met their needs at all, or which have not been priced fairly or sustainably and so have not delivered good value, or which have failed to deliver appropriate levels of service. Just as often, the corollary has also applied, and the industry has failed to identify big and obvious needs or to develop products and services that satisfy them. We think that all these failings have resulted, at least to some extent, from firms choosing to put decisions affecting their customers into the hands of people with little real customer insight or focus.[2]

Second, and more happily, there are good reasons – and in fact surprisingly many – to believe that things are now finally changing, and that marketing is beginning to occupy the kind of central directional role in financial services that it does in most of the rest of the consumer economy. We share some of the research we undertook on this in Chapter 2.

A lot will still have to change to get us there. At this moment, most marketing departments in financial services still play a limited role. Far too many are still unkindly, but often accurately, known internally as 'colouring-in departments'. (Regrettably, our own research among financial marketing professionals indicates that quite a few of them use this term to describe themselves.) The important decisions about what firms should provide to their customers are still resolved elsewhere, and the marketers are then tasked with producing the marketing collateral, the website and the brochures.

And of course far too many of those important decisions still reflect a degree of cynicism toward customers that would make a true marketer's blood run cold. It's not so long ago that one of your authors was working on the launch of a new personal pension for one of the big High Street banks. In a working group meeting, someone pointed out that the proposed product charges would be the highest on the market. 'That's right', said the project leader, 'But you have to remember, this is only for our existing customers'.

Comments like this reveal a horribly misguided view in which marketing is seen as a zero-sum game in which the company can only 'win' if the customer in some way 'loses'. This book is written at a time when we believe that attitudes like this are finally on the way out, and we hope to be able to give them a further shove toward the exit. Our own belief is the exact opposite: by our definition, 'good' marketing can only be marketing that works in the interest of both the customer and the company.

---

[2]In some parts of the industry these tend to be actuaries. One of the old jokes about actuaries says that if you have your head in the fridge and your feet in the oven an actuary will say you're at the perfect temperature. This tells you what you need to know about the average actuary's level of consumer insight.

To be clear about this book's scope, it deals with financial services ultimately delivered to individual consumers, whether they buy them directly from the provider or from an intermediary (and whether that intermediary is an individual, a branch or an aggregator website). To do this, it will embrace the subject of marketing to intermediaries, en route to the end customer. But it won't attempt to deal with financial services delivered to business or corporate customers, or to large collective groups of consumers (such as members of company pension schemes).

It's written from the perspective of two authors who have seen the industry they're describing from the inside, from the outside and from many other angles. Lucian has worked in the marketing services sector specialising in the financial world for over 30 years, during which time he has founded, chaired and eventually sold two creative agencies: a copywriter by trade, he has worked for literally hundreds of financial clients, mostly in the UK, but also across the world. He has written and spoken extensively on the subject for many years.

Anthony also built his initial reputation in marketing services, but has gone on to lead two other careers since then. First, he established (and still chairs) the Financial Services Forum, a membership organisation for individuals in senior marketing roles dedicated to improving marketing in the industry. More recently he has built a reputation as one of the world's leading 'challenger bankers', founding and chairing the highly successful Metro Bank, the UK's first new retail bank for well over 100 years, and going on to found and chair Atom Bank, the first bank in Europe to deliver services via mobile devices.

Altogether, this adds up to a combined total of more than 60 years of financial services marketing experience.[3] From that insider's perspective, we are in no doubt at all that for some time now, the industry has been moving in the right direction. Marketing is getting better, and its importance is becoming more recognised. And consumers are gradually starting to get the kind of quality, value and service that they need in this vital part of their lives.

---

[3] As far as this book is concerned, this is a case of both good news and bad news. The good news is that we can tackle our subject from an insider's perspective: pretty much everything we have to say reflects direct, firsthand experience. The bad news is that inevitably, it means you'll find our fingerprints on a number of marketing initiatives that in some way fall short of the ideal. Nothing too disgraceful – hopefully our antennae were sensitive enough to keep us away from some of the industry's least customer-friendly practices. But, undoubtedly, a good deal of activity could fairly be described as 'colouring in'.

There are many reasons for progress in the field, including increased competition. But if we had to name a single one we would both, unsurprisingly, choose the massive and exhilarating advances in the digital world, which have been gathering pace over the past 15 or 20 years.

In the same way that financial services has been comparatively slow to take advantage of the full potential of marketing, it has also been comparatively slow to take advantage of the full potential of digital, tending, initially at least, to think of it as a way of reducing costs and increasing efficiency rather than fundamentally reinventing propositions and changing behaviours. On a scale of 1 to 10, where 1 represents the pre-digital status quo and 10 represents the eventual total transformation, we'd say that with a few honourable exceptions we haven't yet got much past three. But the snowball is now rolling down the hill, going faster and getting larger as it rolls.

As it gets larger, it becomes increasingly clear that speaking of 'digital' as a singular thing, with a single label, doesn't make much sense or do any justice to its scale. If 'digital' represents a new world, then it's a world made up of any number of continents and land masses. As far as financial services are concerned, some are relatively the well developed: immense efforts and investments have been made, for example, in process automation. Others are largely unexplored: it's very hard at this stage to imagine the kinds of accommodation that financial services will eventually reach within extraordinarily dynamic and fast-changing continent called Social Media, and so far we've scarcely begun to make the most of Big Data. And others again have scarcely been discovered: in the long run, there can't be much doubt that the emerging sciences of Artificial Intelligence and Machine Learning have the most transformative effects of all. To borrow the quote from Carl Sagan 'The future of digital has arrived, it's just unevenly distributed'.

Nevertheless, it's perfectly clear even at this relatively early stage that digital is driving more change in financial services than any other development in the industry's history – and, no less important, that while the processes of change may be difficult, the emerging consumer outcomes have every chance of being largely benign. Digital will transform every industry, but in many cases both the processes of transformation and the eventual outcomes will be painful: in today's world, who would choose to run an offline newspaper or magazine business? But for financial services customers, it just seems to make things better.

By chance, there is at least one other driver of change in financial services that, in our view, could have implications that are almost as dramatic. This is the broad agenda that comes under the heading of Behavioural Economics (BE).

We must admit to some sympathy for the view that BE as a way of think-ing, emerging principally from the US academic community over the past 30 years or so, has less to teach marketers than others in the commercial world. A bit like the foolish hero of the Moliere play *Le Bourgeois Gentilhomme*, who is thrilled to discover that he has been speaking 'prose' all his life, many of the 'discoveries' now claimed by behavioural economists have been well known to marketers – especially direct marketers – for decades. But that's not the point. The point is that these discoveries about the ways that real people think, feel and make decisions are now increasingly owned by economists, academics and senior non-marketing management, and that makes them far more powerful than when they were understood only in the colouring-in department.[4]

This book is about these and many other changes and their implica-tions. We intend it to tell a positive and exciting story, about a huge and historically slow-moving industry that has been through some dark days (or indeed decades) in the way it has treated its customers, and has come under irresistible pressure to change its ways and do things better and differently.

You'll have heard the saying that it is insanity to 'do the same thing over and over again and expect a different result'. We think it would be madness to continue financial services marketing in the way it has been done and expect to get a different result.

We intend to spell out what 'better and differently' will look like. If you're accessing this copy – on screen, or paper or another, newly invented medium – at some distant point in the future, it will be interesting to see how much we got right.

We'd be surprised if you agreed with everything we've written. We didn't even agree among ourselves on all of it, or at least not without some heated debates. But if you work in or around financial services marketing, we hope that some of what you read here will encourage you to question what you're doing and perhaps think differently about it.

If it has, then please do get in touch. Even if you violently disagree with what we've written we'd love to hear from you. You can reach us at www.nosmallchange.co.uk.

---

[4]To take a single, albeit important, example, auto-enrolled pensions represent a way of applying a BE principle to the need to increase retirement savings. It must be very doubtful whether HM Treasury and the Department For Work & Pensions would have committed themselves to this bold and radical initiative if it had been only marketing people who were championing it.

CHAPTER 2

What Is Marketing, And Why Does It Matter?

This is an odd chapter title, especially in a book about marketing that's written for a readership including a high proportion of marketers. It's difficult to believe that an equivalent would be required in a book about any other large corporate department – IT, say, or HR.[1]

In financial services at least, when it comes to the role of marketing this kind of uncertainty is prevalent within firms as a whole, and indeed within marketing departments in particular. In all our research and discussions, we met few marketing people – up to and including some very senior marketing directors – who had a clear sense of what they and their departments were and were not supposed to be doing.[2]

Few, in fact, had any agreed definition of what marketing actually is, shared either within their own departments or within their businesses as a whole. This was a surprise to us, and not in a good way. How can you set goals for marketing if you can't agree on what it is? How can you successfully measure the effectiveness of what you've done if you don't know what you should be measuring?

This is clearly an issue to be tackled sooner rather than later. It wouldn't be easy to write comprehensibly about how marketing needs to change if there wasn't any clarity or consensus on what it is, and what it does now.

We couldn't think of a better starting-point than the definition provided by the professional body for UK marketers, the Chartered Institute of Marketing (CIM).

They've clearly – and necessarily – given it a lot of thought. Reading what they've come up with, it's easy to imagine the workings of the subcommittee of members tasked with coming up with something,

---

[1] Maybe it would. Maybe among those most closely involved with the subject, debate rages about precisely what is, and what is not, included within the HR remit. Do staff contracts properly belong within HR? Or should they be controlled by Group Legal?
[2] Contrast this with a leading FMCG company, the food group Mars, who for many years actually had their purpose – literally engraved – in a tablet of stone, above the entrance to their plant in Slough.

labouring for long hours over working lunches of Pret sandwiches and bottles of Highland Spring water, covering countless flipcharts and sticky notes in their quest for the perfect form of words. In the end, we imagine, they came back in triumph to the management committee with a single sheet of paper bearing the following lovingly-crafted sentence:

> Marketing is the management process responsible for identifying, anticipating and satisfying customer requirements profitably.

And let's say straightaway that we don't think they did too badly at all. Mischievously, we can't resist a little speculation about the drafting process. We suspect, on the basis of absolutely not a shred of evidence, that certain words and phrases in the finished product were absent from the first draft but emerged along the way in response to specific concerns, comments and criticisms:

- *Management process,* for example, is a term that we suspect is intended to imply that marketing is a proper part of business with its own proper process, and not in any way just a bunch of luvvies with their feet on their desks dreaming up wacky ideas.
- *Anticipating* suggests that marketing is a forward-looking activity, not one that's only concerned with the present (or, heaven forbid, the past).
- *Requirements* sounds like a term chosen to blur over the trickiest issue in the definition (to which we'll return later), about whether marketing in financial services should concern itself with consumers' needs, or wants, or both. (Unlike many other categories, consumers may not much want our products but they may need them, or even in a few cases be required by law to have them.)
- And *Profitably* is added at the end for much the same reason as 'process', to emphasize that marketing is a serious, financially responsible part of a business and not simply a cunning plan to spend millions of pounds of the company's money sponsoring golf tournaments and rugby matches that everyone in the marketing department can attend on expenses.

But while speculation like this may be fun, it's not very helpful. True, the form of words does have a whiff of the committee-room about it, but as one-sentence definitions go, it really isn't bad.

We put it to the test in two of the pieces of original research that have gone into this book. We exposed it in the four focus groups that we conducted among senior financial services marketing people who are members of the Financial Services Forum, a membership organisation for senior executives to help improve marketing effectiveness on the basis good marketing is good for consumers. And we also took it into the half-day workshop that we held for two dozen of the best and brightest younger financial marketers, all aged under 30.

All took it as a challenge, looking as hard as they could for ways they could find it lacking. But the truth is that it came through this process of challenge remarkably unscathed, not greatly admired but remarkably difficult to improve on. (It was only later, when we moved on from the high-level definition, that the uncertainties and disagreements that lay below the surface became apparent.)

Inevitably several respondents made attempts to improve on the CIM's form of words. One particularly critical respondent in one of our focus groups, for example, claimed that the great management guru Philip Kotler had said much the same thing, but far better and more memorably. We looked up Kotler's quote afterwards, and in fact he said that marketing is:

> ... the science and art of exploring, creating, and delivering value to satisfy the needs of a target market at a profit. Marketing identifies unfulfilled needs and desires. It defines, measures and quantifies the size of the identified market and the profit potential. It pinpoints which segments the company is capable of serving best and it designs and promotes the appropriate products and services.

Actually, we think the Chartered Institute put it better than the great guru.

Two or three respondents found the CIM's definition old-fashioned and out of date. Some thought it was wrong to imply that marketing is something that's done *by* companies *to* consumers– as one put it, 'rather than with them, or indeed them doing things to us'. Another made a similar point, saying: 'There is a sense that today it's much less about simply telling people, it's about them hearing and then crucially responding to us'.

This idea of marketing as a partnership between firms and their customers has been widely adopted across the industry in recent years, and in some firms has led to some important changes in marketing processes. One of these is the widespread adoption of co-creation, an approach that actively involves customers in development processes rather than tackling all the origination behind closed doors and then testing the output on customers in market research studies.

Others thought that especially in a service-sector business like financial services, but actually in FMCG businesses too, it is important to recognise the importance of building and developing *relationships*. They found the CIM's definition too narrow, one saying: 'This is a very transactional statement, and I don't think we work in a transactional business – it's not about the transaction, it's about the relationship'.

Another made a similar point, saying: 'I think there's a big gap here, and it's to do with the empowered consumer. The notion of the need for a mutually satisfying relationship is not there. And that's something which, increasingly, certainly in the space my business inhabits, is becoming really, really important'.

That said, though, not all our respondents agreed on the importance of relationships. Some (including your authors) approach this subject cautiously. Do customers actually want relationships, or indeed partnerships, with their financial services providers? Might it not be the case that for many people, and for many of their financial needs, what they really want is a brilliantly well-executed transactional service at the moment that they need it?

Faced with the CIM's definition, one radical went a good deal further, challenging the whole concept of a marketing 'function' or 'department'. He said:

> If you take the view that marketing is at the heart of a customer-led organisation, then it should spread through the whole of that organisation. I think that raises a big question about whether there's any need for marketing departments at all – marketing is almost a Diaspora throughout my organisation, so that those who are closest to our customers, in our branches, are the ones who do what it says in your definition, figuring out what the customer requires and how we can profitably fulfil it.

This line of thought created unease among some respondents who enjoy running marketing departments, and it does raise some practical issues. Who is ultimately responsible if something goes wrong? Who should control the budget? Who audits the success (or failure) of the activities?

Meanwhile, in the under-30s workshop, it was a different aspect of the CIM definition that ruffled feathers. There was widespread and serious discomfort with the use of the word *process*. To many of our young participants, this word sounded much too rigid and industrial. Marketing, in their view, should be something much looser, more spontaneous, more creative, just ... funkier. Your authors were a bit sniffy about this, until it occurred to us that maybe our sniffiness meant that we were getting old.

Still, all of that said, given how much everyone in the research would have liked to have improved on the Institute's definition, it held up remarkably well. As one respondent summarised: 'At a high level you just look at it and say, you know, from 10,000 feet it makes a lot of sense. I guess it's missing some of the detail, but then you wind up turning it into a paragraph. Which isn't what it's meant to be'.

It was only when we began our descent from 10,000 feet and looked at the next level of detail that the picture became more complicated.

In our research, we used the best known of mnemonics to explore the main business areas that could be said to fall within the remit of marketing. This mnemonic began in the field of FMCG marketing as the 'Four Ps':

Product, Price, Place and Promotion. Then, when taken from the original FMCG context and applied to the service sector, the list grew from four to seven Ps, with the addition of People, Process, and the slightly awkward Physical Evidence.

To be clear about what we meant by these terms:

The Seven Ps[3]	What They Mean
1. Product	(Or service, obviously.) The functionality of what is provided.
2. Price	What the product or service costs the customer.
3. Place	The route to (and, in these interactive times, from) the market, before, at and after the sale.
4. Promotion	All forms of marketing communication, again before, at and after the sale
5. People	The recruitment, training, motivating and evaluating of the people involved in delivering the product or service to the customer.
6. Process	The journey as experienced by the customer, from beginning to end.
7. Physical Evidence	All forms of customer documentation, correspondence and collateral relating to the product or service – statements, policy documents, forms, websites, apps, wallets, cheque book holders etc.

The central issue is, of course, the extent to which marketers own, or should own, the responsibility for each of these areas.

In our research, opinion among marketers was extremely divided. In fact, more than divided, it was fragmented. A small number of hard-liners claimed responsibility for the whole lot; at the opposite extreme, a similar number believed that only one of the seven, promotion, should fall within the remit of marketing. Most others occupied positions on a spectrum in between.

---

[3] Several marketing writers have introduced additional Ps, and we have a strong candidate of our own. We're strongly tempted to include 'Performance', meaning the measures of what a product delivers in hard financial terms – the rate of interest, the investment return, the excess, the bonus, any guarantees provided and so on. But in fact, we're not going to pursue this: too much of our research concentrated on the already-recognised seven, and introducing an eighth will get confusing.

Amid this uncertainty, it became apparent that many of our respondents weren't at all sure of their own views. Some who began by adopting a hard-line position, laying claim to all seven areas, steadily rowed back throughout their focus group until by the end they were focusing entirely on advertising campaigns and other promotional activity.

In doing so, it seemed to us that they were reflecting a widespread tendency among marketers to believe in principle in the need for a broad remit across the seven Ps but to default, in unguarded moments, to a focus on just one, promotion. For example, your authors recently attended a conference for senior financial services marketing people. Among the speakers' biographies (usually written by the speakers themselves), one described a 'strategic marketer with over 15 years of experience in the full marketing mix including PR, advertising, sponsorship and digital'. Another described a speaker as 'responsible for all aspects of marketing including campaigns, brand management and promotion, sponsorship, advertising, digital marketing and events'. These lists are far from 'the full marketing mix', or 'all aspects of marketing' – they're just lists of promotional activities.

We thought it was important to explore this dichotomy in more depth, so we offered our focus group respondents three options in each of the seven areas. We asked them to make a choice between:

1. taking the lead
2. having an influence
3. leaving it to others.

And we also asked them to contrast theory and practice, by distinguishing between what they thought should ideally happen and what actually happens in their own organisation.

Overall, the large majority of respondents told us that they believed they should have more control or influence in theory than was currently the case. For some the gap was enormous: in theory they believed they should take the lead in all seven areas, but in practice they had little or no say over any of them except promotion.

The enormously wide variation in the scope of marketing is clear from the following verbatim comments. Here is a selection of respondents' comments, showing the breadth of opinion on this crucial issue:

'I think the day of the marketing department that sat there and just generated some big fantastic ad campaign and then went and smoked a cigar are long gone. Most marketers I know are deeply involved in everything that touches the customer, and shaping the pipeline of propositions – everything that's coming through the organisation'.

'My challenge in financial services is that the cake is often half-baked by the time it arrives with me and my department. In our organisation, most people believe that marketing departments are much more about communications, lead generation'.

'Basically, I think your job as a marketing director is to get every customer to put you on a shortlist against your competitors. We marketers create the shortlist, and then it's down to a whole bunch of other things that happen'.

'Marketing is absolutely more than communications to me. It's everything, from the beginning of talking to customers through to making sure they're happy. Communication comes towards the end of that long process'.

'It's important to give marketers permission to do more, but also marketers have to realise that they should do more than just doing the ads'.

'Aligning the organisation around customer needs, and satisfying both stated and unstated needs, and all that stuff – that's my role as marketing director'.

'Really, marketing is there to warm our prospects up, to get us on their shortlist'.

'The company sort of does its thing, and then it's our job to present it to the consumer'.

'Marketing supports your business purpose, and that's its function. I think marketing often gets too big for its boots'.

'I haven't had the difficulty of trying to change the business, we had a very strong purpose and very strong values. My job is to tell the story'.

'I don't think anyone round this table would say marketing is just communication – the influence we need to have is on the products we provide, the service, the experience'.

Of course this fundamental uncertainty about the remit of marketing, and the conflict between those who believe it's basically about doing the ads and those who believe it's about everything that touches the customer, is far from new, and the debate rages on far beyond the world of financial services. The American Marketing Association, for example, supports the broad definition, stating:

> Marketing is the activity, set of institutions, and processes for creating, communicating, delivering, and exchanging offerings that have value for customers, clients, partners, and society at large.

On the other hand, a commentator from a US media company follows the line taken by many marketing services agencies, saying simply:

> Marketing is the art and science of persuasive communication.

But while we're not surprised to see this age-old schism still running down the middle of today's financial services industry, it does seem strange and unhelpful. As we wrote a few pages back, it's hard to think of any other corporate function where a similar uncertainty exists. And big-picture marketers, looking ideally for control and at least for influence across all seven of the seven Ps, must be dismayed to see so many of their colleagues happily reinforcing the colouring-in department stereotype.

The split in self-perception was so significant that we thought we should explore it further. So we included the same questions – on the role of marketing in theory, and the role of marketing in individuals' own organisations – in the quantitative research we carried out among Financial Services Forum members. The key findings are shown in the tables, the first showing what our respondents thought should ideally happen.

Marketers Should Ideally:

	Take Control (%)	Have an Influence (%)	Leave to Others (%)
Product	27	71	1
Price	9	78	13
Promotion	93	7	0
Place	49	50	0
Physical Evidence	64	36	0
Process	58	42	0
People	34	64	1

Note the extremely low scores in the third column: with the single exception of price, virtually no-one thought that marketers should leave any of these areas to others (and even in the case of price, only 13% were happy to do so).

In the second table, respondents told us what happens currently in their own organisations.

In My Organisation, Marketers Currently:

	Take Control (%)	Have an Influence (%)	Leave to Others (%)
Product	10	55	35
Price	7	39	54
Promotion	73	33	3
Place	21	58	21
Physical Evidence	41	45	14
Process	14	58	29
People	12	50	38

The contrast between the figures in the two tables is clear. In respondents' current organisations, the proportion of marketers taking control is far lower. And while the proportion claiming to have an influence isn't dramatically different, the proportion saying they leave the different areas to others is much higher. (At least, in six out of the seven areas it is: the exception is, inevitably, promotion, which only 3% of respondents claim to 'leave to others'. Mind you, even at that very low level, it's an odd figure. Who are these senior marketers who leave promotion to others? And who the hell are the 'others'?)

Finally, in this third table, to get a more accurate fix on the gap between theory and practice, we compare the mean scores given for all seven dimensions. The table shows scores on a scale of 1 to 3, so, for example, in the 'ideal' column a mean score of 1 would mean that all respondents think that marketers should ideally take complete control, while a mean score of 3 would mean that all respondents think they should ideally leave control of the area to others.

The Seven Ps

	Ideal Level of Control	Current Actual Level of Control
Product	1.74	2.24
Price	2.04	2.46
Promotion	1.07	1.30
Place	1.51	2.0
Physical Evidence	1.36	1.73
Process	1.42	2.15
People	1.67	2.26

The middle column in this table tells us that respondents think marketers should have a very high level of control over promotion, and then, in order, slightly lower levels of control over physical evidence, place, process, people, product and finally price. However, in their organisations currently, the right-hand column tells us that they have lower levels of control over all seven areas. Promotion sill scores highest, but at 1.30 against an ideal 1.07, and of the other six areas, only physical evidence scores under the average of 2. There must clearly be a lot of frustrated marketers out there.

This despite the fact that the findings in the middle column actually demonstrate a fairly modest level of aspiration. While respondents certainly think they should ideally have more control, they don't by any means think they should have complete control. Quotes from our focus groups reflect this attitude, and give some clues to the reasoning behind it. For example, a head of marketing in asset management says:

> Product has to come first, you know, you have to be investment-led. You have to think about the return you're going to deliver, how are you going to monitor its risk. There's someone there analysing the risk, so they're really building the product – it's a complex thing.

Such modesty may be endearing, but it doesn't reflect any great confidence in the role of marketing and we don't think you would find it often among the marketing leaders of, say, automotive or IT companies. Acting within the business as the representative of the customer, marketing directors in car companies may sometimes cause friction by asking their engineering colleagues for the impossible – but that doesn't stop them asking. And very often, their customer-based insights are prioritised over the engineers' passions and priorities in the finished product. One of your authors remembers launching a car with advertising which had nothing at all to say about its radical and innovative new suspension system, the engineers' pride and joy, but gave great prominence to its new double cup-holder, which the engineers thought trivial and dull. The marketers were right, though – the target market loved those cup-holders.

Another respondent with a senior marketing role in insurance says: 'Challenging the organization [on behalf of the customer] is the bit which is always an issue—marketing in financial services not really having the standing to challenge is the problem'. Another, running a young and small digital business, says: 'Over the years, one thing I've noticed is that everyone thinks they're a marketer, and everyone likes to fiddle without any particular structure – particularly in financial services, where marketing's beginning to mature now but has a long history of amateurishness'.

And a third, in charge of marketing at a large health insurance company, nails the key point about the experience of marketers to date when he points out: 'Let's face it, there are plenty of organisations in our industry that aren't marketing-led but that are number-one and number-two players in their sector'. It seems to us that everything we have reported on this key issue stems from this one crucial point. So far, on the whole, excellence in marketing has not been fundamental to the commercial success of most financial services businesses. Marketers have usually occupied a second-order role, doing useful work producing brochures and sales aids, and in some firms having fun spending big money on advertising and sponsorship campaigns. But the performance of their firms has depended much more on other factors. All too often, marketers at best have occupied a seat toward the bottom end of the table – and sometimes not even that. In medieval times salt was expensive, and thus served only to those of high rank at the head of the table. Those at the lower end of the table weren't allowed access to the salt, and hence the expression 'below the salt' – the place we think is occupied by many financial marketers.

If that were to remain as true in the future as it has been in the past, financial services marketing wouldn't be a very interesting place to be, and this wouldn't be a very interesting book. That's why it's important – not least for your authors – to consider whether there are reasons why this second-order status quo is really starting to change.

Before we move on to look for those reasons in the next chapter, let's return to those terms we used in our three-point scale – *control, influence* and *leave to others* – and take a view on the place that financial services marketers should rightfully occupy. If the current status of marketing is too low, how much higher should we be aiming?

Frankly, for ourselves, in five of the seven areas, we're not hung up on the distinction between controlling and influencing. It seems clear to us that control over two – Promotion and Physical Evidence – must belong in marketing. These are marketers' core competences, and they simply must have the skills to control these areas better than anyone else. But it's equally clear that the other five areas are all likely to call for some kind of partnerships with other functions. Risk, compliance, IT, HR, operations, legal, facilities, and pretty much everyone else all have a role to play somewhere along the line. If *control* means being able to call a halt or enforce a change when you identify a show-stopper, then control will often belong to someone outside the marketing function. In today's heavily regulated and risk-averse financial world, it's simply not possible for a marketer to override a non-negotiable demand from Risk, Compliance or Legal.

But above and beyond having influence in the five areas not under marketing's control, it seems to us that there's a bigger requirement, to do with setting the overall direction and strategy of anything the business is doing which impacts the customer. If the business aims to be – or become – customer-centric, then it seems to us that by definition it has to be – or become – marketing-centric.

Marketers' fundamental role is to represent the customer within the organisation. To be able to do that, it's imperative that they have a seat at all seven of our tables, and, what's more, a seat above the salt. And while it's neither necessary nor realistic that they should be in charge of every meeting, it is necessary that their voice is always heard.

CHAPTER 3

From 'Best Advice' to 'Satisficing'

Since this book calls for more of something called 'good' marketing, and less of something called 'bad' marketing, we're obliged to say something about what these terms mean – and, particularly, about how they apply to financial services.

We stand behind our big-picture conviction that in a consumer society, marketing – that's to say, identifying and satisfying consumer needs – is fundamentally a 'good' activity. And we strongly support the maintenance of a strict robust regulatory regime that, as far as possible, prevents 'bad' marketing and punishes and penalises those responsible for anything that slips through the net.

But many people argue that for one reason or another, marketing is different in financial services – that there are special considerations, specific problems and challenges, that apply. We want to examine these alleged differences between marketing in financial services and in other sectors. What are they? Do they stand up to scrutiny? And do they make a real difference?

There are four that are highlighted most often, and, simply put, we don't really buy any of them:

1. It's often said that there is an 'information asymmetry' between financial services providers and their customers – or, to put this clumsy expression into plain English, that consumers understand a great deal less about financial services that the companies providing them. This is certainly very often true, but it isn't at all unusual. People understand very little about the workings of computers, or cars, or central heating boilers, or microwave ovens. There is no fundamental difference in the level of knowledge or understanding. However, there is a visible difference in the ability of marketers to make these things accessible to, and usable by, consumers. Very few of us have the faintest idea how ABS braking systems work, but we do know that we can stand on the

brakes on a wet road without skidding. We don't need or want to know how these things work – we just need to know what we need to do to get what we want out of them.

2. Two overlapping points are often made to argue that financial decisions are trickier than other purchase decisions: it's said that they are more important, with more serious consequences if you get them wrong, and also that it's often impossible to tell whether they were good or bad decisions until many years have passed. It's obviously true that some financial decisions are more important than some non-financial decisions – it doesn't much matter if you choose a not-very-good packet of paperclips, but it matters like hell if you choose a not-very-good pension. And it's also true that you often have to wait a long time to find out how well some financial products perform: it takes a lot longer to be sure you bought a good investment than to be sure you bought a good holiday. But neither of these issues is in any way unique to financial services. Getting any big, expensive, important decision wrong is a nightmare – a property, a partner, a business venture. And while plenty of financial products don't have long-term time horizons (motor insurance, credit cards, instant-access savings accounts), plenty of non-financial products do (cars, carpets, pets, thatched roofs, fitted kitchens, spouses . . .).

3. A similar, but separate, point is often made, having to do with frequency of purchase. Consumers frequently buy pizzas and shampoo, it's said, and practice makes perfect. There are several financial products that they buy only once in a lifetime: no wonder they don't know what they're doing. Again, at the extreme – pizzas versus pensions – this is obviously true. But there are plenty of other products and services that most of us buy very infrequently – divorce lawyers, lawnmowers, GCSE coaches, loft conversions. And of course there are some financial products we do buy relatively often – most insurance policies have to be renewed every year.

4. And finally, many people claim that consumers are uniquely unengaged with financial services, finding the whole subject exceptionally boring and confusing and wanting to spend as little time dealing with it as possible.

We strenuously reject this idea for two reasons. First, if they do find us boring and confusing, that's our problem and not theirs, and we can fix it whenever we want to – there's nothing inherently boring and confusing about money (the memory of Margot Robbie lounging in a bubble bath while explaining credit default swaps from the film of Michael Lewis's book *The Big Short* comes to mind).

And second, when people say this, what do they imagine that consumers spend the rest of their time dealing with? Lifestyles of decadent, self-indulgent hedonism dedicated to the pursuit of pleasure? Or days like most of us have most of the time, trying to get a new tyre fitted to the car while still being on time for the school run, booking someone to come and have a look at the leaking shower and querying a horribly high data-roaming charge on the latest mobile phone bill? Frankly, after a day of routine domestic chores, an hour spent planning the home of our dreams or looking forward to our retirement could quite possibly come as light relief.

But there's a fifth alleged difference that is less easy to dismiss, and which we think gives marketers in particular more food for thought.

In retail financial services (in fact perhaps in some sectors more than others) there are important players in and around the industry who believe fundamentally in the principle that consumers must always be provided not simply with a good solution, but with the best possible solution to their particular needs.

The list of these important players include those in and around the financial advice community, for whom providing consumers with the best possible solution is of course the raison d'être. It also includes our principal regulator, the Financial Conduct Authority: trying to ensure that consumers get the best possible solution for their particular needs, whether they've taken advice or not, lies at the heart of the regulatory agenda in the retail market.

And then further afield, there's a much broader constituency of media, lobbyists, consumerists, and indeed many in senior positions in the industry who all believe broadly the same thing – that any process that does not lead to the best possible outcome for individual customers is a process that's fatally flawed.

This point of view clearly depends on a key assumption, that the best possible outcome for a consumer in any given situation is in fact knowable, and measurable against some objective standard. This is, to say the least, a questionable assumption. Best outcome how? Best performance? Lowest risk? Cheapest price? Best fit with needs at the time of purchase? Best fit with needs 20 years after the time of purchase? You might imagine that the enormous difficulty in reaching any kind of definition of 'best' would bring the whole theory into serious doubt. But somehow, it doesn't: those who support it go on to argue that the ultimate aim of the retail financial services industry must be to make sure that this standard is met as often as possible.

Of course if you take this view, you have to conclude that marketing in financial services is indeed very different from other parts of the consumer economy, where customers pay their money and take their choices. There is no other sector in the market economy where the aim is to provide customers with the best possible outcome.[1]

If there is an objective standard of suitability for each customer and for each financial decision, then the role of marketing, and marketers, becomes by definition massively restricted. We effectively find ourselves back in our box as the colouring-in department, concerned merely with the presentation of choices made on our customers' behalf by people with much higher pay-grades.

So how well does this idea of an objective standard stand up to scrutiny?

We can safely disregard the views of those with too much in the way of vested interests. For example, you can see why those in the advice community feel the way they do: for one thing they wouldn't have jobs otherwise, and for another the whole idea of 'best advice' is integral to their sales process and gives them a great way to close the sale. Similarly, it's hardly surprising that those at the Financial Conduct Authority responsible for consumer protection favour the idea of optimal outcomes: they would, wouldn't they?

But as we move into an era much more driven by consumer choice, it's important – albeit difficult – to challenge this assumption, and acknowledge that the concept of the optimal outcome doesn't really make much sense anymore. The outcome that matters now and in the future is the one that appeals enough to consumers to encourage them to choose it over the principal alternative – and more often than not, the principal alternative is not doing anything.

This is a big and controversial point, best made by example.

A few years ago, one of your authors was involved in developing a protection proposition to be distributed by direct marketing. The product was named Well Woman insurance, and did what it said on the tin – it provided life insurance for women, paying out on deaths resulting from a list of illnesses suffered only, or predominantly, by women. Premiums were very affordable, and the cover offered a lot of peace of mind, especially to women with children. It sold well.

Industry commentators hated it. They pointed out that the conditions it covered were uncommon, and accounted for only a small proportion of deaths: the product, they said, lulled women (and their families) into a sense of false security. The product should be banned, they said. Instead, women (and men) should be encouraged to buy comprehensive life insurance.

---

[1]Perhaps the closest you'll find might be a quasi-medical sector like eyecare, where there is an objective standard of suitability as far as the prescription for a customer's lenses is concerned. But even so, there's still huge scope for choice and personal preference around the customer's solution as a whole – glasses or contacts, varifocals or not, light-sensitive or not and of course hundreds if not thousands of styles of frames at price points ranging from a few pounds to thousands.

A phrase that comes to mind remarkably often in financial services marketing is that 'the great is the enemy of the good'. It may well have been that objectively, our target market would have been better served with a comprehensive life protection product. On the other hand, it would have been a good deal more expensive – for many, unaffordably expensive. And, no less importantly, it wouldn't have been possible to promote it with the kind of highly targeted, emotionally engaging direct marketing communication that Well Woman was able to achieve. Objectively, our target market might have been better suited by a different kind of product – if they had decided to buy it. If they hadn't decided to buy it, they'd have had nothing, and it's hard to see how they'd have been better suited by that.

Take another example, and one that in fact has to do with an advice business. Over the years, both of your authors have had a great deal to do with the marketing of the leading wealth management firm St. James's Place. St. James's Place is a firm that has been the subject of controversy in the industry, partly for historical reasons that needn't concern us. Currently, the criticism most often heard is that compared to other firms, St. James's Place's charges are high. Consumers, it's said, could get better value elsewhere.

There's plenty of room for debate about the figures, but let's set that aside. The more important point is that St. James's Place clients are delighted with the service they receive, and, almost without exception, happy and proud to be clients of the firm. Hardly anyone has ever made a complaint about value for money. St. James's Place is unashamedly a premium brand, and in much the same way that you can stay in hotels a lot cheaper than the Connaught, you can probably get financial advice cheaper than from St. James's Place. If you believe there is an objective standard of suitability in financial advice, and that cost is an important component of that standard, then you wouldn't choose St. James's Place. But hundreds of thousands of SJP customers, whose needs are met supremely well, would strongly disagree.

In fact, as far as premium pricing is concerned, our criticism of today's world of financial services is not that some firms' prices are too high – we'd argue that there is currently nowhere near enough of it. In a world where huge numbers of consumers choose to pay premium prices for products that– in reality or perception, or both – offer a better experience and therefore better value for money, financial services offers exceptionally few opportunities to do so. Few of us go out of our way to eat our meals in the cheapest possible restaurant, or to drive the cheapest available car (something called the Dacia Sandero, by the way) or to wear the cheapest available shirt. Most of us have some perception – even if a fairly hazy one – of the spectrum of prices available, and choose a price level somewhere in between the lowest and the highest. Some will choose the cheapest, and some will choose the most expensive. Some think the Dacia Sandero offers outstanding value. Others think the same of the Rolls-Royce Phantom.

What we're saying here is that within a tough regulatory framework that keeps the cowboys at bay, we think it's necessary to get over the old-fashioned, paternalistic idea that the experts know best and the customers should do what they're told.

Of course we welcome the existence of experts, whether they're providing one-to-one advice or something much more widely available. (We suspect that Martin Lewis's Money Saving Expert brand has probably saved consumers more money that all the IFAs in the country put together.) We also welcome the way that digital, and in particular social media, makes it so much easier for customers to reality-check their financial decisions. And if people want to meet the cost, in both time and money, of taking individual advice that will arguably lead them to what is objectively the single most suitable product or service on the market, then good luck to them.

But on the whole, this isn't how we go about making our buying decisions. For one thing, as in our examples above, our decision-making doesn't just reflect objective criteria. We are happily and proudly subjective. We're looking for emotional benefits and satisfactions just as much as rational ones – indeed, often much more.

And anyway, most of the time, most of us just don't care that much. The great American polymath Herbert Simon coined the word 'satisficing', a hybrid term crossing 'satisfy' with 'suffice', to explain the way that most of us make most of our choices: simply put, most of the time life's too short to aspire to perfection, so we make an investment of time and effort that seems sufficient to give us a good prospect of a good outcome (and a very unlikely prospect of a catastrophic outcome), make our decision and move on. This way of working doesn't sound right to classical economists, who believe (or did until recently) that we are rational beings whose natural inclination is to achieve so-called 'optimal' outcomes. But most of the time, in the real world, we aren't, and we don't.

This kind of pragmatic decision-making doubtless causes great distress to experts, not just in financial services but in every field. It must grieve IT experts to see us buying the wrong computers, and holiday experts to see us choosing the wrong hotel in the wrong destination at the wrong time of year. We drive the wrong cars, live in the wrong houses and very often marry the wrong people and have the wrong number of children. At the same time, we also get literally hundreds if not thousands of smaller choices wrong, eating and drinking the wrong things, going to see the wrong films, buying the wrong clothes, washing our hair with the wrong shampoo.

Yet, somehow, we more or less muddle through. We enjoy most of our holidays. Our cars get us from A to B. Our families give us pleasure and happiness most of the time. Our hair doesn't look too bad. This is how consumer-driven markets work. As financial services move in this direction, it's increasingly how they'll work, too.

CHAPTER 4

Why Not Then? And Why Now?

We've put forward two of the main planks of this book's argument in previous chapters, and in this chapter we look at them more closely. They are:

1. The retail financial services industry has enjoyed much success over many years with little need for marketing (and even less need for good marketing).
2. Things are changing, and we're convinced that good marketing will be much more important to ensure continued success in the future.

Itemising the factors that support these propositions means making two lists that are at least to some extent mirror images of each other. For example, the first list will say that for many years the regulator wasn't much concerned about marketing, so various bad practices could continue: the second list will say that these days the regulator is much more concerned about marketing, so much of the bad is being driven out by good. Still, the factors are interesting, varied and important enough that a little repetition may be no bad thing.

In Chapter 2, we discussed the growing importance of marketing from the point of view of financial services providers. With the help of the CIM, we defined marketing as the set of processes that enable firms to develop an understanding of their customers, and so to provide products and services that meet their wants and needs.

Exactly the same story can be told in terms of the benefits it offers to the customer. From the customer's perspective, if marketing is the set of processes that delivers products and services that they want or need, it must enable them to make good financial decisions and manage their financial lives successfully.

There's nothing extraordinary about this. You might say it's a statement of the bleedin' obvious. Marketing has, after all, played just this role in almost every other part of the consumer economy. What's odd is not so much that we see a need for more marketing in the future of financial services. What's odd is our contention that it hasn't been much needed in the past. With good marketing offering such important benefits for firms and consumers alike, our assertion that the industry grew strongly over many years without needing very much of it sounds unlikely.

But it seems to us that there were good and clear reasons. Across financial services, many other factors were at work, enabling firms to find buyers for their products and services, and consumers to find more or less the financial products and services they needed. Here are some of those 'other factors':

- The further you go back in time, the more important it is to recognise that people simply had less money. Over the past 50 years, average incomes after tax have very nearly doubled in real terms, and personal savings have increased by over 500% to a total in excess of £1.5 trillion. People needed far fewer financial services to look after what they had simply because they had so much less.
- The same is true of financial services connected to what is now the most important financial commitment for most people: home ownership. That means not just mortgages, but also types of insurance, investments used as repayment vehicles, loans secured on property and eventually, in some home-owners' later years, equity release. (Largely as a result of affordability issues, in England the level of home ownership actually peaked at 71% of households in 2003 and has now fallen back to 64%. That's still a high figure by historic and by international standards, but it will be interesting to see if it continues to decline especially among the young, and if so what the financial consequences will be.)
- In the past, family traditions and regional ties were much stronger. Anthony grew up in the north-east, so his family were Northern Rock customers. Lucian grew up in Surrey, so his family were with Abbey National. Our first choices of mortgage lender had nothing to do with marketing. Our fathers introduced us to the managers of the appropriate local branches – who, provided that we had maintained passbook savings accounts for the past few years, might with luck be willing to grant us a mortgage.
- In a similar way, in sectors like banking where access to branches was important, branch locations mattered. Lucian grew up in a village where the only bank branch was Lloyds, so it's no surprise to discover where he opened his first savings account. The bank with a branch nearest his college at university was NatWest, so guess where he opened his first current account. (Branch locations mattered, because other methods of dealing with your bank were limited. Telephone banking wouldn't have been a good option in Anthony's earlier years: he can remember the

excitement when the very first telephone was installed in his Newcastle street, at the doctor's house.)

- For many, over many years, employers played a key role in providing financial services as employee benefits, particularly in pensions. There were no personal pensions in the UK until 1988: those who had pensions were members of an employer's group scheme.

- At the same time, in the postwar period more people were more content to depend on the State without making private provision. For some years from the late 1940s, the new Welfare State seemed to have all the answers: if you paid your taxes and your National Insurance, in return the State would provide you with education, healthcare, unemployment benefit and in due course a pension. Perhaps because of lower standards of living and lower levels of income during working lives, or perhaps because of higher levels of confidence in State benefits, or both, far fewer people felt the need to supplement these benefits with private provision.

- The market for general insurance was much smaller because people had less to insure. Fewer owned cars and homes, and most had less need for home contents or travel cover. Car insurance was a legal requirement, and for homeowners home insurance was more or less required by mortgage lenders – no need for marketing to stimulate demand. And in any case, the market was largely controlled by brokers, whose customers would usually accept whatever cover they recommended. (In fact, though, as we'll see, this market sector was arguably the first to start feeling the winds of change.)

- General insurance was by no means the only market controlled by intermediaries. In most sectors, one of the most important reasons – perhaps the most important – for the limited role of consumer marketing over many years has of course been the central and continuing role of face-to-face salespeople of one sort or another. At every level, and in almost every part of the market, financial services has been an exceptionally sales-driven industry. Salespeople can do even better when supported by consumer-facing marketing, but they can do well enough when there's little or none. For decades, the industry chose to spend billions on motivating salespeople with commissions, not on marketing, to win business from its customers.

- As a result, while relatively little marketing activity was focused on consumers, a great deal was and still is focused on intermediaries. Much of it, though, has been very poor marketing indeed. Whether you look at grotesque levels of commission (investment bonds routinely paying 8% of the customer's capital to the person selling them) or at dangerous gimmicks designed primarily to give salespeople seductive stories to tell (the old Equitable Life's unaffordable retirement income guarantees), what was good for advisers in the short term was often very bad indeed for their clients in the longer term.

- Many of the bad sales practices that persisted for so long were the result of a lack of focus on the part of the regulator. Looking back on the sequence of regulatory interventions on the processes of sales and marketing, you can't help remembering the comedian Eric Morecambe's famous line that as a musician he played all the right notes, but not necessarily in the right order. For example, introducing the requirement for financial advisers to 'polarise', choosing whether to become 'tied' or 'independent', some 24 years before acting to eliminate sales commission does bring an expression involving the words 'cart' and 'horse' to mind.
- Much marketing activity responds to change, and in financial services much change is driven by government in legislation or fiscal policy. By today's standards, there was relatively little of this over a long period. (In hindsight the mid-1980s look like a turning point. The Thatcher government was highly active in the field of personal finance, launching many initiatives with major implications, some positive and some negative, for consumers. These included the big public sector privatisations; the introduction of Personal Equity Plans (PEPs), the tax-privileged precursors of today's Individual Savings Accounts (ISAs); the launch of personal pensions; and the abolition of Life Assurance Premium Relief, which dramatically reduced the role of life assurance policies as savings vehicles. All this happened within the space of three or four years – and at the same time, the government set about reshaping the entire industry with its Financial Services & Markets Act, passed in 1987. Directly or indirectly, all these initiatives triggered new waves of marketing activity.)

Taking all these factors as a whole and looking back, say, 40 or 50 years, it's easy to imagine how individuals could have made journeys through the financial world, acquiring an array of financial services, while scarcely engaging with any marketing activity at all.

While still young, someone growing up in a middle-class family might be introduced by a parent (in those days usually a father) to a full set of key financial services providers – bank and building society manager, insurance broker, stockbroker or financial adviser. He or she would likely have chosen a bank branch on the basis of its location; taken a mortgage from the building society and arranged motor insurance via the broker; joined an employer's pension scheme and taken the employer's death-in-service benefit; relied on the NHS for healthcare and State schools for children's education; in later years taken advice to save regularly in a PEP or later an ISA; and then at retirement enjoyed a generous final salary pension provided by a benign employer.

In less affluent families the cast of characters might be different – not so much of a role for the stockbroker, but more for the home-service Man from the Pru and his famous bicycle clips – but the nature of the journey would be much the same. Individuals would have little need for good marketing to help them through their financial lives.

Eventually, though, things did start to change. We identify the mid-1980s as a time when the gathering of pace was noticeable, but you could make a case for other key dates. Some might suggest a much earlier date - maybe 1966, the year when Barclays effectively broke the gentlemen's agreement among the big High Street banks to avoid the expense of competing with each other by advertising on television. In fact, Barclays' first TV commercial paid lip service to this agreement, partly by advertising its brand-new credit card, Barclaycard, rather than a pure banking service, and partly by going out under the name of its wholly-owned Scottish subsidiary, British Linen Bank, which must have rather mystified English TV viewers.[1]

By the turn of the millennium, financial services marketing had grown enormously. The expenditure figures for its most visible and easily measurable manifestation, media advertising, tell us that by the year 2000, financial services was by some distance the highest-spending of all sectors – more even than food, drink or even automotive.

However, the quality of much of this activity was poor. Many of the propositions expensively advertised on television were triumphs of style over substance, offering poor customer experiences and failing to meet real needs. And there was often a lack of integration, with no real thought given to the need to manage customer journeys from initial awareness, often created by all that advertising, through to the purchase and use of the product. Few providers had really come to terms with the enormous difficulties in engaging most consumers with financial propositions, in a sector where most consumers' dominant attitudes and behaviours are apathy and inertia. From an era where little was happening, we advanced into an era where a great deal seemed to be happening – but it wasn't making an awful lot of difference.

At the same time – around the turn of the millennium – another highly-visible change in retail financial services was becoming apparent. Those years were of course the years of the first dot.com boom, and the change in question was the rapid evolution of the Internet. Over the space of three or four years, dozens of new digital financial services propositions emerged – some start-ups, many new arm's-length brands launched by major players. Many were backed by very large marketing budgets. But the large majority of them had very short and unprofitable life spans.

---

[1]This campaign marked a watershed in another respect, being not only the first time that a UK bank had advertised on television, but also the launch of the very first UK credit card.

From today's perspective, it's obvious that in every way, the Internet is supremely well-aligned with the world of financial services, to the benefit of both providers and consumers alike. It fits perfectly with the financial world's intangibility, with no need for delivery vans, drones or even 3D printers to deliver what it offers. It provides near-total accessibility – long gone are the frustrations of 9.30 to 3.30 bank opening hours. Thanks largely to social media, it's rich in opportunities for consumers to tackle what the FCA calls 'information asymmetry' – it's easy to overcome the lack of understanding which has so often disempowered them in their dealings with the industry. Social media, of course, also level the communications playing-field between companies and customers. The era in which 'communication' described a one-way process in which companies say things to their customers has now come to an end.

And from a pure business perspective, compared to any other alternative, digital offers unbelievably low-cost interactions between firms and their customers – one online bank claims to be able to process transactions at one-fortieth of the cost of branch-based processing – and with costs at such low levels companies have no problem either offering customers much better value, or making a lot more profit. Or, very probably, both.

In the light of all this, you'd expect that financial services would be one of the first sectors of the economy to be transformed by digital technology. But in truth, nearly all of those first-wave dot-coms failed – and since then, on the whole really transformational change has been slow in coming. There are hundreds, if not thousands, of small, innovative start-ups, but almost all of them are struggling for customers and for funding.

There has certainly been a great deal of substitution – consumers and providers alike now do all sorts of financial things online that they used to do by post, on the phone or in branches. But at the time of writing, we'd say that the only new major mass-market financial services business model to have achieved real success in the digital age has been the aggregators, or price comparison sites – and if we were feeling particularly churlish, we'd say that anyway, when it comes down to it these sites are only remote brokerages. (If we were feeling less churlish, we'd also add peer-to-peer lending as another sector to have been fundamentally enabled by digital, but at the time of writing you couldn't really call it 'major' or 'mass market'.)

There are many reasons for this. One that stands out especially for that first wave of dot.coms back at the turn of the millennium was a failure to recognise the limitations of the technology. It really wasn't viable to move consumers' personal finances onto the Internet in the era of painfully slow dial-up modems.

But we also think that the often-limited role of marketing has had a lot to do with it. If there's one clear requirement of the digital economy which hasn't always received the attention it deserves – even though it's a requirement that applies to consumer-facing digital businesses generally, by no means just to financial services – it is that digital businesses require good marketing to achieve lasting success.

How so? Let's reprise our Seven Ps table one last time:

The seven Ps	How they're relevant to digital
Product	Clear and meaningful propositions are essential. Digital products and services can't possibly succeed, or even survive for very long, unless their target market is absolutely clear about what's in it for them.
Price	Digital consumers are often value-conscious and price-sensitive. They want to understand the value proposition of what's on offer, and, often, to compare it with others. And they will tend to expect to pay less for digital products and services than their offline equivalents.
Place	Obviously, by definition, online. But it's not quite that simple. For one thing, optimisation for different devices is important – and for another, many financial services will require integration with other channels such as telephone, online chat or even possibly face-to-face to provide a total experience that satisfies customers.
Promotion	Crucial, and potentially a major obstacle for many new and innovative digital financial services. Without adequate promotion, the target market simply won't know it's there – and 'adequate' promotion rarely comes cheap.
People	Not always relevant, but potentially an essential part of the proposition when telephony, chat or face-to-face are integrated.[2]

(Continued)

---

[2] As we move further into the era of AI, robo-advisers and chatbots, we may need to find a new word beginning with the letter 'P' to shorthand one-to-one interactions which may or may not be with a real person.

The seven Ps	How they're relevant to digital
Process	Also crucial. The quality, clarity and simplicity of the online customer journey is an absolutely critical success factor. Arguably more online services fail because of poor customer journey management than for any other reason.
Physical Evidence	Important in that the online experience itself is a kind of physical evidence – and, of course, amid the abstractions and intangibilities of financial services, as the only clear evidence that the customer has actually bought or done something.

By our reckoning, three of the seven – product, promotion and process – must invariably be excellent if a new digital service is to have any chance of success, and depending on the nature of the service and the expectations of the target market any or even all of the other four may matter as much.

Returning to our story of the first dot-com boom around the turn of the millennium, this analysis helps explain what went wrong. Perhaps unsurprisingly, at such an early stage in the development of digital services, these first-wave players scored poorly in most, if not sometimes all, of these seven areas. In hindsight, most also suffered from shaky digital functionality – these were, more or less, the digital equivalents of the Wright Brothers' aeroplane and the Model T Ford. But some, at least, might have overcome these limitations – after all, Amazon, eBay and Google all did – with better and more focused marketing (or, to put it another way, with a stronger focus on consumers).

That's one big reason why we believe that, of all the changes affecting the financial services industry in recent years, the exponential growth of digital is the one that makes the greatest demands on the quality – and actually very often the quantity – of marketing. Digital services give bad marketing – or, even worse, no marketing – nowhere to hide.

With this massive change in mind, let's review that list of factors that limited the role of marketing over the years. To what extent do they still apply today?

1. As incomes, savings and most of all borrowings have grown, so has the range of financial products and services available. Fifty years ago, there were a couple of hundred unit trusts and investment trusts: now there are nearly 9,000. Other categories didn't exist at all – in the years since Barclaycard, the UK's first credit card, arrived in 1966, over

a thousand others have followed. The marketing challenge required to build and maintain a consumer franchise in such overcrowded markets is gigantic.

2. The huge increase in home ownership has caused an explosion in the number of products and services available to – and needed by - consumers. The number of mortgage products on the market has actually declined slightly since the peak just before the financial crisis of 2008 – not quite so many options for sub-prime borrowers – but there are still over 6,000.[3] The same point about the struggle to compete for a consumer franchise applies.

3. Family traditions still count for something, but, not least because of the Internet, much less. Most younger people, including the much-discussed Millennials, don't see any reason to stick with the providers chosen by their parents and grandparents. According to Derek White, of global bank BBVA, their customers spend an average of two hours a year in bank branches, compared with 45 hours on their mobile banking app. They want services designed to meet their needs, optimised for mobile and drawn to their attention by digital channels and networks, and with a look and feel and customer experience to match.[4]

4. Geography is history, as the saying goes, thanks again mainly to the Internet. Regional building societies struggle to maintain families' allegiances across the generations, and a dwindling number of people care where the nearest branch of their bank is located. Choices are made on the basis of marketing, not local presence. What's more, there has been a significant change in regulatory policy. Local building societies were established so that people living in, say, Rotherham could save with their local Rotherham building society and then use those savings to obtain a mortgage in Rotherham. The UK regulator now believes that this causes 'concentration risk', so the Rotherham building society is encouraged to use the savings of the people of Rotherham to enable people living pretty much anywhere other than Rotherham to buy a home. . . .

---

[3] The gigantic increase in the amount of personal wealth now held in the form of property assets now expands the market in many other ways – for example, it's the most important reason for the similarly vast increase in the value of inheritances, and so many financial services aimed to help beneficiaries deal with these.

[4] This isn't absolutely always the case. When the MD of the stockbroking firm Killik & Co was asked to explain why, despite its relatively progressive approach and young age profile, its offices are so chintzy and old-fashioned, he shrewdly replied that the individuals in the firm's target market felt comfortable in offices that reminded them of their fathers' studies.

5. In personal finance, one of the most significant developments of recent years has been the rapidly-increasing reluctance of employers to guarantee the retirement incomes of their workforces.[5] At the time of writing, hardly any final-salary pension schemes in the private sector are still open to new members (although of course it's a very different story in the public sector, where final salary pensions still represent a colossal drain on the public finances). This trend has created such a crisis in retirement savings that the government has been obliged to take action, compelling employers to offer workplace pensions on the basis of auto-enrolment. With contribution levels remaining low, the very high initial take-up of these schemes reflects a triumph of behavioural economics rather than marketing. But as contribution levels rise sharply over the next few years and the temptation to opt out increases, we suspect this may well change, and marketing may have an increasingly important role to play in encouraging people not to opt out of schemes either at the outset, or over the years as financial pressures increase.

6. As the quality and availability of State-funded services have continued to decline (or at least to be perceived to decline), and as people's expectations of the kind of treatment they want for themselves and their families – for example, in education, in healthcare and in old age – continue to increase, the amount of money people choose to divert into private provision goes on increasing too. Some of this goes into dedicated financial products, like private healthcare and long-term care insurance: much just goes into mainstream savings and investments.

7. We've seen dramatic and continuing change in general insurance, and perhaps most of all in the biggest category, motor. With car ownership continuing its long-term upward trend, with insurance still compulsory and annually renewable, and with most consumers rightly or wrongly feeling confident about serving themselves without an intermediary's involvement, the direct-to-consumer sector began to show growth as long ago as the mid-80s and has carried on growing and evolving since. Dozens of direct writers have followed in the footsteps of Direct Line, the original pioneer - and of course the coming of the Internet resulted in the next generation of consumer services, the aggregators or price comparison sites (now spanning a much broader range of sectors, but with

---

[5] Many factors have combined to cause this reluctance, but the single most important has been the increase in cost resulting from our ever-lengthening life expectancy. Back in 1881, when the Prussian chancellor Bismarck introduced the first state pension payable at the age of 70, male life expectancy from birth was little over 50. Today, when the UK state pension age is 65 (although soon to increase), life expectancy for men is just under 80, and for women just over 83.

a core strength in car insurance). Today, just as when the direct writers emerged over 30 years ago, this sector is worth close scrutiny once again for signs of really disruptive, breakthrough innovation: with scores of insurtech start-ups already piloting radical ideas and new technologies such as telemetry, it can only be a matter of time until some start to get real traction.

8. Face-to-face selling is still important in some sectors of the market, but it is under attack from all quarters. Gradually, regulation, in its strange and rather random cart-before-horse kind of way, has stamped out many of its worst excesses, especially in the area of long-term savings and investments and to a lesser extent in mortgages. Commission has gone from many sectors of the market, and with it commission bias. And the required standard for the suitability of advice is now so high that the face-to-face advice process has become too long and complex, and so too expensive, to make sense for consumers with modest amounts of money. Meanwhile, financial services providers have had their own reasons to move away from face-to-face advice: as well as the regulatory risk, all that face-time does take a big bite out of their profits. As a result, the number of financial advisers has fallen dramatically, from some 250,000 at the peak to about a tenth of that number today, and as a result millions of consumers have to make financial decisions on the basis of their own judgement. (In many other sectors, though, such as banking and life and health insurance, sales practices continue largely unchanged.)

9. The recent influence of regulation on financial services marketing – now mainly involving the Financial Conduct Authority (FCA) and previously the Financial Services Authority (FSA) – could fill a book in its own right, although not a particularly enjoyable one. While our regulators have recognised sales processes as a key source of consumer detriment for many years and tried to tackle the most damaging with frequent rounds of intervention, it's fair to say that broader marketing has only moved more recently toward the centre of their field of vision. As a result, many of their interventions so far – arguably most – while well-intentioned, have suffered from unintended consequences and have often proved counterproductive. So far, it would be difficult to argue that the regulator has done much to support or encourage good marketing.

10. The effects of changes in legislation and taxation continue to increase from each year to the next. A large proportion of marketing initiatives are driven by legislative or fiscal change, with tax being still by far the most powerful tool in the public policy toolbox to change or manage people's financial behaviour, where it plays much the same role that commission used to play among advisers. The quantity of tax-related legislation on the statute book continues its relentless rise.

Many changes in tax rules bring about huge changes in the shape of marketing activity. An initiative such as the Pensions Freedoms introduced in George Osborne's 2014 Budget on an extremely tight timetable triggered a wave of new product and service launches right across every company with any kind of stake in the retirement sector. It's simply impossible to calculate the number of millions of person-hours, and investment pounds, triggered by those few short sentences in the Budget speech. More recently, the same can be said of the EU's PSD2 legislation, ushering in the era of so-called Open Banking – at the time of writing, we wait to see the kinds of new marketing initiatives that this will bring about.

It's true that we're biased, but it seems to us that over a long period all the important trends have been pointing in the same direction.

Once upon a time, the financial services industry was able to succeed, and consumers were more or less able to find their way to the products and services they needed, without much need for marketing to build connections and relationships between them.

For many years now that has been changing, slowly at first but at an increasing pace, especially during the period of the explosive development of digital services. Marketing now has a critical role to play, both in enabling firms to develop and promote propositions that clearly meet consumers' wants and needs, and in enabling consumers to navigate their way around a large and complex industry that has a key contribution to make to the quality of their lives. Marketing has been changing – for one thing there's a great deal more of it, and for another there are some examples of extremely good practice. But taken as a whole, there's still a long way to go. Too much of financial services marketing is still superficial, lacking in insight, unrealistic in its objectives and inadequately measured and evaluated. In this book we propose a number of specific areas where no small change is required.

A NOTE ON SELLING VS MARKETING

Over the course of this chapter, astute readers may have noticed an apparent contradiction. On the one hand, we've said more than once that financial services firms have succeeded over the years without relying much on marketing. On the other hand, we've also said they've relied a great deal on face-to-face selling. But isn't selling a sub-set of marketing? And if so, can these statements both be true?

Our answer is that the contradiction is more apparent than real, and the reason is to do with a wide gap between theory and practice. Selling should be seen – and, more importantly, experienced by the consumers on the receiving end – as a part of the discipline of marketing. Exactly the same process, of identifying, meeting and satisfying consumer needs, should apply. However, far too often in financial services over the years, the sales function has actually operated in a sort of parallel universe, managed separately and engaging with consumers on the basis of its people's own analysis and insights on how best to make the sale.

The most effective sales-driven companies make no secret of this. The management team of one of the very best and most successful says quite explicitly that its sales force are its 'primary target audience' – that meeting and satisfying their needs is absolutely the management team's most important priority. At this firm's annual conference, with all staff present, there's a key moment when the sales people are asked to stand and everyone else in the company loudly applauds their achievements. The marketing people, of course, are among the seated applauders.

In companies which are both sales-driven and siloed in this way, the sales team are likely to have the authority to impose their analyses and insights on their marketing colleagues, in particular requesting sales support material of one sort or another which is based around the story as they want to tell it. What has happened in companies like these – and there are many – is that the priority has been reversed, and marketing has effectively become a sub-set of sales. In this situation, the marketing department is frequently known by the lesser term 'marketing services', which means 'not really proper marketing at all'.

It's possible to be misled on the reality of current practice within a firm by the existence of a single individual in charge of both areas, very often a Director of Sales & Marketing. Surely this must mean a coherent and integrated approach, giving due weight to both functions?

In our experience, on the whole, not really. The clue, we'd suggest, is in the order of the terms in the job title. As far as we can recall, this is always 'Sales & Marketing' and never 'Marketing & Sales'. We think that when push comes to shove, this pretty much always indicates that the priorities of salespeople, in terms of designing products and expressing their propositions in whatever way makes it easiest to achieve sales, will come ahead of the priorities of marketing and marketing people.

CHAPTER 5

Retail Financial Services How?

This book's first pages touched briefly on one of the trickier issues we've had to grapple with: that arguably there isn't really a single, homogeneous thing that can be called 'retail financial services', and therefore there aren't really any generally applicable ground rules to tell us how they should and shouldn't be marketed.

Obviously if we accepted that argument it would be difficult to proceed further, so we don't. We think that despite its enormous size and diversity, there is a thing that can meaningfully be described as 'retail financial services', and there is a lot than can sensibly be said about marketing in it.

However, precisely because it is so very large and diverse, we feel an obligation to provide some kind of guide to the territory – a list, in other words, to make clear what's included and what isn't.

For two or three reasons, this isn't a completely straightforward exercise. For one thing, it feels uncomfortable to include a chapter that is so blatantly industry- and product-centric in a book that is supposed to emphasise the paramount importance of putting consumers first. Beyond that, a chapter that is basically a list could be extremely boring to write and indeed to read. And beyond that, we have had to ponder a number of decisions about what should and what should not be included. For example, is gambling a financial service? Or the huge personal car finance market, which is causing so much concern to the regulator at the moment? What about financially oriented media? How about estate agents? Or online utilities switching services?

Arbitrarily, we've decided that for the purposes of this book, none of these is included under the heading of 'retail financial services'. You may disagree, and to be honest on a different day and in a different mood so might we, but there it is. Far be it from your authors to make any comparison between their humble efforts and the great English dictionary of Dr Samuel Johnson, or indeed the strange and disturbing occult dictionary of the sinister Ambrose Bierce. But both those famous books share a principle we intend to copy: their authors didn't hesitate to include words, and exclude others, for no better reason than that they felt like it – or, perhaps, more accurately, because they had something they wanted to say about them.

And then there's one other complication that we feel obliged to explore: in today's retail financial world, what exactly is the distinction between a 'product' and a 'service'? In this book, we tend to refer to the industry as the financial *services* industry, but also to the *products* this industry provides. What's going on here?

Historically, both on a commonsense basis and in the academic literature, the difference between a product and a service was fairly obvious. A product was a manufactured and tangible thing, made to a consistent specification and available for repeated purchase and consumption. A service was an intangible thing, delivered by a person or people and so not completely consistent in delivery, and available only at the moment of consumption. A bottle of shampoo was a product: a haircut was a service.

In truth it was never quite that simple. Many service providers ultimately provided a product: the process of being fitted for a Savile Row suit may be a service, but the suit itself is clearly a product. And many product providers also provided (and often made most of their money) from services. A new car is clearly a product, but what's the word you use to describe what it needs at the garage every 10,000 miles? Exactly.

Today, though, it seems to us that in the financial world the meanings, and defining characteristics, of the two words have become so blurred that it's hard to find any sensible distinction. Some might have a vague sense that a bank account, say, or a mortgage, or an insurance policy has some of the characteristics of a 'product', while financial advice or tax planning would be considered 'services'. But it's very difficult to explain this distinction. All of these things are intangible, unrepeatable as a whole and prone to inconsistency, which would make them services: on the other hand, increasingly none of them is necessarily delivered by a person or people, and are made up of elements increasingly delivered digitally and therefore entirely consistent and replicable, which would make them products.

All in all, we can't see any clear or meaningful distinction between financial products and financial services. In this book we may have a slight tendency to use the word 'product' to describe a packaged, defined and named entity, and 'service' to describe entities that are more open-ended and variable in the consumer experiencer they offer. But actually, we use the two terms pretty much interchangeably.[1]

---

[1] One other point on this. Following a practice we've maintained over many years, when we're discussing what the industry offers from the perspective of its customers, we'll try hard *not* to use the word 'product'. We don't believe that most consumers make much sense of the idea of a financial 'product', a word which to them still has connotations of something that is tangible, physical and manufactured. Does the average customer see an investment fund as a 'product'? Or an insurance policy? Or a bank account? Some may, but on the whole we don't think so.

Having clarified these ground rules, the rest of this chapter is made up of the list of what we have decided to include, in alphabetical order. And in an attempt to make it more interesting to write and to read, we've added some notes about some of the more interesting marketing issues and challenges currently arising in each category.

There's no getting round the fact that all this does result in some extremely product-centric pages: one proof of that is to be found in the generic names used to describe them, many of which are both opaque and unappealing. (It's difficult to believe there were many marketers in the room when terms like *permanent health insurance* and *deferred annuities* were invented.)

But after this blast of product-centricity, don't worry – the rest of this book is customers first, all the way to the end.

ANNUITIES

How are the mighty fallen. Since the Pensions Freedom changes, introduced in 2014 and fully implemented in 2015, sales in this once-gigantic category, providing lifetime income for some 300,000 people retiring every year with defined contribution pension pots, are down according to the Association of British Insurers by some 80%. The at-retirement market has turned its back on annuities, and it's not just advisers – it's consumers, too. Somehow, the word 'annuity' has broken through consumers' customary barriers of ignorance and apathy and established itself as a bad thing, roughly on a par with other bad financial terms like 'PPI', 'mis-selling' and 'pensions black hole'.

The funny thing, of course, is that if you offer the very same people at the point of retirement an income that's guaranteed for the rest of their lives, perhaps with an option to index-link it and provide a continuing income for their spouse on their death, they'll bite your arm off. This is exactly what they want. Of all the words in the financial lexicon, the word 'guaranteed' is the single most popular. And 'guaranteed for life' is the gold standard of guarantees.

You have to say that this dichotomy sounds very like a marketing challenge. On the face of it, the issue is all about managing perceptions, use of language, telling stories, all the things we're supposed to be good at.

But before we start getting excited, we do need to recognise a couple of complications. One is a consumer issue: although people like the 'guaranteed for life' part, they genuinely don't like the way that annuities operate on the cusp, so to speak, between investing and gambling: die young, and you lose. (There's a convincing Behavioural Science explanation for why people feel like this, mainly to do with loss aversion.)

The other is that regardless of what consumers think, a great many people in the industry have fallen massively, and we strongly suspect permanently, out of love with annuities too. From an adviser's point of view, a cynic might suspect this is at least partly because they don't provide much of an opportunity to deliver an ongoing service, and so to raise an ongoing adviser charge: arranging an annuity tends to be a one-and-done transaction, while a drawdown plan, needing annual reviews and rebalancing, offers a much clearer route to locking in that 0.5% (or in some cases even up to 1%) per annum. But it would be too cynical to suggest this is the whole story. The industry's distaste for annuities is also symptomatic of a broader problem, which is its not-infrequent tendency to undervalue, or even disregard, benefits that are genuinely important to consumers.

In investment, this applies particularly to benefits that are to do with consistency or reliability. These qualities really matter to consumers, partly for rational reasons but also for highly emotional reasons to do with loss aversion (see Chapter 12 on behavioural economics for more on this).[2]

People in the industry, on the other hand, don't like guarantees, primarily because they know that there's always a price to be paid. Most take the view that when it comes to long-term investing, you're better off (literally) taking your chances, and giving time in the market the chance to do its work. This takes us to the heart of one of those wants-versus-needs ethical dilemmas raised in Chapter 4. If a consumer is taking financial advice, then the adviser should give an honest opinion, and it's for the customer ultimately to decide whether to take it or not. But outside the context of advice, is it helpful for the industry to show reluctance to provide, or promote, propositions which appeal to consumers and powerfully meet their needs? At the moment, the industry and its customers have formed a tacit agreement to play down the case for annuities. It's debatable whether that agreement really works in customers' interests.

CARDS

Credit cards are the only financial services category with significant 'badge value', because it's the only category that is highly visible. People across the restaurant table or at the checkout counter can see which product you own.

---

[2]It's this combination of rationality and emotion which explains why consumers are so keen on the idea of with-profits investment, at least when they have some sense of what it is (another of those opaque category names). From their point of view, it's fantastic that bonuses, once allocated, can't be taken away.

They are also one of the biggest, most crowded, most complex and fastest-changing financial services categories (and, in turn, part of the even bigger, more crowded, more complex and faster-changing payments market): and, frankly, a category that is now so steeped in some strange and not-very-customer-friendly habits that it's hard to see how it can mend its ways.

The most important of these habits is a business model in which clients who are revolvers (who maintain balances from month to month) are highly profitable, while transactors (who clear their balances every month) are loss-making. This simple if strange reality means that marketing activity is hugely tilted toward recruiting and retaining revolvers (all those endless balance transfer offers), and also of course means that the rates they pay are enormously much higher than rates available elsewhere in the lending market. And God help you if you are a day late with a payment on a balance transfer card ...

Meanwhile, the market as a whole feels like the middle fish in that well-known picture of a little fish that's pursued by a bigger fish that's pursued by yet a bigger fish, and so on. Cards, with the help of technology advances such as contactless, have recently overtaken cash as consumers' preferred form of payment, but in turn are coming under increasing threat from a shoal of emerging new competitors – mobile may be the biggest, but then there's PayPal and Alipay, and behind them the emerging world of virtual and crypto currencies.

Amid all this turbulence you'd imagine that this would be an exciting sector from a marketing perspective, but at this moment there's a continuing sense of phony war or perhaps more accurately a calm before the storm. Marketing communications activity is in fact sharply down from its peak, and a good deal of what still goes on consists of dreary balance transfer promotions. In terms of value propositions, too, card providers seem currently more concerned to trim benefits and improve margins than to develop new stories for their target markets.

Finally, cards also present us with one of the category definition problems that are endemic in this stupid idea of producing a gazetteer of retail financial services: should we include those would-be challenger banks, like Monzo and Starling, which at the time of writing are able to offer only prepaid cards? Let's just say for now that some of these, most notably Monzo, are undoubtedly achieving impressive traction among their young millennial target market, and are achieving a kind of emotional engagement completely different from anything the big legacy banks can hope for. But then again, some would argue that achieving emotional engagement isn't much of a trick when you're running a fundamentally unprofitable business model and giving away a suite of outstanding digital money management services.

Inevitably, sooner or later, it will become necessary either to cut back on the added value or to start charging for it.

CRITICAL ILLNESS INSURANCE

The same set of problems and indeed opportunities as Life Assurance (see below), really, only with three additional challenges to overcome:

1. Very few people have ever heard of it (and it's another opaque and unappealing name, if a little better than the term used when the first products were introduced, the mind-blowingly terrible *Dread Disease Insurance*)
2. Unlike life assurance, prices don't generally turn out to be much lower than people think they'll be
3. Most people think it won't happen to them (although of course many of them are wrong).

All of these challenges add up to explain why there's virtually no direct-to customer (D2C) market for this product, which is still dominated by intermediaries. If the new financial services marketing is all about delivering propositions that meet customers' perceived wants and/or needs, it's going to be very hard work persuading more than a small number that this is one of them.

CURRENT ACCOUNTS

Another big, complex, difficult and fast-changing part of the market is current accounts. These are important for many reasons, but especially these two:

1. Current accounts are perceived by both providers and consumers as the 'cornerstone' product in people's financial lives, and the basis for their biggest, broadest and longest-lasting financial relationship
2. At the same time, they're usually the richest available source of customer data and therefore the most powerful opportunity for providers to develop their customer relationships further.

In much the same way as cards, the reality today is that current accounts have driven a long way down a business-model cul-de-sac, and reversing all the way back to the main road is far from easy. The trouble began many years ago, when the then-Midland Bank (now part of HSBC) first offered free in-credit banking and stole the market. All the other leading banks were obliged to respond, and although all was more or less well during the period of relatively high interest rates – banks could make a return on customers' credit balance or 'free float' – it's a different story with rates not far from zero.

Banks have adopted various strategies, not all of them hugely consumer-friendly, to combat this margin pressure: examples include packaged accounts, where customers pay fees for add-on services, which many don't really want or need, extremely high charges for additional services such as foreign payments, and sky-high rates of interest on unauthorised borrowings.

None of this has endeared big banks to their huge current account customer bases, and in recent years the list of challengers excited about the potential for growth has lengthened rapidly. Hitherto, despite attempts by the regulator to remove some of the obstacles to switching, consumer inertia has largely prevailed: everyone knows the cliché that individuals are more likely to change their spouse than their bank. At the time of writing, we're rapidly approaching another market intervention that may finally change the dynamic – the so-called Open Banking Project, or more properly PSD2 Payment Service Directive is an EU initiative that will make it much more difficult for banks to maintain exclusive control of their customer data, and therefore will open the market to a new level of competition. On the one hand we've heard stories like this before and nothing much has happened: on the other hand, as in the fable of the boy who cried wolf, it's important to remember than in the end there *was* a wolf.

EQUITY RELEASE

With such a high proportion of so many people's assets invested in property, everything about equity release makes perfect sense except the numbers, which tend to be quite painful to contemplate. Still, for many older people the instinctive desire to remain in their homes is strong, and for many of them equity release is the only game in town.

That being so, it remains a curiously undeveloped concept, chosen by only 37,000 people in 2017. One small reason for this may be its remarkably unattractive and uncommunicative name. For many, the word 'equity' means little, except perhaps as the name of the actors' trade union.

FINANCIAL ADVICE

We write at length elsewhere about the extent of change affecting the world of financial advice, most of it driven by regulation while technology also plays its part. In short, the advice industry is getting smaller (in the number of advisers at least), better and less dependent on one-to-one personal contact between adviser and client.

These are all important developments. But there is another potential development, also important and also welcome, that's proving very slow to gather momentum in this fragmented industry – the emergence of a small number of large, strong advice brands. In terms of any widespread level of consumer awareness, financial advice is still an almost entirely unbranded market.

Many of us have been anticipating that this must change for decades, and can cite a long list of compelling reasons why it should have started to change long ago. But we're still waiting. The main obstacle is, quite simply, the personalities of the country's financial advisers: independent-minded, stroppy, unwilling to take orders, determined to do things in their own way. This poses a management challenge on a par with organising the similar number of London black-cab drivers into a single coherent organisation.

There are several other formerly fragmented retail, or intermediary, sectors in the consumer economy where large national brands have emerged. For example, hundreds of opticians are organised into the Specsavers brand; bookshops with Waterstones; and coffee shops with Starbucks. What's interesting, though, is that in all these cases, very few of the branches of the national brands are staffed, or managed, by former owners of small independents. Starbucks managers didn't formerly run Italian espresso bars, managers of Waterstones typically didn't own local bookshops, and Specsavers managers are mostly young opticians either newly qualified and/or qualified in other countries. There's reason for this: those in charge know that if a national brand is to stand for anything then it must stand for a consistent customer experience, and achieving any kind of consistency among a group of people who've spent years doing things in their own way is much harder than starting at the beginning, with people who've never run a branch before.

At some point, the same kind of trend must emerge in financial advice. There are, obviously, tough training and compliance issues to tackle, but they can't be harder than they are for opticians. But until then, in the absence of any firms combining consistency of proposition with scale, there is little opportunity for marketers. As we said in the introduction to this book, some level of consistency in the delivery of a product or a service is the *sine qua non* for marketing: without it, there's simply nothing to be done.

FUNDS

Where do you start with retail funds? This huge, sprawling, massively over-crowded industry could only have developed the way it did in an era of high-charge, commission-driven intermediation: and now that commission has gone, and intermediation is changing in nature, it's an industry that's almost completely unfit for purpose. We simply don't need several hundred firms managing retail funds, or a total universe of over 9,000. We don't need the level of charges still taken by active fund managers who regularly underperform their benchmarks. We don't need the millions of words of market commentary that they pump out on a daily basis. We don't need their almost entirely generic and undifferentiated investment propositions. And we don't need their distant and patronising attitude toward the individuals who entrust them with their life's savings. The industry now feels about as vulnerable to change as the industry that had grown up to serve American travel by horse and stagecoach – stables, feed suppliers, livery yards – must have been at the time when railways first crossed the continent.

Still, it's unlikely that it's going to uninvent and reconfigure itself overnight, becoming dramatically much smaller, better value for money, more differentiated and more focused on what individual investors really want and need, so we're going to have to get to where we need to be gradually, over time. The familiar rebuilding-the-aeroplane-in-mid-flight metaphor seems to apply.

This puts a huge and very challenging responsibility on marketers, both to map out the course and to manage the journey. It won't be at all easy, because fund managers, and fund management firms, hold marketing in particularly low esteem. Even more than other financial services sectors, it's here that marketing is known, almost invariably, as the 'colouring-in department'.

Frankly, this is at least in part because marketers have too often been intimidated by the people running the money. One of your authors remembers working on a brand development project for a very well-known retail fund manager some years ago. On the basis of a thorough strategy development process, with plenty of research among investors and intermediaries, the marketing team agreed that the brand should stand for the idea of 'accessible expertise'. In real life, this brand promise was compromised perhaps just a little by the fact that at that time, the investment team were so arrogant, aloof and thoroughly inaccessible that people from other parts of the firm had to prove they'd booked an appointment before they were allowed to get out of the lifts on the investment managers' floor.

It isn't easy for marketers working in intimidating environments like this to venture far beyond colouring-in, especially when most members of most firms' senior management teams come from fund management backgrounds (and virtually none comes from marketing), but it is a crucial challenge.

To be fair, there is some evidence that the funds industry is starting to change for the better, rather than just becoming ever bigger and more shapeless. Welcome trends include:

- The growth in the number and market share of passive funds, taking much less in charges than their actively managed counterparts, while outperforming well over half of them;
- The increasing readiness of fund managers to assemble and maintain the entire investment solution in the form of multi-asset and other 'non-single-strategy' funds, rather than leaving the crucial role of asset allocation to someone else (adviser or investor) much less well qualified to fulfill it;
- The use of investment platforms to make buying, selling and managing portfolios of funds cheap and easy.

But there's still a great deal more to do to reform and restructure what is probably still today the least customer-oriented and most self-indulgent sector of the retail financial services market, and it looks likely that the next big push in this direction will come from the regulator. The FCA's Asset Management Market Study, published in 2017, can only be described as a damning indictment of much of the industry as it now stands. It's impossible to believe that its publication hasn't started the clock ticking on a process of massive reform.

GAMBLING

Your authors have thought long and hard about whether gambling is within the scope of a book about retail financial services. The truth is, it's very difficult to find a good reason why it isn't, but we don't much want it to be. If you want some detail on the subject, we recommend the comprehensive review that you'll find in Professor Adrian Furnham's excellent book *The New Psychology of Money*. Also, in Chapter 12, we note that behaviours to do with betting have always been a primary focus of behavioural science: we'd expect to see well-thumbed copies of the works of Kahneman and Tversky on the bookshelves of all marketers involved in these sectors.

It's hard to justify our decision in the light of what we've said about consumer wants being just as valid as consumer needs, and the industry having a duty not just to offer consumers only what it *thinks* they ought to have, but there it is. If you're reading this book because you're looking for some interesting *apercus* of the marketing of gambling propositions, we apologise.

If you haven't folded any page-corners over, perhaps you can still get your money back (or double down on your bet …).

Inevitably our choice then raises related questions about Premium Bonds, and about the spectrum of niche financial products which operate on the borderline between investment and gambling – CFDs, spread betting, derivatives trading. We don't have a lot to say specifically about these, but they are undoubtedly a part of the world we're describing.

INCOME REPLACEMENT INSURANCE
(Misleadingly Named Permanent Health Insurance)

Many protection professionals say Income Replacement Insurance is the Cinderella of the protection product suite, and if only consumers had any sense it's the one that they'd take to the ball. Its big problem in terms of consumer perception is that it sounds very much like PPI, which isn't at all a good thing to sound like.

Never say never: a great product and brilliant marketing can achieve the impossible (for instance, everyone said Apple was sure to flop with the iPad). But we don't think that bright and ambitious financial services marketers will be setting off celebratory fireworks if they draw Income Replacement in the Marketing Challenge Sweepstake.

LIFE ASSURANCE

Life assurance is widely perceived (even by many working in the area) as a flat and depressing corner of the industry, where a dwindling number of insurers seek business from an intermediary market dominated by a small number of specialist firms, largely on the basis of endless rounds of price-cutting.

One big current success story, though, makes you wonder whether the fault lies in the category, or in the people working in it. Vitality is the protection brand (providing both life and health insurance) that rewards people for leading healthy lifestyles, an idea that's appealing at two levels. From an insurance perspective, it makes obvious underwriting sense. But from a marketing perspective, it surfs what looks certain to be a big and long-lasting wave in the *zeitgeist*. For a large and growing segment, staying in good health is not just an objective, it's a complete lifestyle – with profound effects on what people do, where they go, how they eat and drink and even what they read. If Vitality can become the default insurance choice for this segment, it will become a classic example of a strong niche brand – and as such, we'd suggest, an important role model for firms across financial services that haven't yet grasped the idea of targeting.

At the opposite end of the protection market, there is another niche – this one specifically to do with life assurance – that is reasonably well occupied. This consists of the segment of much older consumers who are targeted with so-called Over 50s Plans (the large majority, it has to be said, being a very long way over 50). If the hallmarks of the new financial services marketing include a target segment with a clear want or need, a focused proposition, a simple process and highly visible and engaging communications, then this belongs on the list. However, the fifth hallmark is that the proposition should offer consumers acceptable value for money and, if you'll forgive the mixed metaphor, that means these plans fall at the last fence.

Whether you look at protection as a whole or life assurance in particular, it seems very odd that there is such a large expanse of empty ground between Vitality, at the young and healthy end of the market, and Sun Life, promoted by the likes of veteran journalist and TV personality Michael Parkinson at the other end. There are literally dozens of other equally attractive niches available and still unoccupied.

Part of the problem is that most people don't understand the difference between insurance and assurance. You insure against a possibility, you assure against a certainty – and eventually, we are all going to die. ...

For some time now, we've been eagerly awaiting the arrival into the market of a horde of innovative, consumer-focused new players, the so-called insurtechs. There have been rumours of sightings in other markets, particularly the US. A much copied conference slide shows the names and logos of many dozens of them. But here in the UK protection market, the impact of these players has so far been minimal, and the status quo remains largely un-disrupted: the handful of new players to have emerged so far have made modest impacts, and the established major players have suffered few sleepless nights. We're all certain this is going to change, but we're not quite so certain about when.

LENDING

Lending is a great big core sector in the financial services market, worth over £200 billion in the year to June 2017. There are various ways to segment it – secured versus unsecured, prime versus sub-prime, short-term versus long-term. It represents good news and bad news as far as the national economy is concerned – good in the sense that the flow of new credit keeps consumer spending up and the economy going, bad in that if for any reason the wheels start wobbling, let alone falling off, the consequences can be devastating for individuals and for societies as a whole.

And apart from this, we can't think of anything very interesting to say about lending.

MORTGAGES

It's a cliché to say that for most homeowners, mortgages are their biggest-ever financial commitments. They're also commitments that, while usually benign and manageable, can turn nasty and become very difficult to manage remarkably quickly, when rates rise rapidly and/or when property prices fall. You'd imagine, therefore, that borrowers would choose mortgages extremely carefully, and that questions about their long-term affordability would loom large. On the whole, though, they don't. Experience tells us that consumers are driven by the answers to two questions: 'Can I afford the monthly payment?' and 'How quickly can I get an offer?' Particularly if they use the services of an intermediary– and some 70% do in the UK – mortgages have become an increasingly transactional product, with borrowers expecting to switch at two-year intervals as their special offers run out, a bit like a person crossing a pond using stepping-stones. Switching mortgages from one lender to another is lucrative work for intermediaries, too, with so-called 'procuration fees' playing a very similar role to initial commissions.

This doesn't make for very interesting marketing, but there are more opportunities for innovation when you examine consumers' needs in more detail. For example, only a few lenders seem to have taken on board the fact that the first-time buyer market is now almost entirely intergenerational, for example, with parental or grandparental support now more or less obligatory in many parts of the country. And the buy-to-let sector is ripe for further innovation: with so many retirees expecting to use property to generate some or even all of their retirement income, there must be opportunities to package buy-to-let borrowing with pension decumulation investment.

Elsewhere, too, we comment on one of the more disappointing (but also instructive) recent examples of financial product innovation, the curious case of the offset mortgage. For millions of people looking to manage both savings and borrowings, these are simply brilliant products, delivering huge financial benefits: yet sales have always been modest, and even when people have taken the plunge, they've largely failed to make the most of the benefits available. Some cite this as an example of consumer apathy and lack of engagement, but – as we hope we've made clear – we don't subscribe to the concept of blame-the-customer marketing. If people don't get it, either we have to tell the story better or – as is probably the case here – tell a simpler story.

MOTOR INSURANCE

As we've said, motor insurance was the first category in retail financial services to adopt a marketing-led approach. It's well over 30 years now since Direct Line first came into view, with a proposition that brought together all the key elements: clear targeting, simple process, competitive pricing, good service, and high-profile and engaging promotion. Since then, of course, Direct Line has faced huge competition not just from other insurers, but also from a whole new category of competitors in the form of the price comparison, or aggregator sites (discussed below).

With some ups and downs along the way, considering both the number and the intensity of these challenges, Direct Line has maintained its market position well. But the market continues to change, and yesterday's dynamic young challenger can very easily become today's (or tomorrow's) sleepy old dinosaur.

Three issues come to mind:

1. The biggest and most serious: do some of the practices of this category mean it's a mis-selling scandal waiting to happen? The fact is, in much the same way that product providers and intermediaries used to collude to take money from customers in the regulated sector, today a larger collusion involving some insurers, repairers, car rental firms, personal injury firms and others are doing the same in motor insurance. Policyholders would be astounded if they knew the proportion of their premiums diverted into heavily padded repair costs, grossly inflated car rental charges and completely bogus personal injury claims: the bottom line is that it's no-one's job even to try to look after policyholders' money. Can this continue? Could a new kind of challenger tackle this kind of institutionalised bad practice?
2. Not far behind in terms of bad practice toward customers (and also, it has to be said, very bad marketing practice), can insurers continue treating their most loyal customers so badly? The current position on renewal pricing is an absolute disgrace, and insurers deserve a great

deal more criticism than they get for it. From consumers' point of view, the only sensible strategy is to switch every year. This is absolutely ridiculous, and again must create opportunities for a new breed of challenger.

3. Finally, it's clear that the relentless advance of technology presents major new opportunities (or challenges, depending on your point of view) now and into the future. So far at least, telematics is reminding us of the curious behaviour of the dog in the night-time. ('But Holmes, the dog did nothing in the night-time!' 'That, Watson, was the curious behaviour'.) Then there's the initiation of peer-to-peer car rentals, arguably doing to cars what Airbnb is doing to accommodations. How far away are we from the really big innovation, driverless vehicles? No doubt all today's insurers have plans for these developments. Change creates opportunity, and there's a lot of change on the way.

PAYDAY LENDING

Enter the industry's pantomime villain, with green strobe lighting, dry ice and claps of thunder. Financial services people, especially prosperous ones, love to heap abuse on the payday lenders, and it's certainly true that many deserve all they get. But for all the right and proper anxiety about frequently appalling business practices – stratospheric rates of interest, strong-arm tactics and a business model that thrives on trapping people with little money into endless cycles of debt – payday lenders do absolutely meet a real and often desperate need in society that no-one else will touch with a bargepole. When people run out of money, have no way of getting more until tomorrow or the day after and have children who need a meal, they face the choice of dealing with a payday lender or going hungry.

If payday lenders exploiting this need were making unreasonably large amounts of money, it would be right to condemn them for their heartlessness and greed. But generally, they aren't. Several have gone out of business, and others report continuing losses – running costs, including of course bad debts, are horribly high.

It's difficult to believe that payday lenders offer much potential to expert proponents of the new financial services marketing, unless they have plans to broaden either their product mix or their target market. But we do think the less disreputable ones could use some help with their public relations – as a starting point, they could point out that over 30 days, an unauthorised overdraft from a High Street bank can cost significantly more.

Meanwhile, increasing pressure is brought to bear on them, not least by the regulator who unsurprisingly isn't keen.[3]

PEER-TO-PEER LENDING

Are we seeing the early stirrings of a whole new parallel financial services industry – we're almost allowing ourselves to use the word 'paradigm' – that could in time do what the Model T Ford did to the big banks' horses and carts? Or are we seeing the brief flowering of a seriously overhyped fashion, a frighteningly unregulated and dangerous environment that will end in tears as soon as we reach the inevitable crisis in which a lot of people lose a lot of money?

We don't know, and we're not sure if anyone else does. The category remains hazy and poorly understood (so much so that it's arguably wrong to describe much of what's on offer as 'lending' at all): what's more, it's extremely diverse, with firms adopting all sorts of lending models and hugely varying levels of risk. Frankly, many individuals who are involved haven't chosen to ask too many questions. At a time when mainstream savings rates are so extremely low, alternatives purporting to offer returns several times higher are hard to resist. What's missed by many consumers is that this is not 'banking.' Peer-to-peer lenders do not have banking licences, and consumers are not protected by compensation schemes.

The fact that more people haven't shown more interest may reflect sensible risk-aversion and a recognition of the famous aphorism that if something looks too good to be true then it probably is – but we think there's another reason. Like so many new digital categories, most peer-to-peer lending firms seem to have launched on the basis of business plans that allow for little, if any, consumer marketing communication. There isn't a single firm that has any significant level of awareness, and indeed even the category itself remains virtually unknown. For as long as firms are happy to target a very small segment of highly engaged, sophisticated consumers

---

[3]When it comes to being less than keen on expensive services for people with little money, the regulator has previous experience, having taken much the same view of industrial branch sales forces. These organisations, whose business was to visit clients in their homes every week or two to collect insurance premiums, were rightly criticised for offering poor value for money: the cost of the home visits was high relative to the modest amounts collected. But when they were regulated out of existence, it became apparent that they hadn't been all bad. Many of their customers were unbanked and appreciated the premium collection, saying that it forced a savings habit upon them which stopped when the services ended.

(which, in any case, is what the regulator wants them to do), this probably doesn't matter. However, if we're talking 'early stirrings' rather than 'brief flowering', that's going to have to change. As discussed at some length in Chapter 19 the idea that in the digital age you can achieve all necessary marketing communications tasks free of charge, using various readily available online tools and formats, is wrong. Sooner or later, someone's going to have to start spending some money.

PENSIONS (ACCUMULATION)

Pensions are a part of the market in slow-motion transformation as a result of huge changes affecting pensions in the workplace. The gradual fading away of defined benefit, or 'final salary' schemes, where employers bear the risk of providing a pension defined as a proportion of the employee's earnings, represents a huge change not just for retail financial services but for the people of the UK. That short golden age in which millions of people could expect their standard of living to remain more or less unchanged throughout their retirement is gradually coming to an end.

For the time being, the view of the industry and the government is that auto-enrolled defined contributions, or 'money purchase' pensions, where the individual employee is ultimately responsible for building a pot of money large enough to provide the desired level of income in retirement, represent the best available alternative. This very much depends on what you mean by 'best available' – if you mean 'incredibly much worse', then it's probably correct.

The whole question of funding retirement is so big and difficult, and extends into such deep and turbulent socio-political waters, that it feels out of range for a book about marketing. For the time being, while the £1 million DC pot cap remains, there's clearly a need for further retirement savings options for high earners: as for those whose savings can be comfortably accommodated within the cap, it seems that workplace schemes will provide most, if not all, of the solution.

Since the introduction of Pensions Freedoms in 2015, enormous changes have already taken place. We've seen massive increases in the amounts invested within pension wrappers (and, by the way, decreases in the amounts invested in everything else), a growing level of excitement about the potential of transfers from Defined Benefits (DB) schemes to Defined Contributions (DC), viewed with great caution and concern by the regulator, and, of course, the highly successful early stages of workplace auto-enrolment. But despite all this activity, it still feels as if the new pensions era has hardly begun.

PENSIONS (DECUMULATION)

It was in April 2014 that the then-Chancellor, George Osborne, astonished pretty much everyone (including, it's said, most of his colleagues in the Treasury and the Government) by announcing his Pensions Freedom measures. These, to be fully introduced just a year later, in April 2015, effectively brought to an end a situation in which the very large majority of people retiring with defined contribution (DC) pension savings were effectively obliged to use the money in their pots to buy an annuity, which would provide them with an income for the rest of their lives. The reforms also gave people unrestricted access to their pots from the age of 55 (57 from 2028).

The more you think about these changes, the more you realise how absolutely transformational they were. From the age of 55, the whole business of managing your long-term savings becomes a wide-open question, in which any number of options are now available at any moment for the rest of your life (and, actually, beyond, because more changes transform the role of pensions in inheritance planning). For millions of people, the new rules create the clearest and most important requirement ever for financial advice. And they create similar requirements for new solutions, both in retirement and actually for many years before (the right accumulation strategy looks very different when you're not working toward a moment in time when you aim to annuitise).

On the whole, though, the industry's response to all of this has been disappointing. To meet the need for income of retirees remaining invested ('going into drawdown') rather than annuitising, there has been a new wave of new income-producing investments of one sort or another (including a small handful bearing that magic word so loved by consumers, 'guaranteed'), and firms that didn't have a credible drawdown proposition have hurried to introduce one. But that's about all. We haven't seen any dedicated advice propositions, very little that's new to enable DIY customers to explore or manage their own retirement finances, and very little creativity or imagination in product design.

To be fair, the timetable set by the Chancellor was so tight that firms were struggling to get any kind of response in place by the initial deadline. But amid all the overwhelming flexibility and complexity of the retirement saving and retirement income choices now available to everyone with a DC pension, there remains an enormous need for clear-sighted marketers to come forward with propositions that demonstrably meet individuals' needs and give them a sense of direction in a frighteningly featureless landscape.

There are fairly good excuses available to explain why this hasn't happened in the immediate aftermath of the changes – but the excuses will get thinner and thinner as time passes.

PRICE COMPARISON SITES

The big retail financial services marketing success story of the digital age: in some categories, first and foremost motor insurance, their market share has gone from 0% to around 75% in the space of less than 30 years. And also, pleasingly from our point of view, a textbook example of a marketing-led development. Price comparison sites tick almost all the boxes in our list of the Seven Ps ('almost' because they have nothing special to offer when it comes to Physical Evidence), and it's reassuring to see a substantial market sector where the stuff we prefer actually seems to be working.

That said, it's not all good news. We suspect that consumers would be surprised and indeed angered if they ever came to understand the workings of the algorithms that promote and prioritise sponsored content. And in another sense and at a broader level, you can argue that the sites' success highlights the marketing failure on the part of the product providers featured in their listings. The fact that so many consumers are ready to make their purchase decisions primarily, or even entirely, on the basis of price reflects the high level of commoditisation in several sectors, or to put it another way the failure of most firms to achieve any meaningful differentiation.

As marketers, we find it easy to admire the few brands that, so far at least, have chosen to stand aside from the price comparison frenzy (notably Direct Line and Aviva in insurance, still the most active sector). For those that have succumbed, it's difficult to imagine there's a way back out again. For new brands still to emerge, price comparison seems like a fate to be avoided if at all possible, except of course for those few which emerge on a lowest-cost producer, price-based proposition.

It'll be interesting to see how much further price comparison sites are able to extend their scope. In terms of market share, so far insurance represents by some distance their most successful category, with a long list of others – energy, savings, cards, loans and so on – following on behind. There's clearly huge growth potential in these categories, but it's worth considering what others might be seen to be commoditised enough to be added to the list.

PRIVATE MEDICAL INSURANCE

As insurance product categories go, PMI is something of an enigma. It's a sector that has seen a good deal of innovation over the years, especially with a view to making the cost of cover more affordable. It provides a range of solutions to a big problem which everyone recognises, namely the increasing inability of the National Health Service to meet all our healthcare needs. And it also occupies a patch of highly emotionally charged territory at the intersection of the three things which, according to research, we care most about in our lives: our money, our health and our families.

Yet despite all this, market shares remain low, sales remain flat and the sector would scarcely exist if it weren't for Group schemes. (Not only are most policyholders covered within Group schemes, but a significant proportion of individual policyholders are Group scheme leavers.) It's also curious that one big brand – BUPA – is a household name, but while a number of well-known insurance companies include PMI products in their portfolio, there is no other well-known provider specifically associated with the category.

What's going on here? It's certainly true that health is a sensitive and emotional area, where strong and dangerous undercurrents and riptides lie in wait for the unwary: for example, many of us Brits are so passionate about the poor old NHS that for many, buying private insurance feels like a kind of betrayal. But still, it's impossible to believe that there isn't good potential for better – and indeed more – marketing. In recent years, most providers have relied on Group schemes (and Group scheme leavers) for most of their new business, taking it for granted that the individual market isn't going to work for them. Given some more product innovation, some new ideas about partnership between private and public sectors and some powerful and well-targeted promotion, we think that negative view can be proved wrong.

ROBO ADVICE

Does 'robo advice' deserve a heading of its own, separate from advice? And what to do about the fact that this term describes a lot of do-it-yourself (DIY) investment services that don't actually offer advice at all?

Let's not overthink it. Let's use this heading as a term that, regrettably, seems to have established itself as the descriptor for predominantly online DIY investment services, where consumers can buy, sell and manage investments that they can choose in ways that meet their needs – in other words, services that offer a degree of bespoking over and above just buying and selling a fund manager's funds. From a regulatory standpoint, some of what's on offer does constitute 'advice', some is 'guidance' and some is 'execution only'. But hardly anyone—and virtually no consumers—understands the boundaries between these three subcategories, so let's think of it as one.

Many think of it as the shiny new exciting future of retail investment, and particularly as the best way to fill the 'advice gap' caused by the unaffordability of one-to-one advice for the millions of consumers with relatively modest sums to invest.

We must admit we don't really share this view. What is clear is that insofar as this market currently exists, in the UK it's already dominated by one massively successful and capable organisation, Hargreaves Lansdown. Their target market is the segment of something like 1.5 million people, give or take, who are active DIY investors – mostly, although not entirely, upmarket middle-aged and elderly men, living in the south of England, who spend a lot of time and take a lot of pleasure from looking after their investment portfolios. (These same people, by the way, also tend to maintain close and active relationships with advisers, in much the same way that people who enjoy working on their own cars also tend to have close contact with one or more mechanics, and people who like cooking also often eat out in restaurants, but that's another and slightly confusing story.)

These 'hobbyist' private investors have always been there, and no doubt always will be there (not literally the same people, of course, although sometimes it seems like it), and they do whatever there is to be done at the time. Thirty years ago they clipped the coupons in M&G press advertisements. Then they bought from Fidelity on the telephone, and then they used the Interactive Investor or Hargreaves Lansdown websites: next it'll be a risk-managed ETF portfolio accessed via an app on their phones. These people are easy to engage and quite easy to recruit, although their price sensitivity can be an issue: the problem, of course, is that unless they're very happy and comfortable (as indeed most are at Hargreaves) they're also very easy to lose to the next interesting new proposition. (As the Eagles put it in a very different context, 'They'll never forget you till somebody new comes along'.)

For as long as both of us can remember, and we have to admit that means over 30 years each, retail investment firms of one sort or another have been trying to broaden the DIY market beyond this inner core. One of the first attempts we can remember was sparked by the big 1980s privatisation campaigns, where the idea was that ordinary non-hobbyist investors would be so pleased with the performance of their British Telecom and British Gas shares that they'd be inspired to go out and buy shares in Marks & Spencer and ICI. Instead, however, the large majority of them just sold their British Telecom and British Gas shares. Thirty-odd years later, nothing has ever happened.

Maybe things are finally changing, and robo-advice will crack open a broader direct investment market segment. A lot of organisations strongly believe this, and are vigorously launching new services on an 'if we build it, they will come' basis. One big bank, Barclays, believes so strongly on the potential of the 'new investor' segment that they've refocused their DIY investment service toward them and away from those established active DIYers, much to the annoyance of many of the active DIYers. It'll be interesting to see if they're right.

SAVINGS

What is there to say about savings accounts? It's fortunate that one of the most powerful biases identified by the behavioural economists, loss aversion, doesn't seem to take account of inflation. With the differential between inflation as measured by the RPI, and the rates available on all mainstream savings accounts, almost all savers are currently losing money in real terms. It's fortunate, too, that there is a segment of consumers with such a deep and unshakeable urge to save, because there isn't much of a proposition for anyone else.

With margins so tight and returns so miserable, there's terribly little room for any kind of creativity or originality – even the usual levers affecting rate, such as duration, access and amount, can only offer marginal differences. In this situation, it's surprising that we haven't seen more gimmicks, or bells and whistles: one that stands out, taking its cue from NS&I's Premium Bonds, is the Family Building Society's Windfall Bond, where all savers are entered into a monthly draw and can win prizes of up to £50,000.

Some of the category's other marketing practices have attracted negative attention from the media and the regulator. It's one of the industry's favourite rip-offs, unsustained lead-in interest rates, that have caused the most trouble: after a lead-in period of a year or sometimes even less, some institutions have been cutting the rate back to an unbelievably measly 0.01% per annum, which equates to a return of 10p a year on a £1,000 balance. It's tempting to laugh at the sheer mean-spiritedness of this, but we're determined to resist the temptation and say that financial services marketing won't emerge from the Dark Ages until this kind of thing comes to an end.

In this gloomy landscape, there is still at least one much-praised and indeed awarded ray of hope, shining all the way from the other side of the world – a vivid demonstration of the fact that there is always opportunity for marketers smart enough to observe, and then to act upon, big, original customer insights. We refer, of course, to Aussie bank Westpac's Impulse Saver account, an app-based product that takes the form of a big red button on the screen of your phone: one press on the button, and a pre-set amount (anything from one Australian dollar to as much as you like) is transferred to your savings account.

This is not just a highly successful product, but also at another level probably the most effective pushback ever made against the irresistible force of our credit-driven consumer society. Impulse Saver doesn't fundamentally change the balance – what could? But in the age-old conflict between spending and saving, it does make sure the spenders don't get it 100% their own way.

TRAVEL INSURANCE

Well over a decade ago, in the early days of both digital and mobile, one of your authors did some work on a travel insurance startup where the big idea was that you switched the policy on when you set off on your travels, and switched it off on your return. This seemed like an obviously brilliant idea, providing a combination of simplicity and value for money that couldn't be matched by either single-trip or annual policies. But the startup didn't get funded, and as far as we know the product is still not available in the market. Is there a good reason? Or is this just another rather slow-moving backwater of the insurance industry, where providers are reluctant to explore the opportunities available for innovation?

TRAVEL MONEY (FX)

Hitherto something of a happy hunting ground for bad marketing – a sector in which attractive messages like 'commission free!' and 'buy-back guarantee' have distracted consumers' attention from the shockingly large spreads they're being charged.

Over the years, and across the channels, consumers have never been treated well when it comes to foreign currency. Travellers cheques, credit cards, bureaux de change and indeed banks making foreign currency payments have all taken advantage of the fact that travellers – especially holiday-makers – suffer from that dangerous combination of ignorance and apathy when it comes to what they're paying.

But digital may be changing things in this sector a little more quickly than in many others. A new wave of providers, including Transferwise, Revolut and Airmoney, offer much better deals and often better service than the leading players. It would be nice to think that, with some more visible and intrusive communication drawing people's attention to the far better deals available, this will be a rare example of a market where it's the good (travel) money that drives out the bad.

WEALTH MANAGEMENT

As the headline said in one of those great 1980s Albany Life advertisements, still one of the very best campaigns in the history of UK financial services advertising, 'I never had money problems until I had money'. As a proportion, there aren't many people in the UK who have money, but those who do need a lot of help managing it. In recent years, organisations of all shapes and sizes have flocked to offer their services under the 'wealth management' banner, a term virtually unknown until around the turn of the millennium. Now, the category is made up of all sorts of firms, including those that might equally be described as stockbrokers, private bankers, financial advisers, not-so-private banks, family offices, investment managers, discretionary asset managers, accountants, tax advisers and no doubt many others.

Intense rivalry and a good deal of snobbery separate these different sub-species, but in the end what unites them is much greater than what divides them: they help affluent people to look after their money, almost always with styles of services that are commensurate with high fees. This makes them quite fun from a marketing point of view, at least if your idea of marketing fun is taking affluent people to Glyndebourne.

And with that, we complete our stroll around a selection of the stalls in the retail financial services market. If there were some areas where we didn't linger, it was only because we didn't find much of interest to comment on.

No doubt you'll have been struck by the diversity of what's on offer. As we said at the outset, the range of product types, target groups and propositions is so wide that some say it makes no sense to talk about a 'retail financial services market' as a homogeneous entity at all.

But from a marketing point of view, we remain convinced that they do have much in common. For all sorts of reasons, and in all sorts of ways, the need for a new, stronger, more effective and much more customer-driven kind of marketing is something that's shared by all.

CHAPTER 6

Real People, Real Lives

The new financial services marketing requires us to make a lot of changes. Many of them are detailed in the following chapters. Some are changes that need to happen within marketing departments, and in the way that marketing people think and act. Some – generally the more problematic ones – need to take place more broadly, across financial services firms as a whole. They affect other departments, sometimes even all departments. And a number affect the thoughts and actions of senior management.

But the way we look at it, there's another kind of change that's needed. It's a kind of change that isn't really about specifics, although specific examples can be given. It's a change in the way that retail financial services people need to think about their customers, and about what it means to do a good job for them. It's a need to reconsider the balance of power, or the balance of authority, between industry and customer – a need, in the simplest and clearest terms, to recognise that in a genuinely customer-centric industry, the people on the inside really cannot go on acting on the basis that consumers are ignorant, stupid and prone to foolish behaviour, and therefore can be patronised, and treated with little respect, and need protection from the consequences of their own folly.

Few if any financial services firms – or individuals working in them – are likely to acknowledge that they think of their customers in this way. On the contrary, the very large majority say just the opposite. It's hard to find a firm that doesn't claim to be 'focused on our customers and their needs', or, more succinctly, to 'put its customers first'. We think there's often not a lot of truth in these claims. But even when there is, we still think the industry is prone to putting its customers first in a remarkably patronising way.

Back in the Mad Men era, legendary advertising man David Ogilvy warned the industry about its tendency to patronise with his famous comment: 'The consumer is not a moron, she is your wife'. Sixty years later, the gender bias in his words doesn't read well, but otherwise it's still a point that needs making to many in financial services. In a similar way, a present-day agency that has worked with one of your authors calls itself Mother, to remind its people of its raison d'etre. Would they be proud to show their mothers their work?

Several of the ideas that appear in this chapter also appear at various points elsewhere in the book. Even so, we think it's important to bring them together in one place to make one point with the maximum possible impact: we must not continue on the assumption that when our ideas are out of line with our customers, we're right, they're wrong and it's incumbent upon us to change their minds. If good marketing is about anything, it's *about taking customers as we find them, and working with them as they are*, not wishing – or, even worse, wrongly imagining – they were otherwise.

If it means anything, taking people as we find them must first mean getting to know and understand them well. Very often, this is made harder by the fact that our customers aren't much like us. Most of us in financial services earn much more than most of our customers, for a start. (Sometimes, of course, the reverse is true – the clients and prospects of some wealth managers and private banks earn very much more.) We start off on the wrong side of an empathy gap that takes some bridging. See if you can figure out what's going on in this anecdote.

A number of years ago one of your authors was working with Yorkshire Bank, trying to solve a mystery. Even during the busiest periods, many customers would join long queues in their branch to withdraw cash rather than use the ATM in the wall outside. Bank and agency staff couldn't understand it. Was it the Yorkshire weather? The friendliness of the counter staff? The length of the queues outside? It was none of these: the reason was that the machines dispensed only £10 and £20 notes and customers, managing their money carefully (particularly toward the end of the month), wanted to withdraw precise amounts – say £12 or £17 – to avoid overdrawing. That was possible only at the counter.

What follows is effectively a critique of a few of our most sacred cows, for which – since killing seems rather out of keeping with the spirit of our times – it would be a good idea to see if we can find new homes a long way from the industry.

1. Customers are absolutely right not to trust us.

Actually, it's not just us. They're right not to trust more or less everything and everyone, except on a very limited and highly selective basis. That doesn't mean to say that everything and everyone is untrustworthy, but the risk is high enough that people are wise to stay on their guard. As the late, great Groucho Marx said, 'The most important thing is trust. If you can fake that you can fake anything'.

Chapter 14 deals with the subject of trust in more detail, and develops the idea that trust comes in several different shapes and sizes. But for now, let's just say more generally that when we talk about 'restoring consumer trust in financial services', what we really mean is 'restoring consumer trust in *our* financial services'.

A moment's thought brings home the unlikeliness of this. If, say, a customer is (rightly) suspicious of every telephone call or e-mail purporting to be from a financial institution, why should any one company's messages be exempt? And, more important, would it be a good thing if they were? If scammers found a way to circumvent that institution's security process, the consumer's lack of trust would be the last line of defence.

And anyway, people in the industry don't really mean that sort of trust. They mean they want people to accept unquestioningly that the propositions they're putting forward would be good for them. Consumers would indeed be idiots, given previous experience, if they believed that.

2. Education isn't the answer.

Many people in financial services – including many marketers – have spent much or even all of their careers dealing with professional and/or business customers. You can often engage with groups like these in a fairly sophisticated way. They may well understand your propositions as well as you do – sometimes, even, rather dauntingly, better than you do. The engagement with them can be (or at least can seem to be, which isn't quite the same thing) a left-brain affair, an intelligent conversation dealing with the facts of the matter.

When people used to this sort of engagement find themselves dealing with mainstream consumer audiences (by which we mean anyone, young or old, affluent or not, who is *not* a member of the small segment who are exceptionally engaged with financial matters), the culture shock can be enormous. Suddenly, they're dealing with people who don't understand any of the concepts that could be taken for granted among the professionals. It's not just that these people don't understand the jargon – they don't get any of the simplest financial concepts. They don't know what a percentage is. They don't understand the idea of a share, or a bond or a dividend. They've never heard of an excess on an insurance policy.

It's not surprising if the first thought of industry insiders exposed to real people like these is that if only they could just be taken away for a few years and educated about all this stuff they don't get, then they could come back and we could start having a sensible conversation.

However, this simply isn't going to happen. Dealing with consumers means dealing with them as they are, on their terms and at their level, not waving a magic wand so that you can address them on yours. Consumers understand financial services about as well as they understand computers, phones and cars, and maybe a little less well than they understand food, travel and electrical appliances. None of these sectors engages with consumers perfectly – we don't subscribe to the view that everyone's brilliant at engaging with consumers except those of us in financial services. But they all fundamentally understand that the solution does not lie in getting their subjects added to the national curriculum so that future generations will know what they're doing.

On the whole, people get satisfactory outcomes when they venture into other market sectors like these mainly because those responsible for interacting with them do so on their customers' terms. Computers are probably a lot more complex than pensions,[1] and so understanding how they work would be a lot more difficult than understanding how a pension works. But understanding how to get a computer to do what you want it to do is generally a great deal easier than understanding how to get a pension to do what you want it to do – and that's because of what the IT industry has done to connect with its customers, not what customers have done to connect with the IT industry.

There's nothing wrong with education, and nothing wrong with seeking to improve financial literacy among young people (although judging by the difficulty we now have in remembering what we learned at school about photosynthesis and inert gases, we wonder quite how accessible people's learnings about, say, mortgage repayment vehicles would be at the moment when they needed them maybe 10, 20 or even 30 years later). But education is emphatically *not* the way to make our customers easier to engage with.

3. The expression 'Financial services are sold and not bought' is hugely misleading.

To be clear, as things stand it *is* often the case that financial services are sold and not bought, especially those financial services that don't meet an immediate or obvious practical need, and/or are very complex (like pensions). But even though it's often factually correct, there are two reasons why the expression is so hugely misleading.

First, it creates the impression that this is some kind of natural order of things – the sky is blue, water is wet and financial services are sold and not bought. It isn't a natural order of things at all. It's a choice

---

[1] Although, that said, the highly respected actuary Paul Bradshaw, until his untimely death one of the most brilliant thinkers in financial services and the man single-handedly responsible for many innovations in the field of pensions and investment, told one of your authors that he depended heavily on a financial adviser to look after his pension because he couldn't make head or tail of it.

we've made in the industry, to make these products available more or less entirely through salespeople, and to make them so complicated and difficult to understand that very few consumers have the confidence, expertise or indeed stamina to buy them without help.

The second and more infuriating reason why the statement is hugely misleading – indeed damagingly so – is its underlying assumption about human nature and human motivation. It's not explicit, but there's a clear implication that we don't choose to buy these things because we're feckless wastrels. We need the intervention of noble and clear-sighted financial salespeople to focus us on what really matters and save us from our profligate natures.

This may be good for the self-image of salespeople, but in every other way it's absolute rubbish. The idea beloved of financial services people that our customers are ill-disciplined hedonists and spendthrifts, foolishly flinging their disposable incomes at hard liquor, gambling, foreign holidays and immediate gratifications of one sort or another is a travesty of the truth. Very few people live their lives in the same way as that hugely talented but equally hedonistic footballer George Best, who of course famously said: 'Most of my money went on women, booze and fast cars. The rest I just wasted'. Most people spend most of their incomes on the absolute essentials of daily living – food, utilities, running a car, rent and mortgages – and a big chunk of what's left on necessary evils like getting the car serviced, new shoes for the kids, work-related travel and prescriptions from the chemist. If a small fraction of the family's income is spent on a meal out, and/or a holiday, and/or a Sky subscription so that the family's football fans can watch a game together, is the financial services industry really so joyless as to say that's wrong?

This is another of the big respects in which we look at the consumers in our marketplace, judge them and find them wanting. We will never be able to rise to the challenge of marketing the products and services we have for them until we stop doing this.

The next two sacred cows are smaller relatives of this very big and troublesome one.

4. <u>No financial service – not even life assurance – is an unquestionable good.</u>

This is to do with an idea that falls directly out of the previous one, and so is just as mistaken. In the industry, there's a remarkably widespread belief – arguably more than a belief, almost an article of faith – that many of the propositions we have to offer (life assurance is the example most often cited, at least for families with dependents like young children) represent a completely different and indeed objectively better kind of expenditure than any of those hedonistic pleasures to which consumers so often succumb. Buying life assurance isn't a choice or a preference: it's a duty. You're not discharging your responsibility to your family if you don't buy it. Some say there should be a government campaign encouraging or even possibly compelling people to do the right thing by their families, just as there has been for smoke alarms and seatbelts.

Sorry, but, again, rubbish. Life assurance is a perfectly good product. It has the advantage that it's one of the few financial services which, according to research, typically costs a lot less than people expect. There are undoubtedly examples of families for whom a life assurance payout was hugely beneficial at a terribly difficult time. And the strong consumer suspicion that life assurers will do everything they can to wriggle out of making payments is completely misplaced – a tiny proportion of claims is declined. All in all, we have nothing against life assurance at all.

But in a world of strain on household budgets, the idea that it somehow belongs in a different category of expenditure from kids' shoes, a family holiday or a Sky subscription makes no sense to us at all. All of these items, and countless others, represent choices about how to use some of the available money – to use the old-fashioned language of classical economics, about how to optimise utility. As in all consumer markets, you can find a segmentation to explain the choices that different people make. It may be that the particularly risk-averse forward planners put life assurance at the top of their list. Those who choose the family holiday may be . . . well, they may be hedonists, but they may just be people who work long hours and worry that they're losing touch with their children. And what if those 'kids' shoes' are actually new football boots for a child selected for a trial in the County under-13s?

Accurate figures are not available, but the number of parents aged, say, under 40 who die in any given year is tiny – a small fraction of 1%. (For a more compelling statistical argument, forget about life assurance – younger parents are much more likely to need Critical Illness or Income Replacement.) The real reason that many in the industry prioritise life cover is that it's a nice easy sell and it's not very expensive for healthy young people: any half-competent salesperson should be able to wind up the emotional temperature so that prospects would feel intense guilt if they declined. But the reality is that it's just another direct debit fighting for a place on the consumer's bank statement.[2]

---

[2] We don't think this way about products like motor insurance, which provide protection against occurrences that (a) happen frequently and (b) can do harm to entirely innocent third parties. There aren't many of these, but they do genuinely fall into a category which is different from family holidays and Sky subscriptions.

5. The huge majority of people will never voluntarily put enough into long-term savings.

Of the items in this list, this is probably the most widely recognised. But it's still important to draw attention to it – both for itself, and also because of what it says about our evasiveness and reluctance to level with consumers and tell them how things are.

The reality is that even if everyone now in an auto-enrolled pension stays in it as their contributions increase up to the maximum level of 8% in 2019 – and we strongly suspect that opt-out rates will increase quite sharply as people realise the implications for their incomes – it's still likely to fall a long way short of providing the sort of income in retirement they want and expect.

Of course the outcomes for individuals will depend on what happens to that cluster of ageing-population issues that include retirement age, investment growth, life expectancy and the cost of care. But still, on any reasonably imaginable assumptions, it's true. And, by the way, over the next 30 or 40 years or so, while millions of people are coming up to retirement with pots that are half-full, quarter-full or even less, outcomes will be a good deal worse. We haven't served consumers well in helping them envisage the reality of retirement in the new era of Defined Contribution pensions and rising life expectancy and healthcare costs, and it seems sure to lead to a lot of trouble.[3]

6. We have to get better at understanding what customers really value from us.

When we think no-one's looking, we've shown a remarkable ability to snaffle large amounts of our customers' cash in return for things that no-one – or at least very few people – value. PPI compensation is coming up toward £40 billion and counting. Some of the charges we've levied on banking, insurance and investment products – while never tripping over into full-scale mis-selling scandals – take the breath away.

But if we could just get a bit smarter, understand our customers better and segment our markets more intelligently, we could create far more positive, win/win situations where customers get something they value and we get to make money as a result.

PPI is in fact a good example. Lurking beneath the overpricing, opaque sales practices and mis-selling to customers ineligible to claim on their policies is a perfectly good product. A significant proportion of

---

[3] As a somewhat simplistic but nevertheless dramatic illustration of the problem, in the UK today the average DC pension pot at retirement is about £29,000. This will currently produce an income of about £1,500 per year.

borrowers would value this kind of insurance and would be quite happy to pay a fair price for it.

Elsewhere, we're convinced that there are great opportunities in many financial categories for premium products that offer high added value at much higher than average prices. We can hardly think of a consumer market where this isn't the case, and which can't be represented as a classic triangle where a large number of consumers buy at lower prices on the lower slopes, and a small number of consumer pay top dollar at the top.[4]

We're not thinking here specifically about services for people who have a lot of money. Of course there are plenty of these, especially in the areas of investment and wealth management. Of course there are examples of premium financial services brands, and some are very well known. You'd expect an account at Coutts to cost more than a High Street bank, and indeed it does. But there aren't many. If you draw up the pyramids for the various sectors of the market, you'll discover that the bases are very broad, and the peaks very narrow.

There's a reason for this, which is that a lot of influential people in financial services seem remarkably uncomfortable with the idea of a premium brand. The clearest example of this discomfort is probably vertically integrated advice firm St. James's Place. If you asked people in the industry to characterise the firm in one word, they would probably choose 'expensive' (or in two words, 'too expensive'). If, on the other hand, you surveyed a sample of St. James's Place customers, scarcely a single one would mention price. Instead, 98% would say something extremely positive – SJP has what may be the highest client satisfaction scores of any firm of its kind. What's happening here, as with so many of the points in this chapter, is that people in the industry are determined that they're right and consumers are wrong. We wonder if the same industry figures would also encourage people to stay in the cheapest hotels, eat in the cheapest restaurants and drive Dacia Sanderos.

In this particular case, the industry's insistence that it knows better than its customers is costing it a fortune. On the whole (with some exceptions), premium products sold at premium prices are more profitable than vanilla products. By failing to recognise consumers' preference for

---

[4]Where there are exceptions – and there a few – it's usually that the pyramid is upside-down, with the larger number of people choosing the premium product and the smaller number the more basic option. The premium BMW 3-series outsells the vanilla Ford Mondeo.

something better than the basic, we're depriving them of what they want – and ourselves of some good business.[5]

7. If it's not easy enough, it's not good enough.

A lot of people who work in financial services, especially in senior roles, are financially very sophisticated. Some, indeed, are actuaries. This means that their brains work quite differently from ordinary people's. It means they are capable of getting the best out of complex financial products that baffle and alienate most of us.

The same issue arises in every highly technical field. In the early days of home computing, when software as we now know it didn't exist, if you wanted your primitive Sinclair ZX80 to actually do anything – perform simple arithmetic, say, or play a game of noughts and crosses with you – you had to start by writing a programme to tell it how to do so. Most of us found this difficult, boring and far more trouble than it was worth. After a couple of failed attempts to write the 20-or-so lines of code in the noughts and crosses program, we put our primitive machines away, vowing never to even look at them again. It wasn't until several years later that Bill Gates came along and invented Windows, and we started to get interested again.[6]

The problem was obvious in hindsight. The capabilities of the machines were far too inaccessible for any more than a tiny segment of people to appreciate. If we'd all been cleverer, or keener, or had less of a life, we could all have had a lot of fun writing BASIC code and playing noughts and crosses to our hearts' content. But that's not how it was, and very, very few of us wanted anything to do with computers until clever Mr Gates, and equally clever Mr Jobs, made it easy enough for us to cope with (at least most of the time).

The same applies to many of our most ingenious ideas in financial services. The best single example is the flexible, or offset, mortgage. We're not going to get into an explanation of these clever but very

---

[5]It's not necessarily the ideal formulation, but even an obvious failing in the vanilla service can provide a basis for a premium proposition. At a number of UK airports, the queues for security are so long that the operators charge up to £5 for a premium fast-track alternative. The fact that the existence of the premium option creates an obvious conflict of interest for the airport operator is a bit troubling, but no-one seems too bothered. There's an obvious analogy here for organisations operating call centres.

[6]At the same time there were a few nerdy boys at school (it mostly was boys) who loved this program-writing business and while we were all wanting nothing more to do with the stupid things went off and wrote the first versions of Super Mario and Grand Theft Auto.

complicated products – too many readers will glaze over, or, more likely, just give up and go check their phones. But, believe us, for most people who need a mortgage and also have savings, an offset mortgage is an absolute no-brainer. Over the course of a year, it will leave you hundreds if not thousands of pounds better off. There is no downside.

Except . . .

They're complicated. Offset mortgages are hard to get your head round. There's weird new jargon involved, like *overborrowing*. And when you've mastered that, you have to do stuff. You have to move money in, and out again, on a regular basis. You can't just leave it and set up a monthly direct debit. You have to work to make money.

So, inevitably, most of us can't be bothered. We have a look at a brochure or a website, don't get it, don't understand these overborrowings, and decide we'd rather have an ordinary mortgage.

8. On a similar subject, we really could start using language a lot better.

It's not just all the jargon, and all that dreadful, stilted, dead financial language. Firms have at least been trying, with some success, to get rid of the worst of that for a long time now. But to be honest, what has taken its place isn't much better. It's always dangerous for authors to embark on the pot/kettle challenge of criticising writing styles, but can anyone think of a single firm in retail financial services that really uses words well? Can you name one whose writing you could describe as a pleasure to read? Or even one that has a consistent tone of voice that you'd be able to recognise?

To be fair, there is an emerging generation of digital services making fresh attempts to tackle this problem, and the result is a new kind of digital writing that is fairly different from the old-time off-liners – more conversational, more natural, shorter, smarter. Only thing is, again, within its category, it's all the same. It's difficult, or indeed impossible, to distinguish the tone of voice of any one of these new digital brands from any other.

9. Digital comes first, and mobile comes first within digital.

Talking of emerging digital brands, this point isn't news to them – but it's still big news to many others. Overwhelmingly, with only a few exceptions, the established players in the industry still conceive of financial services on paper. Even when they aim to make them accessible digitally, they still typically envisage digital pieces of paper. Think of an online bank or card statement: most are just offline bank statements viewed on a screen. The coming of digital was about more than saving money on stamps.

While that's been apparent for a long time, the supremacy of mobile is emerging with great speed. Too many firms are still starting on paper, then optimising for computer, then optimising for phone. Going forward, it has to be the other way round.

Some readers will have found little that's new in the mini-harangues in this chapter. 'For goodness' sake', we hear some saying, 'does anyone really think education might be the answer'? Sorry if you were one of them. But even if you were already up with the individual points, or most of them, we think that together they still deliver a collective message: that if we're going to get better at marketing, we really do need to think more honestly, more realistically and more perceptively about our customers.

Research shows a widespread sense among consumers that the financial services industry really doesn't 'get' them – that while the front-line staff in branches and call centres are often pleasant enough, the people that you don't get to see belong to a slightly different species that may have been quite well briefed on ordinary life but hasn't actually experienced it.

This feels uncomfortable to consumers, and it must also have damaging consequences for the industry. Some of our biggest and smartest ideas can just miss the mark, go off half-cocked, never really find the market for whom they were intended.

Going forward from here, getting rid of that gap between industry and customers is going to mean getting rid of a long list of the clichés, assumptions and items of received wisdom which shape so many of our thoughts about real people living in the real world. Tackling the small selection in this chapter would be a good place to start.

CHAPTER 7

Cutting in the Middle Man

You can't make much sense of the UK retail financial services market and the changing role of marketing in it, past, present or future, without considering the role of intermediaries – and, specifically, intermediaries giving one sort or another of financial advice.

Over the years, intermediaries like these have played a central role in most sectors of the market, the only major exception being retail banking.[1] And as a result, the defining relationship at the heart of most of personal finance has been a triangle, in which the three corners are represented by manufacturers, intermediaries and consumers.

Those with any knowledge of game theory will react with immediate suspicion to any sign of a triangular relationship. A key principle is that in any game where three parties are involved, two will usually gang up on the third. And in a market where consumers don't have much power or authority, and where costs and charges have historically been opaque, many won't hesitate to take a view about who'll be doing the ganging up – and on whom.

We'll come to that. But let's start with three general points about the intermediated shape of the market.

1. In principle, there's nothing very unusual about it. You could say exactly the same about the way that most other sectors of the consumer economy are organised, except that instead of the word 'intermediary' you'd probably use the word 'shop'.
2. Even within the most intermediated sectors, there are, and always have been, firms that distribute directly to their customers. For example, ever since the days of the famous 'Man from the Pru' (Prudential), who came round on his bicycle to visit his policyholders and collect their premiums every week, a number of so-called 'industrial branch' insurance, life and pensions companies were for many years, as we now describe it, 'vertically integrated', playing the role of both manufacturer and intermediary.

---

[1] It's very different in business banking, which is heavily intermediated. Brokers and accountants play important roles.

3. And when there are triangular relationships between provider, intermediary and consumer, they can vary enormously just as they can in other parts of the consumer economy, and don't lend themselves well to generalisation. Imagine an analogy from a completely different industry – say, for instance, bread and baking. All sorts of firms bake bread, from machine-made white sliced to hand-crafted sourdough; all sorts of 'intermediaries' make it available to the public, from supermarkets to specialist bread shops to sandwich shops and restaurants; and all sorts of people buy it and eat it. There's at least as much variation in the world of pensions, or insurance, or mortgages, and this chapter will over-generalise about 'intermediated' markets – it won't be difficult to find exceptions to almost every point it makes.

The first question about intermediated markets is why they're structured in this way at all. On the face of it, the intermediary is just an unnecessary complication, a link in the value chain that could perfectly well be dispensed with. Why don't more product providers deal more directly with their customers?

Apart from the fact that some indeed do, the principal answer to this question is one of those sweeping over-generalisations: on the whole, intermediaries have established their position in the value chain on the basis of their ability to add value to both the other parties involved. End-customers perceive that intermediaries help them find a way through the complexities and technicalities of confusing and worrying market sectors. And product providers rely on them to help them find customers, and then sell their products to them. In a sales-focused industry, they've been the best salespeople.

As we said back in the first couple of chapters, the industry's enthusiasm for selling largely explains its lack of enthusiasm for marketing. Sales and marketing can and indeed should work seamlessly together, but more often than not they're seen as alternatives. When it comes down to it, for many product providers it's a choice between business models: do you spend the available margin on motivating salespeople (that is, more often than not, intermediaries) to sell, or on encouraging customers to buy?

As a result, it seems to us that the industry's reliance on sales-oriented intermediation has largely acted as a brake on marketing, at least as far as end consumers are concerned. But as we shall go on to discuss in this chapter, we think that intermediation is changing – both in itself and in the relationships between intermediaries and manufacturers – and that as a result of these changes we're evolving into a very different kind of intermediation that is much less sales-driven, and where marketing to end consumers, both on the part of manufacturers and indeed on the part of intermediaries themselves, has a much greater role to play.

THE INTERMEDIARY MARKET TODAY

The UK intermediary market, which dominates the distribution of pensions, investments, life assurance and mortgages, is a very odd place.

In a country with an adult population of around 50 million, it's odd that a mere 24,000 or so financial advisers should maintain such a tight grip on the distribution of regulated financial services. The intermediary channel still accounts for something like 70% of mortgages, and similar proportions of investments and life assurance policies.

(To put the same point the other way round, it's odd that by contrast, the country's largest consumer-facing financial services providers, the banks, have so little business in these areas. For example, in continental European markets like Germany and Italy banks have hugely dominant market shares in the field of investments, while in the UK they are minor players.)

It's odd that the cost of the financial advice process required by the regulator is so high that by common consent it's only sensibly affordable for something like the most affluent 10% of the population.

Especially in view of these cost pressures, it's odd that advice is still delivered almost entirely face to face, and not either remotely (for example by telephone) or digitally. One to one, face-to-face advice is the most time consuming and therefore expensive way you could possibly distribute financial services – surely it can't make sense to rely on it so heavily?

It's odd that the number of financial advisers has fallen so sharply in recent years, from well over 200,000 just 30 years or so ago – especially during a period in which prosperity has increased and, crucially, individuals have experienced an ever-increasing obligation to take responsibility for their financial well-being.

It's odd that today's advisers almost all work as either self-employed individuals or in tiny micro-businesses employing small handfuls of people. Businesses that may look substantial from a distance, like Openwork, Sesame, Tenet, Intrinsic and St. James's Place, turn out on closer examination to be structurally much looser than they appear. Most are so-called 'networks', providers of centralised services of one sort or another to their huge numbers of micro-business 'members'.

It's odd that there are no specialist advice brands with any kind of significant consumer awareness.

It's odd that while the coming of digital has had a big effect on advice firms' processes, so far it has had very little effect on the structure of the industry. You might imagine there would be close parallels between financial advice and a longish list of other sectors made up of small firms that have been completely transformed, and not usually in a good way, by digital – examples like perhaps travel agents, recording studios, bookshops, even opticians. But so far, advice remains remarkably untransformed.

And finally, it's odd – at least at first thought – that very large and sophisticated product providers, including the large majority of the country's life companies, asset managers and mortgage lenders, should have been ready for so long to depend on such extraordinarily fragmented, mostly amateurish and ramshackle distribution.

Unpicking all the reasons why the distribution of regulated financial services is the way it is in the UK would be a big, complicated task some distance beyond the scope of this book. We'd need to consider the evolution of the industry over a long period of time: it is what it is today because of what it used to be in the past. But – again as a sweeping generalisation – a single key reason stands out: over the years, this has been a sales-driven industry, where successful sales have been rewarded by commission.

Commission-based selling is a tough way to make a living, and not many people can do it well. It's also a relatively solitary way to make a living: good salespeople need some admin support and backup, but they don't generally fit well into corporate structures, even if only because they want their remuneration to be based on their own personal performance. And needless to say it's a role that requires a great deal of personal, one-to-one contact with clients – very little of it can be done remotely or online.

Factors like these go a long way to explaining why the industry grew up as it did. There's one key reason why there are so few successful advisers, why they tend to work on either a self-employed or micro-business basis, why so much of their work is face to face and, indeed, why these people still command such dominant shares of their key market sectors: these are all important characteristics of commission-driven sales. And for about 50 years, from roughly the mid-1960s until 2014, the large majority of financial advisers were remunerated almost entirely by commission.

This is not to say that commission was ever the only club in the product providers' bag: they always had other means available to seek intermediaries' support. With commission rates tending to converge, and also with the regulator starting to display an increasing interest in the quality of the advice given and the suitability of the products recommended, these 'other ways' increasingly included a number of forms of intermediary marketing. Building unique benefits into the design of a product, for example, has often proved an effective way to motivate advisers to recommend it over its competitors. And there were opportunities to achieve competitive advantage to be found across all of the seven Ps – Product, Price, Place, Promotion, People, Process and Physical Evidence, as you'll doubtless remember.

Some of the intermediary marketing strategies adopted by providers worked powerfully to the benefit of consumers, but it has to be said that the benefits to consumers were often marginal and the benefits to advisers frequently much greater. Sometimes this was simply because the benefits on offer were designed with advisers' needs uppermost in mind: all other things being more or less equal, for example, it's not unreasonable for an adviser to prefer to recommend a product from a provider known to offer particularly smooth, efficient, error-free administration. On other occasions the benefits in question worked ostensibly to the benefit of the adviser's client, but actually served to provide justification for the advice, in case it was ever needed. Critical illness insurance, for example, went through a rather silly period in which providers offered to insure longer and longer lists of increasingly obscure conditions, not really because anyone was very likely to fall ill with dengue fever but more because an adviser recommending that provider's product couldn't be criticised if someone did.

A great deal of marketing communication was also deployed to support intermediary distribution. Much of it of course targeted intermediaries themselves, and an extraordinarily large and vigorous sector of trade media emerged to soak up the intermediary advertising budgets of the dozens of providers vying for their attention.

Some firms also spent large amounts of money targeting intermediaries' end-clients, on the basis that intermediaries were more likely to recommend firms whose names were known to their clients (and it was even better if from time to time a client actually requested a product from a particular provider by name). From the point of view of advertising agencies creating these campaigns, though, it's regrettable that no hard evidence to prove the effectiveness of this strategy has ever become available.

Meanwhile, in one large market sector, intermediaries steadily lost market share from the mid-1980s onwards. This was general insurance – motor in the first instance, and home and other smaller categories like travel and pet insurance subsequently. Their market share was taken by a rapidly growing group of telephone-based direct insurers, led by Direct Line, leaving brokers in a position of strength only in the small non-standard sector. As we argue elsewhere, this was one of financial services' greatest marketing triumphs, with propositions that competed effectively across all seven of the Seven Ps. But elsewhere, it was more or less business as usual for another 30 years.

Looking back on this lengthy era, it's hard to know quite what view to take. There's no doubt that many consumers were and still are well-served by their financial advisers, who helped them maintain their personal finances in very much better shape than they would have done otherwise. It's also true that even more consumers believed they were well-served by their financial advisers and expressed high levels of satisfaction when asked about them, which can be a very different matter: one of the key skills of the best salespeople is to build confidence among their clients.

On the other hand, it's also true that a lot of consumers were badly served by advisers, who pocketed unjustifiable quantities of their money in return for questionable advice, often involving the recommendation of not-very-suitable products paying high commissions.[2] Overall, the commission era was one in which end-customers paid very high charges to providers and advisers alike, and there was very little price competition in any part of the market. Those suspicions among game theorists that the market basically involved providers and advisers ganging up on clients seem widely borne out by the facts.

And of course while many advisers' clients received poor value for money, a much larger number of people received either no advice at all, or very little. Not unreasonably, the advice industry has never had much interest in serving individuals with little money.

In the end, the FSA's[3] concerns about the danger of commission bias, and more generally about the quality and suitability of advice, led to the package of reforms required by the Retail Distribution Review (RDR) and implemented at the start of 2014. The most notable of these was the banning of commission on investment products, and its replacement with so-called Adviser Charges to be paid by the end-client.

Some have argued that even this hasn't really made much difference. They point out that the levels of Adviser Charges are very similar to the average levels of commission paid previously (typically 3% of the value of the investment up front, and then an ongoing charge of at least 0.5% p.a., and often more). And they also point out that clients' awareness of these charges remains low, mainly because they don't actually have to pay these amounts personally. The rules allow so-called Provider-Facilitated Adviser Charging, which basically means that the charges can be deducted from the value of the client's investment and paid to the adviser by the provider. Clients typically see no more than a line of detail in a statement that they probably don't read anyway.

All this is true, but it misses the point. The point is that at a stroke, by switching the responsibility for remunerating the adviser from provider to

---

[2]In particular, the enormous sales of lump-sum investment bonds through financial advisers were widely suspected to be a consequence of the stratospheric levels of sales commission available, often up to as much as 7% of the client's investment.

[3]The process that led to the introduction of the changes required by the Retail Distribution Review (RDR) in January 2014 was originated by the Financial Services Authority (FSA) but completed, following the shake-up of UK financial regulation, by its successor the Financial Conduct Authority (FCA) which came into being in April 2013. We refer to the FSA when discussing events pre-April 2013, and the FCA when discussing events occurring later.

client, the new rules removed the principal lever that providers had used to manage and control the adviser market. In fact, forget 'levers' – it was as if the steering wheel had been removed from the car.

So far our story has focused on the role of sales commission in shaping the nature of the intermediary market, and maintaining a sales-driven model in which individual advisers took control of their remuneration effectively by choosing what to sell and to whom.

But in fact its abolition coincided with other important developments that also played an important part in helping a new financial services distribution framework to begin to rise, like a slow-motion phoenix, from the ashes of the old one. These developments can be found in all of the segments of what used to be a PEST (political, economic, social and technological) analysis, and has now expanded to become a PESTLE (with the addition of legal and environmental factors):

1. In parallel with the RDR, *the FCA has become increasingly concerned about the quality, and particularly the suitability, of investment advice.* This concern has led to new requirements for a much more rigorous and wide-ranging process, exploring the client's needs and circumstances in more detail and analysing the investment marketplace more thoroughly – changes that, while well-intentioned, have inevitable consequences for the cost of the advice to the client, and also for the depth of resource needed by the firm delivering it.
2. At the same time, in the Technology quadrant, *a wave of innovation has recently been transforming the basic processes of advice.* Perhaps the single most important of these is the introduction of investment platforms, one-stop digital services where advisers can buy, sell and manage all their clients' investments and which allow for much simpler, more effective and lower-cost control of clients' portfolios.
3. In the Political quadrant, *2014's Pensions Freedom reforms dramatically changed the advice needs of people at and after the point of retirement,* especially the steadily growing number with some or all of their retirement savings in DC pensions. Whereas previously most had required little more than a relatively simple one-off annuity purchase, the new rules allow everyone to remain invested indefinitely through their retirement years – and therefore raise all sort of big and hugely important issues about what those investments should be. No single rule-change has ever done as much to increase the need for ongoing, rather than transactional, advice.
4. At almost exactly the same time, important *rule changes affecting workplace pensions* have also come into effect. The auto-enrolment initiative has resulted in a huge increase in the number of people contributing

to workplace schemes, and therefore to a huge new potential market for advice in the workplace – a market further stimulated by new rules enabling employers to arrange advice for their employees on a tax-privileged basis, although at the same time arguably somewhat clouded by the fact that the majority of these new pension investors are earning, and contributing, far less than the minimum level likely to attract most advisers.

5. And as chance would have it, at much the same time again, a large proportion of the principals in small advice firms are more or less simultaneously reaching *the point where they're ready to retire*.[4]

Coming together over a short period of time, this complex combination of factors is bringing about major change in the advice business, to reset relations between advice firms and providers and to trigger a period of steady but very significant change in the way that the industry engages with consumers – not least in the nature of its marketing activities towards them.

Inevitably these changes are taking some time to work their way through the system, so at the time of writing it's difficult to predict the shape of the industry in, say, two, five, or 10 years. Still, bringing together some current realities, some clearly established trends and a little bit of crystal ball-gazing leads to some thoughts on how the intermediated sector is developing. From this, the changing role of marketing will emerge.

1. *The advice industry is rapidly consolidating.* No doubt some of the old-style cottage-industry micro-businesses will survive, but on the whole advice is now becoming too difficult, too expensive and too risky for very small firms to provide on their own.

2. *High-net-worth (HNW) individuals will get better advice, better service and better value.* The RDR works entirely to the benefit of people with money. Much greater transparency about charging, the requirement to provide ongoing service in return for an ongoing charge, higher professional standards and more robust advice processes all work to the advantage of this group. What's more, almost every advice firm wants to work for these people: gradually competition will drive quality up and prices down.

---

[4]There is a reason for this. Back in the late 1960s and 1970s there had been a huge spike in the number of young salespeople coming in to the advice business as a result of the introduction of unit-linked assurance and the aggressive growth of direct sales companies like Abbey Life, Hambro Life and Allied Dunbar: now, some 40–50 years later, these people are coming to the end of their careers.

3. *Much less of the whole advice process will happen face to face.* Technology has arrived in the nick of time to tackle the horrendous cost of delivering advice. We're cautious about the potential of 100% digital (or even 90% digital) robo advice, but we're in no doubt that much of the process can be digitised and handled remotely.[5]

4. *It'll all get better and better for DIY investors.* It's already pretty good for the relatively small number of highly engaged individuals who enjoy actively looking after their personal finances. They have a large number and wide range of largely digital services already available to them, some of which meet their needs brilliantly while others offer exceptionally low charges. (There aren't quite so many that do both.) With technology becoming more powerful, and with price pressures increasing across the value chain, the potential is for even better services at even lower cost.

5. *For the majority, the workplace will become the main focus of their financial lives.* Actually, that's not expressed very well. In purely practical terms, it's nothing to do with the physical environment of the workplace, and most people will look after their finances at home. But for many, the workplace pension will act as a core financial relationship, and will also provide access to an online hub, or platform, that can broaden the relationship (and also, in many cases, a source of employer-subsidised advice).[6]

6. *The boundary between 'regulated' and 'non-regulated' advice will become increasingly blurred.* The EU's PSD2 (Payment Services Directive), implemented in January 2018, enables consumers to choose, if they wish, to share their banking data with other financial services firms. For advice firms, in particular, the opportunities of really understanding their clients' financial lives and advising on the basis of far deeper and more insightful analysis is potentially transformational.

---

[5] We're equally sure that most clients will be entirely happy with this. It's often said that it's only young people who are really comfortable with digital services, but actually the same goes for a lot of old buffers like your authors, both of whom lead more of our lives online than our children do.

[6] Actually, on closer examination, this point is more complicated than it looks. With employees' average length of service steadily falling, many financial services (including pensions) will start off with a strong connection to a workplace, but within a few years that connection is likely to be broken. Workplace pension arrangements may be transferred to new employers, but the same is much less likely to be true of other financial products and services acquired during the previous employment. These may well move from the workplace to the employee's personal life, in much the same way that so many individual Private Medical Insurance customers are people who have left Group schemes.

7. *Outside the HNW and hobbyist markets, the separation between 'provider' and 'adviser' will largely disappear.* As providers acquire advice arms, this is already happening. Again this is mostly about money: increasingly, there just isn't enough margin in the process to provide worthwhile revenues for entirely separate manufacturing and distribution businesses. This will often mean that previously 'independent' advisers will have to make the move to 'restricted' status, but the truth is that hardly anyone cares about this except a dwindling number of independent advisers.

8. *The non-advised, D2C market will grow, and will provide much simpler and lower-cost solutions than anything currently available (even from Vanguard).* We fervently hope this is the biggest and most transformational item in this list of eight points. We strongly believe that over many years, the industry made an entirely conscious choice to achieve such complexity that it became frighteningly difficult for most consumers to make decisions and proceed without advice, and so we naturally believe equally strongly that when circumstances change, the industry can make a similarly conscious choice to do the opposite. Currently, the big, inspiring, agenda-setting example is auto-enrolled pensions. Drawing on key concepts from behavioural science, the success of these has much to do with the fact that individuals can expect good outcomes without having to engage with the process or make decisions or choices in any way at all – they can simply default their way through to a satisfactory solution. By comparison, all other direct investment services so far launched are too demanding and too complex (and, as a result, usually too expensive).

We're aware that this chapter, while ostensibly about intermediated financial services as a whole, has focused very largely on investments. The two other main categories where intermediaries play a major role are mortgages, and life and health insurance. The mortgage sector, in particular, has been affected by its own regulatory interventions, notably 2014's Mortgage Market Review (MMR); life and health insurance have been affected by regulatory change to a much lesser extent, being excluded from the scope of the RDR. Nevertheless, even if the particular combination of PESTLE analysis changes may differ, most of the seven points above will still apply:

■ *Consolidation* will happen across the intermediary sector, not only among investment intermediaries;
■ *High-net-worth individuals* will be better served with more tailored solutions that better meet their needs, and with a greater emphasis on ongoing relationships rather than transactional advice;

- *There will be a much greater digital component* to mortgage and protection advice;
- *DIY customers will have better access to a wider range of products and to online tools* to support their decision-making;
- *Employer-provided portals and platforms* will offer mortgage and protection propositions, ad will achieve an increasing share in these sectors too;
- *The same blurring of boundaries between provider and adviser* will certainly appear in protection – less so in mortgages, where lenders are much less involved in vertical integration (although you can of course argue that those with branch networks are in a sense 'vertically integrated' already);
- *The non-advised D2C market will grow*, providing extremely simple mortgage and protection solutions at very low prices.

In the unlikely event that all of these predictions are accurate, the big question is what it will all mean for marketing. In this chapter, the focus of this question falls on marketing addressed to intermediaries.

THE NEW INTERMEDIARY MARKETING

Marketing directed towards intermediaries is changing fast, and it will continue to do so. Two of the seven developments outlined above will bring about the biggest changes:

1. The process of *consolidation* in the advice industry will move the main marketing target away from individual advisers, most of them owner-managers in micro-businesses, and toward people in decision-making roles in bigger businesses. Consolidation, after all, results in large part from the fact that the advice process as defined by the regulator is increasingly too difficult and too complex to be left to the frontline adviser, and should be delegated upwards either to Head Office teams and/or to third-party partners of one sort or another: inevitably this must mean that this much smaller number of more sophisticated decision-makers becomes the primary target market.
2. Similarly, the drive towards *vertical integration* will increasingly reduce the requirement for any kind of marketing (or any kind of external marketing, anyway). When, say, a life, pensions and investments company acquires an advice capability – or, vice versa, an intermediary business creates a strategic partnership with an investment provider – then the aim will invariably be to provide product solutions that are

integrated with the advice process. At this point all sorts of operational and business integration issues arise (and must be tackled under the extremely watchful eye of a regulator who is distinctly dubious about such arrangements), but marketing activity, except in the broadest sense, no longer has a role to play.

The marketing consequences of these two trends are already clearly visible, particularly in the dramatic reduction in the volume of marketing communication addressed to individual advisers. Amazingly, most of the titles filling that magazine rack full of trade publications still exist, but it's hard to understand how some are carrying less advertising in a quarter than they used to carry in a week.

This is not to say that at the time of writing, providers have completely given up on the frontline financial adviser. For one thing, the process of consolidation is still far from complete, and there are still several thousand small firms where the business owners and decision makers are providing frontline advice. And for another thing, while the overall responsibility for product selection increasingly lies elsewhere, individual advisers often still retain some freedom to make the final selection from a buy list.

All the same, there's no doubt that expenditure on marketing to individual advisers has fallen sharply, and the emphasis now falls much more heavily on a combination of low-cost digital activities, and live events that can be closely co-ordinated with sales. At any given moment in the working day, you can be sure there are groups of advisers gathered together in the conference suites of hotels on city ring roads around the country, nibbling croissants or canapes at events at which experts from, or at least paid for by, product providers hold forth on topics like the outlook for the markets, the implications of Brexit, what advisers need to know about new data regulations and (particularly if addressed by one of your authors) how to build advice brands.

But while providers[7] have cut back their marketing to frontline advisers, they're absolutely carpet-bombing their relatively newly constructed and shortish lists of decision-makers – people in the Head Offices of advice firms, members of investment committees, discretionary fund managers, platform fund selectors. To be on these lists means never having to buy a meal or a drink ever again – and to be so saturated with content marketing initiatives of one sort or another that if you spent every minute of every day reading the material that's intended for you, you wouldn't have got through half of it by bedtime.

---

[7]We're using the word 'providers' here in its broadest sense, to include any business providing things to intermediaries and/or their clients, whether products, or technology, or expert analysis, or services of any kind.

This isn't, needless to say, just about communication, although there is a colossal amount of it. It's about a 360-degree marketing effort that starts with product, and reaches out to these individuals from every angle. And when most sectors of the provider market remain as extraordinarily overcrowded as they still are today, the total volume of activity is simply enormous.

Some sectors have become less crowded recently. The number of life and pensions companies is already much reduced – counting only those that are open for new business, for example, the number is down by 75% in 30 years. The number of mortgage lenders has fallen less dramatically, but is still much reduced – the number of building societies, for example, has fallen by just over half since 1990, largely as a result of the financial pressures that have so greatly thinned their ranks. In asset management, though, a combination of fat margins, low overheads and low barriers to entry have kept the forces of consolidation largely at bay – at the time of writing there are over 530 authorised managers of ISAs in the UK, for example – and with the regulator having recently started to take an extremely critical look at the level of charges, and the value for money, offered by asset managers, you can't help suspecting that the Golden Age is now drawing slowly closer to the end.

This will be a good thing for everyone except the fund managers on the wrong end of consolidation programmes, and arguably the providers of meeting rooms in ring road hotels, who will find the number of bookings for meeting rooms and croissants reducing inexorably.

Meanwhile, the problem as far as marketing is concerned is not so much the industry's overwhelming tendency towards herdlike behaviour, but more the sheer size of the herd. It made sense, for example, with the coming of Pensions Freedom, for asset managers to respond to the new need for income-producing decumulation funds – but what makes less sense is the fact that in the last couple of years we've seen the launch of over 300 of them. In the Innovation category in the 2016 Financial Services Forum Marking Effectiveness Awards, discussed at some length in Chapter 19, all but two of the entries were to do with funds like these: it would be fair to say that after reading them all, the judges' main reaction was confusion about which particular multi-asset strategy belonged to which.

The sheer size of the herd is fairly awesome when it comes to new product development, but even more so when it comes to other forms of marketing – perhaps most of all content marketing initiatives. To say, for example, that asset managers publish investment-related White Papers daily would be a huge understatement: hourly would be closer to it. And of course content marketing uses other media too. There are literally thousands of interviews with fund managers on YouTube, and not many fewer podcasts on iTunes – and the consequence of this vast oversupply is clearly apparent, with most of those videos clocking up no more than a few hundred views, and many only a few dozen.

But while a fair amount of this material is more or less relevant to its target group, very little of it reflects the three other key attributes for marketing success. *Very little of it stands out* and achieves really exceptional visibility; *very little of it is differentiated* from all the rest of it, or really contributes to a differentiated sense of what the firm in question stands for; and *very little of it is part of a consistent, integrated programme* intended to build specific, defined perceptions and so lead to specific, defined behaviours over time.

In short, what we think is most needed in provider-to-adviser marketing is a much stronger big-picture focus on *brand differentiation*. Most firms adopt many of the trappings of brands – consistent typography, colour palettes and the rest of it – but very, very few project any distinctive sense of who they are, what they're for and how they're different. As a result, the market is densely and confusingly crowded with vast amounts of activity, but there's very little trace of strategy to be seen.

In this respect, although the implementation is entirely contemporary, the underlying strategic imperative of the new intermediary marketing is a much more traditional one. As marketing plays an increasingly central role in orchestrating relationships between intermediaries of one sort or another and providers of one sort or another, it must evolve from the much more limited 'marketing services' role where its main purpose was to provide material to support commercial relationships based on commission and managed by salespeople. The first responsibility of intermediary marketers going forward is to take responsibility for defining, developing and maintaining their organisations' intermediary brands.

CHAPTER 8

Introducing the New Financial Services Marketing

The first section of this book has made three main points:

1. The retail financial services industry has been very successful over many years without the need for a great deal of marketing.
2. As a result, on the whole the industry isn't very good at it.
3. Things are changing, and the industry is going to have to improve if it's going to continue to succeed into the future.

The second and longer section will go on to paint a picture of what this improved marketing might look like. In this chapter, we briefly introduce the key components as we see them. But first, a summary of the current position as perceived by the respondents in our Financial Services Forum quantitative research.

The first part of the study asked some questions about the respondents as individuals, and particularly about their experience and expertise. Reflecting the make-up of the Financial Services Forum membership, they were a senior and experienced bunch: just over half had worked in financial services for over 20 years. We were impressed, too (and if truth be told, a little surprised) by the extent of their academic qualifications in marketing. Again a little over half told us that they had been educated to degree level (23%) or to postgraduate level (31%) in marketing. An even higher proportion, over 60%, told us that they had other university qualifications in business, 31% to degree level and 31% as postgraduates. We should emphasise that these findings reflect the profile of Forum members rather than the financial services marketing community as a whole, but certainly they suggest that there's no shortage of academic firepower in the industry.

It's also important to note, before we explore the views of respondents on the quality of their efforts, that the large majority work in businesses that target end consumers, either wholly (12%) or in part (63%). Only a quarter work for firms that don't target end consumers at all, mainly because they rely on employers or intermediaries to reach their customers on their behalf.

In Chapter 2, we looked in some detail at respondents' perceptions of the role of marketing, both in theory and in practice, in their current firms. Using the familiar Seven Ps as a way to define the territory, we said that there was no consistent view on the theoretical scope of the role that marketing should play – but there was a somewhat more consistent (and disappointing) perception that in real life, at present, the only one of the seven areas that clearly falls within the remit of the marketing department is 'promotion' – in other words, marketing communications.

This very narrow view was reflected again in respondents' reactions to one of a number of attitude statements that we explored in the research. We asked them to what extent they agreed with the statement 'People in financial companies understand that marketing means much more than just communications'. Only 3% agreed strongly with this, and only 25% agreed at all. The large majority, clearly, believe that their colleagues think of marketing more or less entirely in terms of communications. That old colouring-in department stereotype is still alive and well.

This was part of an overall assessment at least as downbeat as anything we've covered in our earlier chapters. For example, when presented with the statement 'Very few financial services providers are really committed to marketing', 60% agreed and only 20% disagreed (and of those, only one single individual disagreed strongly). And when asked for their response to the statement 'On the whole, the quality of marketing in financial services is lower than in other service industries', those who agreed (54%) outnumbered those who disagreed (27%) by two to one.

At least in part, respondents thought this was for the simple reason that marketing is harder in financial services than in other service industries. They agreed with a statement to this effect by 49% to 28%. And we weren't surprised to find an even more widespread belief that marketing is harder in financial services than it is in fast-moving consumer goods (FMCG) – almost exactly half agreed with this, with only 22% disagreeing. (On the contrary, the figure that surprised us was the 22%. In our view, marketing in financial services is a very great deal harder, for all sorts of reasons, than marketing for products that you can eat, drink, drive, wear or apply to make you smell nice.)

But all in all, our financial services marketing respondents were remarkably critical of the status of financial services marketing, and this view played out consistently in other findings from the research.

Elsewhere in the study, we asked a question about our sample's perceptions of 'financial services providers in general.' To what extent, we wanted to know, did respondents agree that firms are 'close to their customers and understand them well'? Not to any very great extent, came the answer. Only 15% agreed (and of those, only 3% agreed strongly): at 61%, those disagreeing outnumbered them by four to one. Of all the findings in the research, this one seemed to us the most self-critical from the point of view of people in marketing departments: after all, whose job is it to ensure that firms are 'close to their customers and understand them well'?

The finding can only mean one or both of two things: either marketers are failing to do the work to achieve that kind of closeness and understanding, or they're doing the work but failing to share it with their colleagues. That's not brilliant either way.

In the same part of the questionnaire, we provided two more statements that generated similar responses. One proposed that firms 'care about their customers and consistently treat them well': 20% agreed with this, but 45% disagreed. (In hindsight, the question combined two ideas in a way that makes the responses hard to interpret – were our sample commenting on the level of care, or the consistency of treatment, or both?)

The other boldly proposed that firms 'are positively perceived by most of their customers'. Only 11% agreed with this, and 58% disagreed. This and the previous two findings demonstrate that the industry's self-perceptions are at least as negative, and maybe even more so, than the perceptions of customers as we report in our chapter on the subject of trust, Chapter 14.

That said, we make the point in that chapter that consumers tend to feel much more positive toward their own providers than toward the industry as a whole, and the same is true of our sample of marketing professionals. As we said above, only 15% believe that firms in general are close to their customers, and 61% think they aren't: however, when the same people are asked about their own firms, 45% think they're close to their customers and just 32% think they aren't. Similarly, nearly 60% agree that they care about their customers and consistently treat them well while only 12% disagree (compared to the industry-wide figures of 20% and 45% quoted above). And 53% think their own firms are positively perceived by most of their customers, while only 11% think the same can be said of the industry as a whole. It's hard to know what to make of these findings, but there is a well-known research effect in which respondents have much poorer opinions of those around them than they have of themselves. Other studies have found, for example, that the huge majority of respondents believe that they're much better than average drivers, much nicer than average people and so on.

Still, in our marketing professionals study, such glimmers of positivity don't do much to lighten the overall gloom. Elsewhere, we asked respondents to what extent they thought their own organisations were customer-led, and in a finding that clearly suggests one of the most crucial areas for change in the future only 36% said their firms were 'pretty good at it': 52% thought their firms were 'not very good at it'.

And in another finding with obvious implications for the future, while 94% said that in their view a strong consumer brand was important for their business, very nearly half – 48% – believed that their organisation doesn't currently have a strong consumer brand. (Perhaps unkindly, we can't help raising an eyebrow at the 52% who believe their firms do currently have strong consumer brands. Unless these respondents were freakishly concentrated into a very small handful of institutions, we'd suggest there's a great deal of wishful thinking reflected in this figure.)

With 94% of respondents expressing a view that a strong consumer brand is either 'very important' (42%) or 'increasingly important' (52%) for business success, we can presumably expect to see a great deal of brand-building activity in the future.

In short, respondents in this study generally agree that on the whole, retail financial services firms don't have a strong marketing orientation, and haven't made much progress in tackling key marketing challenges like becoming consumer-led and building strong consumer brands.

Many, though, work for firms that have been consistently successful, and so help to substantiate our hypothesis that hitherto, good marketing simply hasn't been essential. If, for all the reasons we put forward in previous chapters, marketing is going to be a far more important component of future success in retail financial services, things are going to have to change.

THE NEW FINANCIAL SERVICES MARKETING

The second part of this book is made up of 12 chapters, each dealing with a key theme that we believe will characterise the new financial services marketing. We introduce each one with a question – a challenging question, asking how much progress in each area you, your team and your organisation have made.

But in providing a brief introduction to the 12 themes, there's one confession we need to make.

It would be nice if most of our themes, or maybe even all of them, came as huge surprises. We'd love it if every chapter heading raised startled eyebrows. But it isn't going to be like that. Few of our themes will be massively unexpected or unfamiliar to anyone with any current level of involvement in marketing, whether in financial services or elsewhere. Some, indeed, are often claimed to be deeply embedded in many firms already. Are we really saying, for example, that there's anything forward-looking or mould-breaking about a commitment to 'put customers at the heart of the business'? It's hard to think of a more clichéd expression. Or similarly, in the very first of our 12 chapters, we discuss the importance of corporate purpose – the need for organisations to be able to express a clear *raison d'être* above and beyond making money for their shareholders. We can hardly claim that's new, either.[1]

At least, *talking* about it isn't new. *Claiming* to have defined a corporate purpose, or for that matter to have made great efforts to put customers at the heart of the business, isn't new at all. We're now several years into a period in which senior managers in many firms – and not just in marketing departments – recognise that it would be kind of embarrassing *not* to make statements like these. These days, it would be a brave company that proudly claimed to take an entirely product-led approach, and to define its purpose exclusively in terms of the return on capital it provides to shareholders.

But of course *talking* and *claiming* are one thing (or maybe two things). *Doing* is quite another. At the moment, in financial services, we're in a curious kind of limbo – a halfway house where many firms publicly espouse many of the practices that go to make up good marketing, but few actually practise them.

(Actually, as we'll see in a moment, some of these practices are more espoused that others, but the general point stands.)

What are we to make of this state of affairs? An optimist would say that we're already halfway to our goal. If senior financial services people with backgrounds in accounting, actuarial, compliance, IT, risk, operations and all the rest of it are happily spouting the jargon of 'customers', 'purpose', 'mission', 'brand' and so forth, then the fact that their words currently lack substance is just the next issue to tackle.

A pessimist, on the other hand, would say that this has all gone horribly and maybe even irretrievably wrong. Non-marketers spouting marketing jargon have made the classic mistake of assuming that it's all just pink fluffiness, and if it goes down well with the media and the analysts there's no real harm done, provided that no-one actually has to change anything. Certainly the next chapter, which looks at corporate purpose, finds some fairly startling disconnects between some organisations' claimed purpose and some of their actual behaviours: it certainly doesn't look as if it has occurred to a lot of people that if the stated purpose is to be achieved, some sort of effort will be required.

---

[1] But that doesn't make it any less valuable. Many long-established theories about aspects of marketing still hold good today. For example, one of your authors remembers, verbatim, a lesson he learned in his first job in advertising almost 40 years ago, that 'the purpose of an ad is to attract and hold the favourable attention of the maximum number of the right sort of people whilst a selling story is told and a desired action or reaction created'. We haven't heard it put better since.

For our part, at risk of sounding boringly balanced about this, we feel sure that the answer lies somewhere halfway in between. There are undoubtedly a depressingly large number of deeply cynical organisations, and deeply cynical senior people within them, who are comfortable enough talking the marketing talk, but have no intention of taking even baby steps towards it.

On the other hand, there's a refreshingly and even inspiringly large number of committed idealists hugely committed to doing the right thing by the consumer, and these committed idealists aren't always the people you'd expect. At a conference recently, one of your authors sat next to a young and very idealistic delegate attending her first such event. She admitted she'd been dreading a series of dull and reactionary presentations by the speakers, all middle-aged men in suits. In fact, as chance would have it, this particular group of besuited middle-aged men all expressed far more radical and progressive points of view than the young delegate had expected. She left the event buzzing with enthusiasm for the industry.

Anyway, the point we're making is that the current phony war – the situation in which many organisations are paying lip-service to many of the big ideas in the new financial services marketing, but few are doing anything much to put them into practice – makes the next part of this book a bit tricky to write. We'll do our best to highlight the differences between pointless posturing, and the real thing.

The following chapters discuss these themes:

1. *How does your firm define its purpose?* We must admit that we're not massively convinced by the many modern business and management theorists who say that consumers are unwilling to engage with brands unless they see a clear sense of purpose that has meaning for them. Some consumers and some brands, maybe. But we're much more convinced that a clearly expressed over-arching purpose can play an important part internally, in recruiting, retaining and motivating people. And even more convinced that it can direct and guide marketing activity, in ways that hugely affect an organisation's ability to build and maintain a clearly differentiated position in the marketplace.

   Purpose doesn't mean much if it doesn't come from the top. When it's expressed in an empty slogan produced by the marketing team, or one of its external agencies, everyone knows it doesn't mean anything.

2. *Do you have a strong and distinctive culture?* Culture is a fairly close relative of purpose, but it's a bigger and broader thing that characterises the particular way that an organisation, and its people, go about doing the things they do. It's an idea that, mainly because of the regulator's focus on it, has definitely made a journey from the HR and marketing departments to the boardroom: C-suite executives may still be fairly unclear

on the subject about what it is, but these days they all know that they're responsible for it.

Our chapter makes some points about the importance of *distinctiveness* when it comes to culture. It seems to us that this is a dimension that can easily be overlooked even in good organisations that care a lot about their customers, and are concerned to meet their needs as best as they can. Marketers, we think, have a particular responsibility for the interface between brand and service that is central to the customer experience: does everyone in your organisation really understand how your way of doing things is supposed to be not just good, but different?

3. *How much is Big Data changing the way you do business?* Being halfway through a revolution is an awkward place to be. Most marketers now believe we're on the way to a future where data will be big enough, powerful enough and low enough in cost that we really will be able to run our businesses in customer-centric ways and achieve that 'one-to-one future' that Peppers and Rogers first told us about well over 20 years ago. To do so, we'll pretty much literally need to turn our businesses upside down and inside out.

But only a very small handful of firms have completed this journey, and many – especially bigger, older and more complicated ones – still have a long way to go. Continuously evolving a marketing approach to keep pace with a firm's data capabilities is far from easy: it's tough enough being half-pregnant, but even harder to be in that condition for what may well be decades.

4. *Do you get the real power of Behavioural Economics?* That may sound like a strange or even naïve question. Some very good marketing people – especially those with direct marketing backgrounds – have a distinctly Emperor's New Clothes attitude toward BE, saying that there's very little in it that a direct marketing guru like Drayton Bird wasn't doing 40 years ago.

At one level that's largely true, but it's completely missing the point. When Drayton said you should put a red flash on the envelope stating 'Respond Before 18th June!' it was just a direct marketing bloke saying so. When Daniel Kahneman says it, it's a Nobel laureate.[2]

Bear in mind the well-established principle that it's not what you say, it's who you are when you're saying it that matters, and you'll realise that the behavioural economist is, potentially at least, the very best friend of the marketing department. Read David Halpern's account

---

[2]Actually, Kahneman doesn't say anything quite so banal. But at least one other premier league behavioural economist does.

of his triumphant presentation to the assembled Permanent Secretaries of most of Whitehall's departments, and just imagine the kinds of budgets he could unlock if you could get him in to present to your Board.[3]

5. *Are you any good at innovation?* We think this is probably one of the book's more useful chapters, intended as a pocket guide to successful innovation, and also no less importantly as a pocket guide to avoiding unsuccessful innovation.

It's very big on ease and simplicity, saying that the trouble with a great deal of financial services innovation is that the people responsible are far too interested in financial services and assume too much enthusiasm and stamina on the part of their target markets. It's difficult to think of any products or services that have failed because they were too simple. It's very easy to think of a great many that have failed because they were too complicated.

6. *Are you really trying to 'rebuild consumer trust'?* It's not easy to say which is the most controversial proposition in this generally controversial chapter: that the loss of consumer trust in financial services is a good thing, that it would be impossibly difficult and expensive to get it back or that we can manage perfectly well without it.

In any event, we go on to argue that the real challenge for marketers is not 'rebuilding trust', but the much more achievable and subtle art of 'managing distrust' – finding ways to engage with consumers, build relationships with them and deliver products and services that meet their needs, while recognising the fact that we'll probably never overcome their deep suspicions and one false move at any moment can lose them forever.

7. *Call that a brand?* As we reported earlier in this chapter, just over half the respondents (52%) in our Financial Services Forum member research believe their organisations have strong brands. We say that unless by coincidence they all work for First Direct, Hargreaves Lansdown and a handful of others, that seems unlikely.

Anyway, for the benefit of the other 48%, we have a lot to say about the value and importance of brands, and some refreshingly straightforward and bullshit-free things to say about how you build them.

And we also pay a lot of attention to an idea that comes up in several other places too: brand, like so many other parts of the marketing agenda, is so incredibly much easier to manage in small, young, simple organisations than in big, old, complicated ones. (Actually, we go a bit further than this and say that in big, old, complicated organisations developing a strong, single master brand is probably impossible.)

---

[3] In his book *Inside the Nudge Unit*.

8. *Whatever it is, can you make it simpler?* In this short chapter, we make an appropriately simple point: that if the new financial services marketing is going to mean anything to consumers, we're going to have to keep it very, very simple. This admittedly overlaps with a key theme from our Innovation chapter (above), but it's a sufficiently important message that it's well worth saying at least twice.

Most of us aren't used to this. Many marketers trying to adapt to the new digitally oriented, consumer-facing world after careers spent targeting intermediaries, business markets and the small niche of highly engaged hobbyists have no real understanding of just how simple their efforts have to be. This isn't just a question of communication. Often it's the underlying concepts that have to be simplified, not just the words used to express them.

Rule of thumb: if you think you've now made it simple enough, you're probably halfway there.

9. *Are you just a little bit boring?* If there's one Achilles heel that most financial services marketers already recognise, it's the issue that we label in our jargon as 'engagement', a rather odd word little used in real life that means something like 'capturing and keeping people's attention'. There are many words that could be said to be the opposite of engagement – confusion, anxiety, lack of interest, impatience, distrust and, perhaps most often, plain and simple boredom.

In a chapter about as short as the previous one, but similarly heartfelt, we make a plea for financial services marketers to be less boring. People don't find money boring, but they do find us boring – almost all of us, and almost always. This is hopeless. Our new financial services marketing can't achieve anything at all if it can't capture and keep people's attention. Doing so is quite literally the first and most crucial challenge that we face.

10. *Does planning your marcomms seem horribly complicated?* As the punchline to the old joke (one of Woody Allen's, as we recall) would have it, only when you're doing it right. At the time of writing, out there in financial services marketing land the themes in these twelve chapters are at different stages of development, and this is already one of the furthest advanced: it's a long time since the days when the marketing communications mix for a financial services firm consisted of a TV awareness campaign, some product direct-mail packs, a suite of brochures and some trade press ads.

As we recall, even orchestrating and integrating that little list wasn't easy, and the list is several times longer today. This chapter reviews the main components, with varying degrees of enthusiasm. (It's probably at its most sceptical on the subject of content marketing, which, it says, as currently practised, is a way of wasting remarkable quantities of time, effort and money.)

11. *Yes, but can you* prove *it's working?* Another chapter making a simple, single, central point: we still need to get a whole lot better at measuring the effects of what we do.

At the moment, a few firms take measurement very seriously, quite a few dabble and many do little or nothing except capturing some irrelevant-but-free internet analytics. This is a situation that's symptomatic of the current status of marketing: if it isn't very important and doesn't have much effect on the business, it doesn't really matter if we measure it or not. But if marketing is now becoming very much more important, then by definition so is measurement.

It's important for two reasons: to guide the direction of future spending and activity, but also to substantiate the role and value of the function to colleagues across the business. Colouring-in departments don't really have much use for measurement. Marketing departments do.[4]

12. *Given the choice, wouldn't you prefer a Sky subscription?* In this last chapter, we take a step back from the financial services world to recognise the broader context in which consumers lead their lives and make their decisions. Understanding this context better must be another hallmark of the new financial services marketing: for as long as we continue to make arrogant and self-serving assumptions like, for example, that in some kind of ill-defined objective way it's actually *better* to buy life assurance than a Sky TV subscription, we'll never really get close enough to our customers.

And as a final thought, the superficially simple task of getting close enough to our customers is really what the new financial services marketing is all about.

That's the short version of what you're in for over the next couple of hundred pages. Here comes the long version.

---

[4] Although not always. One of us remembers working on direct marketing campaigns for a very large building society a few years ago. We had developed an impressively rigorous (and expensive) test-and-learn matrix to ensure we took the maximum learning from everything we did. However, the marketing director was a paid-up member of the JFDI tendency. We learned the lessons all right – but only some time after the next campaign had gone out.

CHAPTER 9

How Does Your Firm Define Its Purpose?

Time was when it wasn't difficult to grasp a company's core purpose – at least, the purpose of a public company with external shareholders. Such firms would invariably express their purpose in terms of their responsibility to those shareholders. Their primary responsibility, the management teams would say, was to deliver shareholder value.

Somewhere in their shareholder communications – perhaps most frequently in their Annual Report – most public companies still say this. And in terms of the formalities of corporate governance, it is of course still true. The first responsibility of a firm's management is to deliver value to shareholders: that is the basis on which the shareholders have agreed to put them, and keep them, in their posts.

Back in the proudly mercenary days of the 1980s, this was more or less all that a firm had to say about its purpose. In his book *Capitalism and Freedom*, economist Milton Friedman, favourite guru of the political right, wrote: 'There is one and only one social responsibility of business: ... to increase its profits'. In the climate of those days, saying anything else could sound feeble. In the heyday of privatisation, state-owned and mutual enterprises that were not driven by shareholder pressure seemed lazy and uncommercial. The introduction of private capital was widely perceived as a bracing, energy-giving development that could only improve performance.

(For some reason this widespread feeling spread right across the UK public sector with the sole, but significant, exception of the NHS. Many people deeply hostile to state ownership continue to believe that the health service must never fall into private investors' hands.)

However, over the years since the Gordon Gecko-driven lunch-is-for-wimps 1980s, things have changed. It has become increasingly clear that defining purpose solely in terms of shareholder value presents two big problems.

The lesser is that it sounds terrible to everyone else. If you take the view that the role of management is actually to try to achieve some kind of positive accommodation between shareholders, staff, customers and other stakeholders, then emphasising one of these constituencies to the exclusion of the other two gives a very bad impression.

But the greater is that in itself, it doesn't of course say anything at all about how this shareholder value is to be achieved. It's absolutely not in any sense directional, or aspirational, or motivational, or inspirational, or any other word ending in –ational. At a certain statement-of-the-bleedin'-obvious level it may remind the firm's management of the need to be financially successful, and perhaps at a slightly deeper level it reminds management that whatever it is that they're doing, have done or want to do in the future they need to be able to claim that it has helped, is helping or will help create shareholder value. But that's about all.

As a result, while creating shareholder value generally remains in place as the highest-level summation of corporate purpose, a considerable industry has grown up around the need to define purpose at the next level down: how is this value to be created? Virtually every firm now has something to say on this subject, and of course a huge amount has been written. One of the first to define this second level of purpose was management consulting legend Peter Drucker, who wrote as early as 1954 that 'There is only one valid definition of business purpose: to create a customer'.

As we shall see in this chapter, though, it remains a problematic area, and perhaps particularly so in the field of financial services. While some firms are certainly driven by clear and strong senses of purpose, many have made distinctly half-hearted or superficial efforts to define and articulate them. As a proof, if you asked a thousand people from a hundred businesses, it would be interesting to know how many of them could state their own business's core purpose. We'd pretty confidently guess that as usual when you ask people things, the outcome could be represented as a classic triangle – a few at the top who can quote it verbatim, a larger group in the middle who have a rough idea and a much larger group at the bottom who either don't know, or state with varying levels of confidence that their business doesn't have one.

What's more, among the verbatim-quoters, we're inclined to think that there wouldn't be an awful lot of difference between the purposes they came up with. Most, we strongly suspect, would consist of highly polished forms of words expressing the firm's determination in one way or another to work for the betterment of humanity, or at least that part of humanity who have become customers.

(And, by the way, if business's purposes are less than apparent to their employees, how much more opaque are they to their customers? You might imagine that if a firm is driven on to do what it does, in the way that it does it, by some deeply-held and passionate commitment to a purpose, some faint sense of what it is might be visible to people who do business with it. However, we challenge any financial services firm to achieve an unprompted customer research percentage score on 'understanding of corporate purpose' that gets into double figures.)

The fact is, there's so much bullshit and lip-service to be found around the area of corporate purpose that it's tempting – very tempting – to believe there isn't anything there of any substance at all. But as we'll go on to argue, there certainly is some substance there. And it's a kind of substance that can make a fundamental difference to the role and nature of marketing within organisations.

Let's start our exploration of this difficult but important subject by considering why it's viewed with so much cynicism and scepticism both outside and very often inside organisations.

The obvious explanation can't be ignored: what's being said so often just doesn't seem to be in any way true.[1] Anthony, who travels a lot, is invariably infuriated when he calls American Express in the UK. It doesn't matter if he's calling at 3 in the morning or the afternoon, more often than not he gets the same message: 'Unfortunately we are experiencing a high level of calls at the moment'. He might believe them once, or twice, but not every time he calls. The world of corporate purpose – and indeed all those other high-falutin' definitions like mission, vision, values, essence and all the rest of it – is full of this kind of obvious and blatant contradiction. In fact, it's rare to encounter an organisation where the level of contradiction isn't immediately and laughably obvious.

Let's play a guessing game. Which company, describing its values, said among many other similar things:

> We work with customers and prospects openly, honestly, and sincerely. When we say we will do something, we will do it; when we say we cannot or will not do something, then we won't do it.

---

[1] This difficulty arises not just with statements of purpose, but with pretty much everything that companies say to us in their 'sincere' voice. A recent study reported that of all the irritating things that firms do when dealing with their customers, the single one that infuriates us most is the endless repetition, when you're kept waiting by the call centre for what can easily be half an hour or more, of the complete and evident untruth that 'your call is important to us'. Of course it isn't, you think. How stupid do you think I am? Is this the way you'd treat me if my call was important to you? If I was the Queen, say, or Kim Kardashian, would you seriously keep me on hold for 37 minutes and counting while listening for the seventh time round to sodding Spring from The Four Seasons? There is what you might not unreasonably describe as a disconnect between what's being said, and what's being done. And given a choice between judging from words, and judging from deeds, there's no doubt at all which provides the stronger evidence. If my call were important to you, you'd employ more contact-centre staff.

Yes, you got it, the corrupt, dishonest and manipulative (and before long spectacularly bankrupt) US corporation called Enron.

Whose mission statement is this?

To produce fashionable products in an ethical way and demonstrate a responsible attitude towards people and the environment.

This of course is Arcadia Group, the business owned and run by that controversial entrepreneur Sir Philip Green.

One more? Okay. Who wouldn't want to be treated at a health-care institution with these fine values?

We deliver personalised care of the highest quality, with the best possible outcomes for users and carers, empowering them to remain independent.

Excellent, but rightly or wrongly you may react with a little scepticism when you know that this is the statement of purpose made by the NHS healthcare trust which runs Stafford Hospital, a few years ago the subject of one of the most damning reports on quality of care ever produced in this country.

That's enough of this game – it's too easy to play. To research examples, all you have to do is think of terrible companies or organisations, and google them together with the words 'purpose', 'vision', 'mission' and 'values'.

So what are we saying here? Are we saying that this kind of rhetoric is in fact completely discredited? Well, actually, no. Just because most of something isn't very good, that doesn't mean it's all bad. And anyway, when you look at what's written in tablets of stone on a company's website, you're looking in the wrong place. If it's just a statement on the website, then it's just front-office flim-flam, designed for public consumption. The real test of a company's priorities happens when you work there, and something's gone horribly wrong, and it's late and everyone wants to go home, and if you just delete a file or two no-one will ever know. Someone once said that your ethics define what you do when no-one is watching. Someone else said, a little less memorably, that a company's true values are the answers to the question, 'What does a person have to do to get on around here?' Ethics and values, granted, aren't the same thing as corporate purpose, but they're ingredients in the same minestrone. If one is cosmetic fiction, they probably all are. And if one is for real, they're probably all real, too.

Let's see if we can devise some background tests – some checks to which customers can submit organisations to get a fix on how likely that stated purpose is to be for real.

BACKGROUND TEST 1: HAS THE STATED PURPOSE BEEN ADOPTED RECENTLY?

If so, then right now it's unlikely to be for real as far as your experience as a customer is concerned. Even if the business's management team want it to be real (as opposed to just wanting something to say on the new website), it's likely to take years to embed the purpose into the beliefs and behaviours of the people in the organisation. If the purpose is significantly different from the previous one (or indeed if there wasn't a previous one), it's going to take even longer, and very likely involve the replacement of staff members too deeply entrenched in the former mindset. But, all this said, we've never seen an organisation admit to being 'in the early stages of trying to live up to a new purpose': firms would always have us believe that they're 100% there already. Can't be true.

BACKGROUND TEST 2: IS THE ORGANISATION LARGE, COMPLICATED AND SILOED?

If so, that's another very bad sign. In fact, a terrible sign. Organisations that fit this description are extremely, exceptionally unlikely to own any shared culture or values at all, let alone something as fundamental as a purpose. Typically more or less the only thing that unites the various parts of organisations like this is a shared and passionate desire to do other parts of the business down.

We're touching here on one of the recurring themes of this book, which is that everything involved in good marketing is incomparably more difficult in large, complicated and siloed businesses. In Chapter 17, on branding, we argue that from a marketing perspective, it doesn't really make sense to think of these as single entities at all, ultimately because achieving change across the entity as a whole is just impossible. It's not just about size: after all, in the end the proverbial supertanker can be manoeuvred, although not nimbly. It's more about lack of cohesion: as a nautical analogy, managing a business like this is more like manoeuvring a fleet of miscellaneous vessels, large and small, fast and slow, each with their own captains and crew and without any effective communications system to tell them which way to go.

There's a slight difference of opinion between your authors here, with one (OK, it's Anthony) preferring to say that achieving change across organisations like these is *almost* unachievable. As an exception, he points to British Airways in the 1980s, where the management team led by Lord King and Colin Marshall did in fact achieve fundamental change across a big, complex, long-established, siloed organisation in a remarkably short period of time. It's a pity that you have to go back 30 years and to a different industry for an example, though, and it may be the exception that proves the rule.

BACKGROUND TEST 3: SIMILARLY, AS A CUSTOMER, ARE YOU DEALING WITH A PERIPHERAL PART OF A LARGE, COMPLEX BUSINESS?

If so, the part you're dealing with is particularly unlikely to share the sense of purpose of the whole. The statement of corporate purpose will almost certainly have been dumped on the business unit in question, whether it makes any sense or not. One of your authors, running a financial specialist creative agency committed to originality and creativity, found himself landed with the need to express a purpose developed by the parent group, essentially to do with achieving excellence in data-driven communications for the pharmaceutical industry. Needless to say, his agency's website displayed this idea in extremely small type.

BACKGROUND TEST 4: HOW IS THE BUSINESS'S RELATIONSHIP WITH ITS EXTERNAL SHAREHOLDERS?

We all know that formally, the first responsibility of the management in a public company is to the shareholders. But what does that really mean? A participant in one of our Financial Services Forum focus groups expresses a commonly held view among business managers, saying:

> You need to have a purpose which ... will lead to sustainable, positive outcomes for your shareholders, otherwise you won't get ... their patience to continue to do it. But that doesn't mean it has to be out of kilter with what's good for customers and for staff as well. To generate real, sustainable value for your shareholders, you have to be in sync with your customers.

This sounds admirably consistent and sustainable. But insofar as there's an unresolved aspect here, it's almost always about time scales. Conflicts between shareholder interests and customer and/or staff interests are usually about the short-term versus the long term. Management typically argues that an action that will pay off for customers or staff in the short term will pay off for shareholders in the longer term: shareholders will not infrequently reply that they'd rather have their jam today, even if there's a little less of it.

That said, some shareholders can be remarkably patient when they're confi-dent that there will indeed be a greater quantity of jam tomorrow. Different investors can have very different time scales – but what none of them likes is when management promises something and then fails to deliver.

BACKGROUND TEST 5: IS THE BUSINESS FINDING IT EASY TO MAKE MONEY?

It's easy to overlook, or underestimate, this rather obvious question. The fact is, the huge majority of deviations from firms' purposes, visions and values happen when the immediate pressure to make a buck gets too great. That infuriating call-centre hold-message isn't exactly a lie: the company really does believe that every customer's phone call is important. So how can it possibly leave calls unanswered for 37 minutes? Quite simply, because it doesn't think it can afford to recruit more staff. (This may be one of those shareholders versus customers, short-term versus long-term issues described under the previous heading, although, in our experience, most shareholders don't like businesses with dissatisfied customers.) Businesses that find it easy to make money don't often have to grapple with this kind of squeeze.[2]

Those five tests should give you an initial fix on the likely credibility of pretty much any stated purpose (or at least, any purpose other than making as much money as possible as quickly as possible, which isn't something you hear often.) At this point we need to become more specific and look at the kinds of purposes that firms may want – hopefully credibly – to claim.

Both of your authors have founded, managed and sold businesses, but only Anthony has done so in a financial services firm. On the basis of this experience, he says, 'No financial services business can claim any kind of commitment to good marketing unless its fundamental aim is to give its customers a better product, service or experience'.

If he's right, this is clearly a hugely important point that begs a hugely important question: how many financial institutions do fundamentally aim to give their customers a better product, service or experience?

---

[2] As a perfect if trivial example of this kind of squeeze in real life, during a prolonged period of falling stock markets, one of your authors was working for an asset management firm. The firm withdrew chocolate biscuits from its meeting rooms when the FTSE-100 Index fell below 5,000, not restoring them till it climbed back above that level again.

One answer comes from our Financial Services Forum members online research. We asked our sample to what extent people in their own organisations would accept Anthony's point.

Only a very small minority of respondents – fewer than 1 in 10 – told us that the point was accepted throughout their organisation. Nearly two-thirds said it was accepted in 'some parts' of their organisation. But one in five said it was accepted only in the marketing department, and one in eight said that acceptance was weak even there.

Our first reaction, especially to this last finding, was astonishment. Can there really be marketers who don't believe that their business should aim to give its customers a better product, service or experience? It's a question that deserves further exploration.

Trying as hard as we can to be fair, we've been considering the word 'better'. 'Better how?' we've asked, in a pale imitation of Joe Pesci's legendary *Goodfellas* scene. Better than everyone else? Better than it was before? Better than what? Maybe we operate in such crowded and competitive markets that to be 'as good as' is enough. Maybe offering a good, or very good, product, service or experience is satisfactory. But we're not convinced.

Anyway, on this more limited basis, we reviewed the forms of words some firms used to define their purpose, starting with the Big Four High Street banking groups.[3] In alphabetical order, Barclays (defining values introduced by Anthony Jenkins) says:

What are Barclays' Purpose And Values?
    At Barclays, our common purpose is to help people achieve their ambitions – in the right way. We'll measure and reward our people, not just on commercial results, but on how they live our Values and bring them to life every day.

HSBC says:

Who we are and what we do
    Throughout our history we have been where the growth is, connecting customers to opportunities. We enable businesses to thrive and economies to prosper, helping people fulfil their hopes and dreams and realise their ambitions. This is our role and purpose.

---

[3] The following details are correct as at September 2017.

Lloyds says:

OUR PURPOSE

Helping Britain prosper

Through our branches and businesses, our Group has the potential to reach every family, business and community in the UK. We place immense value on our purpose, helping Britain prosper, driven by our desire to give back to the communities in which we operate.

And RBS says:

At RBS, our purpose is to serve customers well. We serve around 24 million customers across the globe, and our aim is to consistently meet their needs wherever they find us.

In their unexpectedly different ways, you have to say that these aren't bad efforts. All are clearly anxious about the derision sure to result from an overclaim: it doesn't take a PhD in semiotics to realise that these are organisations aware that they command little public trust and have a great deal of scepticism to contend with. But all try to go at least one step beyond pure platitude, aware that 100% pure platitude generates derision in its own right.

Barclays, perhaps the bravest of the four, tiptoes up toward the suicidally dangerous area of bankers' bonuses with its form of words about how they 'measure and reward' their people. HSBC plays the international card, hinting at its strength in Asia – they tell us they're 'where the growth is', an idea rather more focused on the business than on the customer. Lloyds, on the contrary, describes its purpose in wholly UK-centric terms – they're 'helping Britain prosper'. And poor old RBS, still in the hole to the taxpayer to the tune of £50-odd billion, can aspire to no more than a modest aim to 'serve customers well' and 'meet their needs', neither of which is a thought to stir the spirits.

But the more we think about them, the more we realise that all four run into trouble at not just one, but actually two different levels.

The first is the obvious one: the four banks' recent histories, and the public perceptions currently existing as a result. As we absorb these valiant efforts, we're painfully aware of the extent to which delivery against them has been, well, patchy, to say the least. RBS may promise to 'serve customers well', but newspaper headlines are still reminding us that not so long ago, in the years after the 2008 crash, the Global Restructuring Group in its NatWest business was deliberately driving hundreds of viable businesses into bankruptcy so that it could pick up their assets for a song. The same HSBC that prides itself on 'connecting customers to opportunities' was in fact paying a E300 million fine as recently as November 2017 for connecting some of its more affluent customers to Swiss-based tax evasion opportunities that were proved in court to be criminal. And of course while Barclays was setting about rewarding its people on 'how they live [their] values', a number of its corporate debt traders were at the forefront of the LIBOR-rigging scandal, and four received the prison sentences to prove it.

There is a real issue here: the extent to which any statement of purpose is discredited, or invalidated, by a one-bad-apple episode (and, if so, how long that discrediting or invalidation will last). You could certainly argue that if the stated purpose of an organisation employing well over a hundred thousand people in thousands of locations around the world is discredited by one person in any of these locations doing one bad thing, then the whole concept of stating any kind of purpose becomes untenable.

But to us, this is too simplistic. Given that there will always be bad apples, the real question is how managements react when one or more are found in the barrel. Were they up-front and honest about it, or did they deny it, begrudgingly owning up only when they had to? Did they issue the usual empty platitudes about 'lessons being learnt', or were there any signs of real action being taken to avoid a recurrence? And, perhaps most important, was there any sign of an effort to discover where responsibility lay? Your authors know hundreds of bankers in all of the UK's big banks but have never met one who was responsible (in any way, no matter how small) for PPI mis-selling.

In fact, being seen to deal with a malfeasance effectively can do more than just repair the damage. It's a curious quirk of human nature that it can leave us feeling more positive toward the organisation than if the malfeasance had never happened. On a smaller scale, one large hotel group that had invested heavily in a brilliant housekeeping service was said to make sure that guests would find one defect in their room when they checked in. The problem would be fixed so efficiently and courteously that the guests' perceptions of the hotel's service quality were higher than if their stay had been trouble-free.

But the second level of difficulty with the big banks' statements of purpose is the one that would arguably exist anyway, even without the faintest breath of recent scandal: the problems arising from the big banks' performance against numbers 1, 2, 3 and 4 of our background tests outlined previously. It must surely be the case that all of these banks are far too large, too diverse and too siloed to be able to live up to any kind of corporate purpose across the totality of their businesses, and in any case the stated purposes are far too new and have not yet had anything like enough time to take root inside the organisations. And it's hard to believe they ever will. Even if top management were grimly determined, it would take God knows how long – 10 years, 20 years, 50 years – to convince every salesperson measured in one way or another on their sales performance that they were really and truly to be rewarded 'on how they live our values and bring them to life every day'. It would be like trying to convince lions you were going to reward them on the basis of their kindness to wildebeest. And even if you did ever succeed in achieving this across your own pride of lions, as soon as a new one came in from another pride (analogy for recruiting a salesperson from elsewhere, or of course buying and merging with another sales-driven firm), they wouldn't get it and there'd be wildebeest body parts all over the place again.

As with everything to do with every aspect of building brands, it's all infinitely much more achievable in businesses that are not big, long-established, complex and siloed – in other words, which are small, young and simple. Sticking with banks for a few minutes longer, can you guess who stated this?

> We pioneer banking that makes a positive difference to the lives of our customers and communities.

Not too hard, is it? It's the Co-operative Bank, which of course has become inextricably connected with a level of catastrophic mismanagement and misbehaviour far beyond any of the Big Four's travails – yet, amazingly, to your authors at any rate, its statement of purpose remains basically credible. They may have been chaired by a sex-fuelled junkie, and teetered on the brink of financial disaster, and they may now be owned by a bunch of hard-nosed US-based private equity firms. But at some level, it is still basically credible that they pioneer banking that makes a positive difference to the lives of their customers and communities. They put their money (and their customers money) where their mouths are.

Most financial services providers fit somewhere in between the hopeless fragmentation of a really big complex institution, and the straightforward simplicity of a single-channel niche player.

Here, for example, is another medium-sized bank, TSB:

> We provide local banking for Britain to help local people, businesses and communities to thrive together.

Not quite as powerful or distinctive as the Co-operative Bank maybe, but there certainly is something there.

Here's a statement that works in a different way. What Nationwide does is much the same as quite a few others: it's who they are, as the UK's one remaining large building society, that is special:

Whether you bank with us, save with us or buy a home with us, we always have our members' best interests at heart and provide the great customer service you expect. Run for the benefit of our members, we really are on your side.

Aviva is a large, complex organisation, but does well to define an area of common ground that most of its business units can buy into:[4]

Our purpose is to free people from fear of uncertainty, allowing them to get on with their lives.

And finally Hargreaves Lansdown is able to reflect both the clarity of its proposition, and the focus of its targeting, in this simple and undeniable statement:

We aim to help you make more of your investments by giving you the tools and information to make your own informed decisions.

Let's be clear. The key point is not that in and of themselves, published statements of purpose like these, even when they are clear, credible and distinctive, make much difference to anything. The key point is that businesses that are able to express their purposes effectively, as these examples can, are businesses where marketers stand a chance of doing a great job. There is a basic direction here, a fundamental sense of what we do and indeed what we don't do, that gives a good marketing team something to build on.

Young, simple businesses that start with clear senses of purpose from the outset have a great opportunity to express them in the most visible way

---

[4]Having said that this definition works pretty well from a retail customer perspective, it would be interesting to know how widely it's shared and accepted across Aviva's businesses. We strongly suspect that internally, it's by no means universally popular. It works very well for the group's insurance-based businesses. But although it's something that could be said of Aviva's investment businesses, we wouldn't mind betting that the investment people aren't keen on it– 'Much too insurance-y'. And the people running more niche and specialised business units like the Aviva investment platform won't be keen on it at all – 'What the hell have we got to do with fear of uncertainty?'

possible – that is, in their choice of name. You might think that Mother is a rather silly name for one of the UK's leading independent advertising agencies, but the word actually reinforces and reminds us of an idea that's understood by, and vitally important to, everyone who works there: that they should always ask themselves whether their mothers would be proud of what they've just done. The same was true, in the experience of one of your authors, of the direct insurance business MORE TH>N (in fact a semi-autonomous business unit within the RSA Group). Another odd name, but with another strong rationale: the intention was that whatever anyone in the firm was doing, they should always be able to explain how it offered customers *more than* what they would find elsewhere.

Both these firms embedded important aspects of their purpose in their names. That's a powerful thing to do, but it isn't always possible or practical. A clear purpose can still act as a positive and inspirational guide to behaviour even when a firm has a name as boring as, say, for example, Hargreaves Lansdown.

To emphasise this important point once more, imagine that you're in charge of marketing at RBS, and at Hargreaves Lansdown (seems unlikely you could do both, but we're just imagining). You look to the organisations' prominently displayed statements of purpose for guidance on the kind of direction you should take. RBS's says (remember?):

> At RBS, our purpose is to serve customers well. We serve around 24 million customers across the globe, and our aim is to consistently meet their needs wherever they find us.

Hargreaves Lansdown states:

> We aim to help you make more of your investments by giving you the tools and information to make your own informed decisions.

It really wouldn't be difficult to come up with a dozen ideas in twenty minutes that could reinforce and demonstrate that purpose of Hargreaves Lansdown's – but it would be very difficult indeed to think of anything that would do the same for RBS's.

We don't make this comparison to be unkind to RBS. In their circumstances, we have no idea what they could say that might be better. We're just saying that marketers should be able to do some great work at Hargreaves Lansdown, but it's going to be extremely hard going at RBS.

This distinction is so important, and so fundamental to what follows in this book about good marketing, that it's worth examining in a little more detail. Why exactly is it that Hargreaves Lansdown's stance gives marketers a great starting-point, while RBS gives them a very poor one?

At its simplest, it comes down to one of the marketing world's longest-established formulations, a three-question framework that, it's said, helps to reduce a proposition down to its simplest possible form. Those three questions are:

1. Who wants it?
2. What is it?
3. Why should they bother?

And the more clearly and distinctively they can be answered, the stronger the proposition of a business as a whole, and/or a particular product or service.

On this basis, here's a stab at Hargreaves Lansdown's purpose:

▪ Who wants it?	People who want to manage their own investments
▪ What is it?	The tools and information to make informed decisions
▪ Why should they bother?	Because we'll help them make more of their investments

Here's a stab at RBS's statement:

▪ Who wants it?	24 million customers around the globe
▪ What is it?	Service that consistently meets their needs
▪ Why should they bother?	Not stated. Presumably they like having their needs met.

Hargreaves Lansdown's formulation gets off to a flying start by reflecting such clarity about the people for whom the service is intended. We return many times in this book to the need to focus on the customer – to really focus on the customer, which is difficult, rather than just claiming to do so, which is easy. Hargreaves is an absolutely customer-centric business, and that's what's really good and special about it.

Across large swathes of financial services, though, this is still distressingly unusual. There's a remarkably simple test of customer centricity that delivers unscientific, but highly indicative results: visit organisations' websites, and see if they feature pictures of any of their customers.

Some sectors perform much better than others. Most building societies do show pictures of customers. Asset managers are terrible. At the time of writing, we've visited the websites of 16 large UK-based asset management firms' websites. Two showed images of customers. (It may or may not be significant that these two were Fidelity and Legal & General, two firms that appear to be somewhat more customer-focused, or at least customer-aware, than other asset managers.)

The truth is that this people-picture test may be more revealing than the lofty statements of corporate purpose. If you believe – which more or less everyone does these days – that it's what you do, not what you say that matters, then this almost complete failure to enter the customer's world is significant. It makes it look as if this simply isn't a place where the firms belong.

And of course for most asset managers, the simple truth is that it isn't. Although asset managers ultimately manage money for private individuals – a point which they frequently shorthand by referring to the end investor under the patronising and arrogant generic term 'Mrs Miggins' – very few people working in the firms have had any contact with private individuals at all. Most firms manage much more institutional money than retail, so they spend much of their time operating in a rarefied atmosphere occupied by pensions fund consultants and group scheme trustees. And of course even in the retail market the very large majority of relationships with end clients are intermediated – it isn't actually necessary to meet Mrs Miggins, Mr Miggins or any other members of the Miggins family.

A few consulting firms have done good business trying to narrow the gulf that exists between people working in firms like these, and the millions of Mrs Migginses whose money they're actually managing. Brilliant innovation agency WhatIf? have a wonderful habit of taking very senior financial services clients a million miles out of their comfort zones, for example – there's a story which we fear may be an urban myth, although we'd love it to be true, that they once organised a meeting of a big bank's main Board in a social housing flat at the top of a tower block, where no room was big enough to accommodate them all so half sat in the lounge and the other half sat on the bed. For most, this was no doubt the first and last experience of ever visiting a place like this. It would be nice to think it left a lasting mark.

By contrast, whenever one of your authors is addressing groups of financial services executives on any subject to do with investment for people who are not affluent and who are not at all engaged with investing (a surprisingly common conference theme these days), he always starts by asking how many of those present have a Hargreaves Lansdown account. The answer is pretty much never fewer than half. 'There's your problem right there', he tells them. 'Not a single member of your target audience has ever heard of

Hargreaves Lansdown, and not a single one would have the faintest idea what to do with their website if they ever stumbled upon it. Now, what was it you wanted to sell them?'

This is, of course, a single example of a much bigger and broader problem: the breadth of nthe gap that exists between most senior people in most financial srvices firms, and most of the people they have, or want to have, as their customers.

The simple fact is that it's infinitely much easier to be good at dealing with customers, and having real insight into their wants and needs, if you personally (or, if not you personally, then a fair proportion of your colleagues) aren't so very different from them. But while the financial services industry doesn't do too badly on issues of diversity overall, it still doers dreadfully badly at senior, decision-making levels. Check out the Business Class lounges, for example, at Heathrow and Edinburgh airports on Monday mornings and Friday evenings, when the great and the good from the financial services industries of both cities fly home for the weekend or to the office for the week. We're not quite 100% male, pale and stale – a few may be under 40, a very few may be women and a very few indeed may be people of colour. But do we[5] reflect anything remotely like the diversity of the people we want to do business with? Do we hell?

Of course this sort of gulf is far narrower in other sectors, and in a few it doesn't exist at all. Marketing people are at an enormous advantage when not only they themselves, but also their colleagues across their firms' management teams, have a strong affinity with their customers.

To sum up, we're arguing that a strong, clear and distinctive sense of purpose is an essential attribute for any organisation that aims to be a leader in the new financial services marketing. This sense of purpose may work at one, or potentially both, of two levels:

- It may be so powerful that it genuinely does act as a high-level navigational system for the whole organisation.
- But even if it doesn't, it will still say something important and valuable about the people the organisation intends to serve, and what it is that the organisation intends to do for them.

Either way, provided that the company is willing to live it in both good times and bad, it provides marketers with a starting-point to do some great work.

---

[5]Your authors are well aware that the 'we' in this sentence includes both of them, although Anthony would like to point out that in his case the UK airport lounges in question in recent years were much more likely to have been Bristol and Newcastle.

It seems clear to us that finding a clear focus for a corporate purpose gets harder and harder the bigger, more complex and older an organisation gets (and it's even worse if the organisation is mired in scandal and misbehaviour and can say virtually nothing without risking snorts of derision). Vice versa, we think it's highly probable that the clearest purposes will be owned by smaller, more focused, younger businesses that haven't become mired in scandal.

This point has obvious and important implications for organisational strategy, to which we shall return further on in the book and particularly in the chapter on branding.

CHAPTER 10

Does Your Firm Have a Strong and Distinctive Culture?

Here's a puzzle for you. What organisation, an important player in the financial services world, defines its 'cultural characteristics' like this?

> We want people with *backbone,* who judge situations carefully, are confident communicators and challenge the status quo.
>
> We promote *professional excellence* and we demonstrate it in everything we do, by setting high standards and delivering on our commitments.
>
> We're *curious* by nature. We want to learn and find out more, every day, and we explore the implications of our actions in detail.
>
> We're *already on the case*, thinking ahead and acting with confidence.
>
> We're a *strong team* that celebrates our differences and successes, and we show trust in our colleagues.

If you think about it hard enough, you'll probably get it. First you'll realise that these are not the characteristics of a commercial organisation, or one that serves customers. It could perhaps be some kind of educational body – all that learning and finding out more – but it's tougher and more challenging than that. A government department? Not enough accountability, and maybe a bit too hard-edged.

Have you got it yet? Here's a clue: it is in fact the organisation that has done more than any other to push culture up the corporate agenda, shifting responsibility for it from the HR department all the way up to the boardroom.

Well done, you're there. It's our industry's regulator, the Financial Conduct Authority. And while we can't say to what extent these characteristics are in fact consistently reflected in the day-to-day behaviours of its people, we can say that as an aspiration they work well. We feel happy to engage with a regulator with values like these.

Of course the FCA really does have to be seen to be doing everything it can to manage its own culture, having criticised so many of the firms it regulates and especially their senior managers so sternly for neglecting or mismanaging theirs. The FCA, indeed, has decided that bad culture was more responsible than anything for the financial crisis of 2008. Here's a quote on the subject from a speech given by Chief Economist Peter Andrew, in autumn 2016:

> Culture is a priority for the FCA, one of our seven business plan priorities for 2016/17.
>
> We believe that poor culture played a significant part in the financial crisis and that it is a root cause of many failings at firms. Thus culture is both a major driver and potential mitigant of risk. Our ambition is that firms' senior management lead and foster a culture that has the fair treatment of customers and market integrity at its core.
>
> Hence the main aim of our major initiative, the Senior Managers and Certification Regime or 'SMCR', is to drive cultural change. It does this by making senior managers accountable and by applying baseline standards to all financial services staff.

The FCA wasn't in the chair, of course, during the 2008 crisis – that was its predecessor, the FSA. But anyone who knows anything about what went on during that extraordinary period will know that they aren't kidding when they talk about 'poor culture'. To choose a single example from many hundreds available, here is former Goldman Sachs executive Gregg Smith speaking about the culture of the bank soon after his resignation in 2012:

> It makes me ill how callously people talk about ripping their clients off. Over the last 12 months I have seen five different managing directors refer to their own clients as 'muppets', sometimes over internal e-mail.

As we'll go on to discuss, there is an infinite number of positive variations in the way that firms may choose to define and express their culture (and Goldman Sachs have consistently claimed that Smith's claims were untrue). But we don't think there are any that include ideas like 'ripping clients off' or calling them 'muppets'.

Actually, we must pause to wonder how an investment bank accused of behaving like this could have become, at around this time, the most successful, highest-paying and most highly-regarded institution of its type in the world. It is, let's be honest, a bit of a worry. Every word in this book is based on the premise that going forward, in the retail financial services market, firms will only achieve sustained success by doing the right thing by their customers. Admittedly this Goldman example, and all the many,

many others from the world of investment banking during the crisis, is looking backward rather than going forward; and the worst offenders at that time were institutions focused mainly on corporate and institutional markets, not retail. But it does bother us, all the same.

There isn't any other chapter in this book where we introduce our thoughts on a topic by quoting enthusiastically from the FCA. But on the topic of culture, we think the regulator's point of view is so right on the money that we'll allow ourselves one more quote, this time from a summary of a speech entitled 'What Is Culture in Financial Institutions?', given in Hong Kong by CEO Andrew Bailey in March 2017. The summary says, in part:

> A firm's culture emerges in large part from inputs that are its responsibility. It is for firms to ensure that their desired culture is consistent with appropriate conduct outcomes.

Absolutely. As an executive summary of this chapter, that works well.

Mind you, when it comes to famous and/or memorable quotes about culture, the FCA still has a way to go. In the world of management and business consulting, there are very few quotations that become seriously famous – so famous that literally everyone knows them. There's one on the subject of culture, from the management guru Peter Drucker. 'Culture', Drucker said, 'eats strategy for breakfast'.[1]

Anyway, one way or another, Drucker, the FCA and your authors are all saying that culture is very important. So how exactly does a company get one?

In UK retail financial services, few organisations' cultures are more admired than HSBC's remote banking arm: First Direct. So who better than their former Head of People Experience, Stewart Bromley, to talk about how you do it?

He says it begins with defining values:

> First Direct was the first place I'd worked which had a truly well-defined value system that drove all the culture of the business.

---

[1] Actually, it's possible that this is not quite what he said. Among the many marketing and business books that feature his comment, one specifies a different mealtime, claiming that he said culture eats strategy for lunch. To be honest, whether this strategy-eating took place at the start of the day or in the middle, it's still an odd expression. But maybe that's why it sticks in people's minds. And after all, Drucker was an Austrian who didn't speak English until he was 24.

The founders of the business had really set it off on the right trajectory. Mike Harris and his team had done a fantastic job – the way their value system was originally defined was with a bunch of people in a room thinking, what are the values? They basically set up a bunch of values that were defined in a way that would drive behaviour.

They ended up with four values, but what happened was that we did a big survey among the people experience team and their customers and we realised there was more to the brand than the four values they had defined. So we redefined the value system using six values that really did orientate the behaviour.

Then it's a question of using the values to drive hiring decisions. . . :

'We hired on values, yes, the whole hiring process was designed around those values. Because the thing about values is that if you hire on them, then your culture will to a large degree look after itself, assuming you hire appropriately. It's inherent in how everyone behaves and talks to customers – you know, it's just who you are. It's an identity rather than a belief system, right?'

. . . and taking every opportunity to reinforce the culture in the environment:

'We changed everything, from the signage in the building to the words if you forgot your pass as you came in – it said 'oops. forgot my pass'. We designed new processes and new policies. We redesigned the employee value proposition. And at that time, my job was both people experience and customer experience, because the idea is that if you own both bits, you can create this really tight bond – people *are* it, rather than just knowing what it is'.

And then one of the biggest parts of keeping it alive is to embed the whole subject of culture in your appraisal system – and not just as a detail or an afterthought, but as a core element of the process:

'In our appraisals we mapped people in two dimensions – the what, which is all about what you contribute, and the how, which is about how you do it. And the how is all about values and culture. We measure both those things, and they're equally weighted, so you can be brilliant, but if you're not on values then you're a bit rubbish, right? And if you're completely on values but not delivering, then that's just as bad'.

In this account, one of the most intriguing elements is the very first one – where that initial take on the organisation's intended values and culture comes from. At First Direct, they came quite simply from the business's founder, Mike Harris, and his initial core management team. Thirty years or so later, what drives the business today still flows very directly from the personal convictions of the individual with the original vision for the business'.

Stewart Bromley has since gone on to become Chief Operating Officer for Atom Bank, and the approach here has been a bit different:

> 'At Atom, we wanted a culture that tied in very closely to our customers, so we did a whole bunch of research into that target customer group, who are usually described as millennials. And what you find is that millennials have a very distinct psychology, and a whole bunch of psychological cravings that underpin that psychology, and we defined a value system that directly appeals to those cravings. So even our value system is based on the cultural needs of our target group, right?'

Provided the people in the organisation, from the top down, are willing to live the values, it doesn't really matter where they come from. Whether they represent personal convictions or customer needs (or even 'cravings'), they can provide the basis for something distinctive and valuable.

Note, however, the use of the notorious weasel word 'can' in that last sentence. Relying on Stewart Bromley, with his First Direct experience, for an account of how to build a culture is like asking Gordon Ramsay how to cook an omelette, or Laura Trott how to ride a bicycle. It looks easy when they do it. But when you come to think about what happens in other companies, you realise how easily things can go horribly wrong. Very few firms set out to develop cultures as toxic as Goldman Sachs (even Goldman Sachs probably didn't set out to develop a culture that toxic). But somehow it happened anyway. How come?

We suggest that when culture does go horribly wrong, it usually goes wrong from the top down – like a fish, as the saying goes, it rots from the head. We can think of a whole bunch of different ways that bad management can lead to bad culture:

1. *Just faking it.* In the same way that organisations can fake their sense of purpose (see last chapter), it's perfectly possible to promote a culture that everyone knows full well has no connection with reality. When this is the case – and it often is – the evidence isn't hard to spot. The business, and especially the senior people in it, keep on behaving in ways that are entirely at odds with the alleged culture, and it doesn't seem to be getting

them into any trouble. Off the top of our heads, we can immediately think of:

- a firm that allegedly valued openness that unhesitatingly fired a whistleblower;
- a firm that claims to put its customers first, but that only rewards and incentivises sales success (actually we can think of several of these);
- a firm that celebrates diversity and equality of opportunity, but has a Board made up of eight middle-aged white men;
- a firm that says it stands for empowering its customers, but is lagging far behind its rivals in delivering online functionality;
- a firm that claimed to have put its past bad behaviour behind it, but was then found trying to cheat its customers out of their PPI compensation.

To be honest, although it's fun thinking of examples like these there isn't much to say about them. Everyone working for these firms knows that their values and culture are bogus. And increasingly, people outside – especially their poor bloody customers – know it too.[2]

2. *Window dressing.* This is effectively a variation on faking it, and a particularly cynical one where the idea is to fill the shop window with attractive values that appeal to customers and staff, while behaving behind the scenes as badly as you think you can get away with. Google, though not a financial services firm, comes to mind. Everyone knows the firm's cultural centrepiece, that resonant slogan 'Do No Evil': there may be room for debate about whether the company's elaborate international tax avoidance strategies could fairly be described as 'evil', but not much doubt when it comes to their long-standing advertising sales model which can have the effect of channelling money from major brands to the You Tube channels of terrorists, racists and pornographers.

---

[2]It's such a perfect example that we simply must include it. An element of Lloyds Banking Group's culture, according to its website, is to do with its treatment of its suppliers. It says: 'We are committed to ensuring that all our dealings with suppliers are conducted in accordance with the principles of fair and ethical trading, from initial sourcing to ongoing supplier management'. As we write this page, a friend who runs a company which has supplied Lloyds for years has sent us a copy of an email from Lloyds, telling her that her contract is to be terminated as of April 1st. The date of the e-mail? March 31st.

3. *Sabotage*. This comes a couple of notches down from outright fakery, but is still deeply unhelpful. It happens when someone important – often someone very important – knows perfectly well how their firm defines its culture (and indeed may have participated in creating the definition), but decides that because they're very important, some or even all of it doesn't apply to them. It's when the culture is built around mutual respect, but this person is always late for meetings. Or when it stands for fairness and equality of opportunity, but this person's kids all come in on a placement while other people's somehow can't be accommodated. Just little things – but little things that say we don't really mean any of this.

4. *Mixed messages*. Perhaps another notch down again, this is often what happens when cost-cutting programmes nibble away at cultural strengths. Of course we want our customers to enjoy an excellent experience in a way that suits them ... but for cost reasons, we're going to have to start closing the call centre three hours earlier.

5. *Underinvestment*. Similar, but more systematic. Since we cut down the number of desks in the call centre, call waiting times and abandoned call numbers are rising month by month. But we still stand by our customer service value.

6. And finally, and perhaps the odd one out, *culture of the month*. In today's world of mergers, acquisitions, restructures and rebrandings, some people working in financial services firms are finding themselves reimmersed in new values and new cultures on more or less an annual basis. Frankly, in the circumstances, it's only human nature to let out an audible groan on receipt of the next invitation to an important new values workshop.

But the truth is that while any of these errors and misfortunes can have a terrible effect on culture, probably the most difficult challenge is neither an error nor a misfortune.

So far we've discussed the issue implicitly, at least, in terms of small-ish, youngish, start-uppish businesses, such as First Direct and Atom Bank, where building a strong culture is quite possible provided that nothing terrible happens.

The majority of people in financial services don't work for firms like these. They work for great big complicated long-established firms, based in many locations, organised into many largely autonomous business units and with a heavily siloed history that has resulted in very little trace of cultural glue helping to hold the whole thing together. What then?

Well, to repeat a point we make in other chapters of this book, to put it in plain English, you're a bit buggered. In the same way that we don't think it's possible to build a really strong and cohesive brand across businesses like these, and we don't think it's possible to create a really strong sense of common purpose, we don't think it's possible to build a truly distinctive culture. Business like these are too big, too fragmented, too political and simply too diverse: it's pretty much impossible to imagine what a distinctive culture could be like, beyond some kind of extremely lowest-common-denominator value like 'being helpful' (which, as it happens, was until very recently the core of the culture that big, fragmented, political, diverse RBS Group was seeking to establish).

That's why – as, again, we say in those other chapters, notably chapter 17 – as marketers, we favour an approach that breaks these behemoths down into manageable units, and builds appropriate cultures in each of them.

As we know from our own experience, this can work. By coincidence, both of your authors had a great deal to do with the MORE TH>N direct insurance business at the time when it was being carved out from its parent group Royal & SunAlliance (now RSA). It was a remarkable experience.

MORE TH>N was based in RSA's big operations centre down in Horsham – it occupied the second floor – and the very large majority of its people were long-standing RSA people who had transferred across. But in an extraordinarily short period of time, MORE TH>N built a culture that was as different from RSA's as you could possibly imagine. Under the leadership of its MD Adrian Brown and its marketing director Mike Tildesley, MORE TH>N rapidly established itself as a business that – culturally at least – stood for everything that RSA didn't. It was young, it was hugely energetic, it was positive, it was eager to learn and improve and develop. If you were blindfolded and dropped down into various floors and departments in that large RSA office, you'd know in seconds when you were on MORE TH>N's floor – there was a buzz about it in complete contrast to the stodgy stillness of the other floors.

All of this was in sharp contrast to another 'brownfield' startup within a big company. A couple of years earlier, one of your authors had a good deal of experience with Barclays' 'alternative' investment brand b2. This wasn't a success, and after a couple of miserably unsuccessful years it was wound up.

There were several things that MORE TH>N got right and b2 got wrong, but one that clearly stood out was that while MORE TH>N was staffed by people who were committed to the business and bought into its culture, the b2 team were part-timers – the large majority working for Barclays in the mornings, so to speak, and b2 in the afternoons. This was hopeless. It meant that at best, there was no distinctive culture at all – and at worst, there was a desperately confused group of people, never sure which hat they were supposed to be wearing or which values they were supposed to be espousing at any given moment.

Much more recently, by the way, another big bank found another way to create a cultural vacuum, again experienced by one of your authors. In today's cost-conscious climate, many big institutions are enormously reliant on contractors and temporary staff, especially when it comes to special projects. Here, there may have been 40 people or so working more or less full-time on the project – an online investment service – of whom no more than a small handful were on the bank's payroll. And just to make sure there was no chance at all of any cultural commonality emerging, they were based in at least six locations across the UK, continental Europe and North America. It would be interesting to see what Stewart Bromley would make of that.

Time to move on. So far, we've approached this discussion of culture at a rather abstract level, on the semi-explicit basis that there are good cultures (liked by everyone, including firms' staff, customers, the FCA and us) and bad cultures (not liked by any of the above); and provided your organisations has one of the good ones, then all is well.

However, for those of us with a marketing orientation, that's not quite good enough. There is a word that we've thrown in a couple of times and should now consider more carefully: 'distinctive'.

As marketers, we think this word is crucially important to our particular involvement with the whole subject of culture. As marketers, we worry when we hear others with a stake in the subject – sometimes in general management, sometimes in HR – discuss culture in terms that sound to us alarmingly generic.

In retail financial services, there is a value set, with clear implication for culture, which no-one is going to disagree with. It's characterised first and foremost, of course, by a commitment to *putting the customer first*: it always emphasises the importance of *doing the right thing*, and *working as a team* on a basis of *mutual respect*: there's usually something about *innovation*, and something about *transparency*, and that dreadfully vague and hollow word *professionalism* often makes an appearance. What could possibly be wrong with that?

Well, nothing, except for that all-important point that no-one's ever going to disagree with any of it. Building a culture that's really fully rooted in these values isn't at all easy. But if 12 organisations, or 50, or 100, were able to do so, they'd all be pretty much exactly the same as each other.

And it's for this reason that as marketers, our first responsibility in the development of culture is, of course, to make sure that our firms tackle the task in a way that is ruthlessly and uniquely focused on our most valuable asset, which is to say our brand. With apologies for the longish quote, here's what customer experience expert Vanessa Hamilton, of Smith + Co, has to say on the subject:

> After 15 years in the customer experience business, there's still one sentence that makes me want to run for the hills. 'We need a service excellence programme for our front-line staff.' You don't! You've probably implemented many perfectly good service excellence programmes in the past. What does that tell you about the impact they had? And about the difference they've made?
>
> That's because generic service training doesn't connect your people to your brand. It doesn't help them to understand what your brand stands for, and why that matters. It doesn't help them to explore how they can really bring your brand to life for customers through their actions and behaviours.
>
> If you want your people to deliver an experience that differentiates your brand from competitors, you have to create a branded experience for them too.

Without jumping ahead to our chapter on brand (although it starts on page 216, if you're determined to), creating a properly differentiated, branded service experience , reflecting a deep-rooted, differentiated, branded culture is something that our industry isn't yet very good at.

There are at least two reasons for this:

1. Few financial services firms are very good at creating differentiated brands or propositions, because few firms care much about developing or maintaining a sustainable point of differentiation
2. There are few financial services firms where marketing and HR people work closely enough together.

Here and there, you can find a handful that tick both boxes. Among larger firms – well, medium-sized anyway – Direct Line has made considerable progress towards establishing a brand that's focused on fixing its customers' problems, and at the same time worked hard to start building a culture that actually embodies this value. But this level of integration is still highly unusual. Much more commonly, if, say, a brand is reflected in high-profile advertising, the integration will extend to the home page of the website and no further.

The thing is, distinctiveness at the level of both brand and culture depends on daring to be different – on doing something that's idiosyncratic, maybe even a bit peculiar, but hey, that's how we do things here. (It's not too difficult to find examples in experiential sectors outside financial services – we're sure you'll know the classic case studies, from IKEA to SouthWest Airlines to Zappos to Geek Squad, as well as we do.)

This particular issue, we should make clear, is definitely not one where the smaller, younger players seem to be outperforming. On the contrary, we'd say that in sectors where large numbers of young startups are emerging, brand and cultures are looking extraordinarily generic. There's a wave of so-called robo advisers, for example, offering online investing and all standing for ease, transparency and simplicity. And a wave of challenger banks all built around highly customisable apps. And a wave of remarkably similar-looking insurtechs. We assume that a lot of these young businesses aren't expecting lengthy lifespans – they're only here for a short while before selling out to a big institution that finds it easier to buy than to build, and at that time they'll almost certainly rebrand anyway. But still, the lack of differentiation at any level is dispiriting. Putting in a bar or table tennis table or allowing people to wear casual clothes doesn't make you differentiated. And don't get us started on bean bags.

CHAPTER 11

How Much Is Big Data Changing Your Business?

It's bad form for a book like this to draw too extensively on a single source. And worse than bad form, it's potentially bad business, too – you can use a small handful of short quotes free of charge, but as your level of borrowing starts creeping up from dozens to scores to many hundreds of words the question of payment becomes more and more likely to arise.

Still, we simply can't write a chapter about the hugely important, ever-increasing and totally transformative effects of the irresistible advance of big data without drawing right up to the limit of propriety on the book that first got us all thinking about the subject – Don Peppers' and Martha Rogers' *The One-to-One Future*, first published way back in 1993.

Re-reading the book today, it seems more than ever one of the very most extraordinary examples of prophecy since, well, John the Baptist or even Nostradamus, and even George Gendron is starting to appear a lot less ridiculous than he did at the time.

We have no idea who Gendron is, or was, but the one thing we know is that he's the chap who turned up on the front cover of the US edition of *The One-To-One Future* saying: 'This is not the book of the year or the book of the decade. It's one of the two or three most important books ever written'. At the time, this caused a bit of a stir among fans of Tolstoy, Shakespeare and Proust. But all these years later, it looks as if Gendron may have had a point. *The One-to-One Future* really is a fairly important book.

In essence, it argues that technology is bringing about a massive change in the whole nature of marketing – that we're moving out of an era of mass marketing in which the main aim is to sell products or services to as many customers as possible, and into an era of one-to-one marketing in which the main aim is to sell as many products and services as possible to each individual customer. On this basis, the authors say, the key measure of success must move on from share of market to share of customer.

What's truly remarkable is that the book attributes these developments to the advance of technology – even though almost all the authors' technological predictions never happened, and they missed all the important things that did.

Here are the big things to look forward to in interactive communication, as they saw them in the early 1990s:

- By the end of the decade, many major magazines will offer subscribers not only personalized advertising, but personalised editorial content as well.
- Some newspapers may also offer personalization.
- Fax machines, already found in 30% of Japanese homes, will be found in more than 50% of US households.
- By the end of the decade, airplane seatbacks will come not just with telephones, but with interactive video screens as well, connected by satellite to programming providers and catalog merchandisers.
- Microwave ovens and VCRs will respond to your spoken instructions.
- Nintendo sets will be used for homework, connecting televisions by phones to databases that provide encyclopedias, textbooks and news.

Like most cloudy crystal balls, what makes it funny is not so much that it's all completely wrong, but rather that it's all just fairly wrong. By the end of that decade, the few remaining fax machines were gathering dust in remote corners of offices. Airplane seatbacks did have video screens, but they were never used for browsing catalogs. And kids were using technology to do their homework, but the authors' enthusiasm for Nintendo machines blinded them to the potential of computers.

In fact, writing at the start of the Internet era, the authors make the occasional rather oblique reference to computers, e-mail and websites, but in an oddly tentative way as if they're really not too sure what these things are or where they're going. And of course they have nothing to say about any form of social media – their top tip for dialogue with customers is something called interactive radio.

Their tin ear for technology provides plenty of amusement, but when we stop sniggering we realize it makes the substance of their prophecies all the more impressive. Their big ideas about relationships between companies and their customers were right in almost every detail. Here, chosen not quite at random from different chapters of the book, are eight of the things they have to say about the 'one-to-one future'.

- Mass marketing requires *product* managers who sell one product at a time to as many customers as possible. One-to-one marketing requires *customer* managers who sell as many products as possible to one customer at a time.

- For any [consumer] product, it is possible to make money from the fact that consumers have lifetime values that far exceed the profit that can be made on individual purchase transactions. We have only to know who these consumers are to begin to take advantage of this fact, by offering the consumer something of value.

- It is impossible even to talk about mass marketing without thinking of customers and marketers as adversaries. The jargon of mass marketing itself is the jargon of war. One-to-one marketing is collaborative rather than adversarial. You listen as the customer speaks, and you invite a customer to participate in actually making the product, before asking the customer to take it.

- What people say they do and what they actually do are two entirely different things. The only reliable predictor of actual future behaviour is actual past behaviour.

- Tomorrow's one-to-one marketer will be following the testing and learning disciplines of today's mail-order merchant. The same kinds of strategies and techniques will be applicable, but the *velocity* of learning will be several orders of magnitude greater.

- Organising your company's marketing effort around the task of managing customers is more easily said than done. You need to structure your marketing organization so that each of your customers and prospective customers, individually, becomes the direct responsibility of one customer manager in your firm.

- You should evaluate and reward your customer managers on one, and only one, criterion: the increase or decrease in the total projected lifetime values of the customers in their portfolios.

- And finally, on the whole, marketers are far more prepared to talk *to* customers than to hear *from* them. This is mostly because (at the time of writing) there just aren't any convenient, inexpensive media that allow customers to send messages to marketers. Don't let a momentary accident of technological history convince you that your customers don't have individual feelings they would *like* to communicate to you, if it were as easy for them as it is for you.

They were wrong about the technology, but right about almost everything else. (We say 'almost' because, arguably, they made one other mistake that's commonly made by futurologists. They expected the future to arrive a bit more quickly than it has. The time horizon of Peppers' and Rogers' book was, by implication at least, the turning of the millennium some seven years or so after it was written. Although we still believe in the one-to-one marketing revolution they predicted, we can't deny that large chunks of it are still on the to-do list today. And that's not just in the world of financial services, which is routinely lagging behind when it comes to revolutions. It's in most of the rest of the consumer marketing economy, too.)

To test the truth of this, let's review a small selection of the inbound marketing messages received by one of your authors on the day of writing this. (The author in question is in fact Lucian – as a dedicated online shopper, he has provided the greater quantity of personal data to allow for more targeted one-to-one communications. He apologises in advance if any of his favoured retailers have a negative effect on your perceptions of his personal brand.)

1. An e-mail from online clothing retailer Lands' End announcing a 24-hour discount on the price of jeans. To take advantage of this, Lucian has to click through to the website and choose whether he's a woman, man or child. Having announced himself as a man, he is shown some jeans. Being 6 foot 6 inches in height, everything Lucian has ever bought from Lands' End comes in a tall fitting. There are no tall-fitting jeans available.
2. A reminder from his Audi dealer that his car is due for a service. This relates to his last Audi but two, which he disposed of six years ago. Both of the following cars have been serviced by the same dealer, but they don't seem to have noticed yet.
3. Some specially selected items from Amazon, on the basis of his recent purchases. Foremost among these are some printer ink cartridges, obviously specially selected on the basis that he just bought a dozen of them (for printing more drafts of this manuscript) and therefore can't possibly need any more for months.
4. Programmatic ads for a financial services conference that he has no interest in attending, but whose website he did visit to see if his co-author was speaking at it. (He wasn't.)
5. His weekly review of the investment markets from his bank, which a little embarrassingly is Coutts. Lucian has never bought an investment from Coutts and has no interest in doing so, a point which he would happily confirm if asked.
6. Details of the latest monthly auction of second-hand four-wheel-drive vehicles from a firm called Brightwells. He was indeed once interested in buying a second-hand four-wheel drive vehicle, which was why he subscribed to Brightwells' weekly auction details, and in fact he did actually buy one, although not at auction. But that was 12 years ago now, and he's been discarding these e-mails unopened ever since.

7. An e-mail inviting him to join easyJet's frequent flyer scheme, Flight Club. In principle this makes good sense because he is indeed an easy-Jet frequent flyer and Flight Club offers some valuable benefits. But the e-mail takes a strange turn from the outset. The headline reads *Your Exclusive Personal Invitation to Flight Club,* and introduces a video presented by the CEO, but the first sentence of the copy reads 'Your Flight Club membership is already live so you don't need to do anything'. Huh?

8. And finally, before we all get bored, around two dozen random e-mails from retailers, travel companies and others with whom he presumably did business once, but toward whom he has no particular interest, loyalty or desire to repeat the experience. These include firms called La Marquiere (something French, no idea), Qwerkity (a Christmas stocking filler some years ago), Aspinal & Co (ditto, but a bit more upmarket), something called Grand Prix Legends (can't remember), Dreweatts (an auction house where he bought a signed picture of Michael Owen for his son for his seventh birthday, but now offering him a preview of a Chinese ceramics sale) and Booking.com (cheap accommodation in an almost surreally unattractive selection of places, including – honestly – Caen, Stockport and somewhere called Boryspil in Ukraine[1]).

Actually (Lucian adds), even more finally, on the home page of my browser here's another ad, just served this minute, for that Future of Digital Banking conference, which I would start finding a bit creepy if it wasn't for the fact that I'm in the business and know, at least roughly, how these things work.[2]

Apart from saying that it wasn't terribly interesting, you might raise three objections to this list. You might say:

1. Nobody, not Peppers and Rogers or anyone else since, has ever said that personalized, data driven one-to-one communication will ever completely replace the old mass marketing sort. It may well be that when Lands' End are offering a very chunky 40% discount on the price of

---

[1]Note from Lucian: I think I ought to explain Boryspil. My son Ollie quite quickly outgrew his enthusiasm for Michael Owen, but maintained his love of football, as indeed does his father. In 2012 we went to Kiev to watch a couple of games in the Euro 2012 tournament, and I've been bombarded with offers on travel to Ukraine – a place I confidently expect never to visit again – ever since.

[2]Meanwhile, Anthony points out that the weaknesses of online shopping can arise at the end, as well as the beginning, of the customer relationship. His bete noire is *The Times* newspaper subscription website. Nowhere on the innumerable e-mails he receives or on the website itself can he find the opportunity to unsubscribe.

jeans, that they can enjoy excellent ROI from a simple, single mass e-mail to their customer base, rather than bothering with all the faff of personalizing the offer to target the very small segment of ridiculously tall males. Who cares about pissing people off with irrelevant e-mails?

2. As chance would have it, this was a day when there were few attempts at personalization and the ones that did come through weren't hugely successful – it was bad luck, for example, that the Amazon Special Selection was so obviously irrelevant. On other days, the proportion of wheat to chaff must be higher.

3. The majority of the messages in the list, and especially the two dozen or so under number 8, don't represent failed attempts to do clever things with data – they're just bog-standard follow-on e-mails to random customers or enquirers about whom the retailers know little except an e-mail address.

On the other hand, the sheer quantity of this one-notch-up-from-spam material is a problem, even if only because anything genuinely well targeted and personalized is likely to be drowned out amidst all that noise. And most, if not all of the senders could have cleaned up their data with remarkable ease at any time over the years: the Audi dealer could and indeed should have known that their records are two cars out of date, Coutts should have been able to see that none of their investment e-mails has ever been opened, and after 12 years Brightwells might have been wise to check whether Lucian still has any interest at all in four-wheel drive vehicles, or in driving, or indeed is even still alive.

But if the problem among digital marketing organizations generally is that they're continuing to pump out far too much irrelevant, untargeted and unpersonalised stuff, the principal problem in financial services is still the opposite. Returning to Lucian's inbox for one last time, his last 100 marketing messages include just three from financial services firms – the Coutts market review mentioned above, an extremely boring Terms & Conditions update from Virgin Money and a personal loan offer from PayPal. This may well suggest that he spends more of his online time exploring the world of four-wheel-drive vehicles and planning trips to watch football matches than dealing with financial services, and this is certainly the case. But still, he is an active and current customer of at least 20 financial services providers of one sort or another, and has signed up as a prospect (even if only for work reasons) with at least twice as many more. Really your authors should know better than to base so much of this chapter's content on a research sample of one, but even if the one in question is very atypical indeed a clear point still comes through.

At least, on the upside, this suggests that at present financial services firms need to worry less than many about the danger of perceived creepiness – or, worse than creepiness, thoroughly disturbing intrusiveness – which is starting to reach alarming levels in other sectors. The problem is partly that consumers don't understand how marketers are able to target them so precisely, and so feel uncomfortable when, having bought, say, a pair of reading glasses or a case of Chilean wine on the Internet they're then pursued by ads for reading glasses and/or Chilean wine on almost every website they visit over the following month. Bu actually it's worse than that: even when they do have some sense of how their data is captured and used, many really don't like it very much.

The evidence suggests this is largely a generational issue, and that older people reflect their generally higher levels of discomfort with the digital world in their higher levels of anxiety about personal privacy. But, that said, research indicates overall levels of anxiety so high that younger people can't be immune. A survey among a nationally representative sample of over 2,000 people tells us that 71% don't feel comfortable sharing geo-location data, and 68% feel uncomfortable sharing data from their social media profile, while 45% say they would stop dealing with an organization altogether if they found it was using their personal data in a way they didn't feel comfortable with, and 57% say they don't trust brands to use their data responsibly. On this last point, just over half say they have received communications from firms that they believe have in fact misused their data.

The same research, incidentally, confirms two other points. Only 8% of respondents said that they understood where and how organizations use their personal data, while 31% admitted that they didn't have a clue. And among the separate sample of marketing people, the findings indicated that consumers are currently right to be suspicious. 41% of marketers say they don't understand the laws around using consumers' personal data, and only 35% say their own organizations are transparent in the ways that the collect data. And only 40% say their organizations have training in place to ensure that the current data protection rules are adhered to.

All in all, these aren't hugely auspicious findings for the two hugely important data-related legislative changes taking place at the time of writing. GDPR, imposing new constraints and controls on the use of customers' personal data, and PSD2 obliging banks to make their customers' data available to customers, and through them to third parties, could both result in significant and very positive change. But, although it's very early days, at the moment it does rather look as if industry ignorance of the former, and customers' security fears about the latter, will act as considerable obstacles to progress.

Data protection and security issues are certainly one of the items on the list of difficulties in bringing Peppers' and Rogers' vision to life, but from the fact that 25 years after the publication of their book there's still such a long way to go, you can tell that it's by no means the only one.

In fact, we're in no doubt that of all the challenges posed by the new financial services marketing, moving to a truly data-driven approach is right up there among the very greatest, not just for marketing people, but for their organizations as a whole. It may well be that the available benefits, for firms and customers alike, are the greatest, too: let's hope so, because otherwise it simply wouldn't be worth the effort.

Like many – perhaps even most – of the marketing advances described in this book, this one presents very different challenges for large, complex, long-established organizations, and for small, simple, young ones. And like many – perhaps even most – of those marketing advances, they're much easier for the latter firms to tackle.

If yours is a small, simple, young financial services firm, then arguably you should only have one significant problem in adopting a data-driven approach: you don't have much data yet. It is of course possible to acquire any amount of third-party data, and it's also possible to set about building a significant prospect database (or data lake, as it seems we now like to call it) of your own as an urgent marketing objective in its own right. But, nevertheless, you're still aiming to overcome a disadvantage compared to large, long-established firms with thousands or even millions of customers.

The US market for online investment services provides a case in point. Digital startups like Betterment and WealthFront worked extremely hard from a standing start to build their customer bases, and their efforts in attracting assets under management (AUM) of a billion dollars or more within just five years of launch were widely admired. As the size of the market for this kind of service became clearer, established giants in retail asset management like Vanguard and Charles Schwab launched similar services. With stronger brands and bigger budgets, but above all with data including millions of existing customers and prospects, they overtook the startups' five-year AUM numbers within a week or two.

Schwab and Vanguard were unusual in that they were large, successful firms with big customer and prospect bases but, as relatively young and simple businesses, they were less-than-averagely affected by many of the legacy and complexity problems that afflict so many other firms. Bearing in mind that most of the biggest firms are the result of numbers of mergers and acquisitions, and that mergers and acquisitions invariably create horrendous IT and data integration problems, it comes as no big surprise to hear that some of the biggest are still running up to a dozen separate data platforms, and several are unable to tell how many customers they actually have or what combinations of products they currently hold. For firms in this sort of situation to embrace the one-to-one data-driven future is almost unimaginably hard. Some data experts believe that in this situation, we're moving inescapably toward a two-speed future where smaller, younger businesses with less legacy and newer computers have a sustainable agility advantage, at least until they themselves become bigger and older and carry out some mergers and acquisitions of their own.

Still, in the end, even the firms faced with the biggest, hardest and most complex challenges can only tackle them in the same way as any other – one step at a time. On this basis, we held a workshop with a group of consultants, all with extensive current financial services experience, to identify the biggest issues that the industry is currently tackling. The main 10 points that emerged from this session – in no particular order – were as follows:

1. For most classically trained marketers, the change in perspective and the new skills required in moving to a data-driven basis is likely to be among the toughest challenges of their careers.
2. Successful data-driven marketing requires new levels of co-ordination between marketing and many – if not most – other business functions, including (obviously) IT but also operations, risk, sales, finance and others specific to the sector in question, to manage customers' journeys from start to finish. Few marketers have the authority or skills necessary to manage and control such disparate project teams.
3. Many firms' own data are still very limited, either in terms of what they hold or (at least as often) in terms of what they can effectively access. The growing availability of open source data is important, but nevertheless the ability to access third-party sources is still a key constraint for many.
4. Very often, a key skill is the ability to merge third-party data with firms' own internal sources. For example, you can review publicly available data that doesn't give you individuals' personal detail, but gives you the information you need on, say, their shopping behaviour: the need is then to merge that with the transaction data on your own bank system to create something you can actually use. Those data-merging capabilities aren't easy to develop just now.
5. Similarly, good data-driven marketing almost always involves some kind of merging of quantitative and qualitative analysis; if you go too far down either path you'll miss the bigger picture.
6. Insofar as we continue to overlay segmentations onto individual data, there are good reasons to think that one of the most important will be segmentation on the basis of age. This relates to some extent to the point in the previous section, that on the whole younger customers are less concerned about privacy and 'creepiness' issues than older

customers – but also, more broadly, to the fact that we're at a point in time at which younger customers' journeys are likely to be significantly different from older customers'. (The clearest example relates to the choice of devices. For younger customers it must be mobile and tablet first; for the next groups it's computers; the next group still prefer the telephone; and there's still a surprisingly large proportion of the oldest group who like to clip coupons and write letters.)

7. The IT challenges certainly haven't gone away. The evolving philosophy of the so-called 'data lake', which can be accessed effectively by marketers and others without the need for extensive IT input, makes life easier once the 'lake' is built and filled with data. The big idea, one of our consultants told us, is self-service analytics, meaning that users who would have once needed to form an orderly queue to commission a six-month, six-figure IT project can now DIY what they need straight away. But specifying and building that lake in the first place is a huge task that does require extensive IT input – so the problem has changed shape rather than disappearing.

8. And even more important, there's the single biggest thing that Peppers and Rogers underestimated: the gigantic scale of the data-processing requirement to run your personalised programmes. One of our consultants discussed a project for a leading UK supermarket, dealing with a total of over 200,000 product lines and data that embraces 8 million loyalty scheme members: not even Google, he told us, has a grid big enough to come up with a personalised model for each individual. (The corollary is that data storage and data analytics are becoming so cheap as to be virtually free.)

9. What's more, you're trying to process that stupendous quantity of data in an environment in which timeliness is critically important. A personalised, data-driven communication that is timely is welcome and relevant. One major bank quotes a powerful case history in which it texts an offer of a discount on a personal loan to a customer at the moment he or she is visiting a car showroom or looking online at a car ad. Get the timing even slightly off, and it's probably an irrelevance.

10. In the end, there's no getting round the fact that high levels of personalization mean that we're quite simply going to need to create a lot more marketing stuff. As a participant in our workshop put it, we don't need one big-budget TV commercial any more, we need 10, 20 or even 30 much lower-budget, much more customizable messages that we can target to particular segments and then address to individuals within them. And with so much more stuff being produced so much more quickly and with much lower budgets, you can't help recalling

the famous aphorism of the author Kingsley Amis (in fact commenting on the increasing number of available university places in the UK, but equally relevant in all sorts of other contexts), 'More Means Worse'.

As well as these generic, industry-wide issues, there are specific points relevant to specific industry sectors. Among the most thought-provoking are those that relate to insurance, where it's arguable that the rapid increase in individual customer-level data effectively signals the end of insurance as a concept: by its very nature, insurance depends on the principle of pooling risk, in situations where the overall level of risk across the pool is quantifiable but not the individual level of risk run by each individual within it. When we have data that defines each individual's level of risk with ever-increasing levels of accuracy, it's difficult to see how risk-pooling as a principle can survive. At the time of writing, the industry is still maintaining moratoria in a couple of specific areas, not using genetic data in the pricing of life assurance and not making full use of flood risk data in home insurance. But it's difficult to believe that either of these policies will last for long – and meanwhile other sources of data are having an effect on life assurance underwriting (with, for example, the highly successful firm Vitality offering discounts for people maintaining high levels of fitness), and on motor insurance, particularly with telematics, the in-car 'black boxes' that allow individuals' driving styles and behaviours to be reflected (or controlled in the case of 10 p.m. curfews for young drivers), for better or worse, in their premiums. The impact of ever-increasing and ever-improving data on the concept of insurance underwriting is a subject beyond the scope of a book about financial services marketing, thank goodness, but it's very difficult to see how insurance as we know it can last much longer under these growing pressures.

We've come a considerable distance in this chapter without yet mentioning either Artificial Intelligence (AI) or its close relative Machine Learning (ML). Given the truly vast amounts of money being invested in developing these capabilities, and the much vaster amounts that will be required to implement them across the industry, this feels like a major oversight.

In one sense that's certainly true. In another scale-and-complexity point underestimated by Peppers and Rogers, the delivery challenges of data-driven marketing are so immense that it would be quite impossible to achieve the scale required if they ran on human brain power alone. At every point in the customer journey – but perhaps most of all at the points where the customer actually wants to interact directly with the organisation – computers with the ability to learn from their interactions and deliver an ever-more personalised service are the only possible solution. We have now reached a point where, in well-designed processes, chatbots can now do an acceptable job of maintaining the necessary dialogue with the customer (although there's little doubt that for some while to come, a bail-out to a real person will be necessary when things get complicated). As marketers, your authors aren't too embarrassed to admit that we haven't the faintest idea how the technology works, but we're happy to recognise that it works increasingly well – and that for the data-driven future ever to arrive, it's essential that it does so.

Up to a point, this kind of technological ignorance is acceptable, and indeed inevitable. It's not possible for everyone to know everything. But there are dangers that emerge when subject areas become so complex that only a very few specialists really claim to understand them – probably the all-time best-ever example being the area of derivative-based complex financial products during the 2008 crash, some of which were said to be so complicated that actually no-one understood them, or what could happen when they went wrong. At the time of writing, the data-driven marketing equivalent is the area of programmatic advertising, where it seems that hardly anyone involved at any point in the process understood that the way the system currently works, the appearance of ads for blue-chip grocery brands, charities and government publicity campaigns on sites featuring jihadist bomb-making videos is an inevitable consequence.

It would be a brave person who would predict how the current concerns in this area will develop in the future, but it seems clear that the biggest reason for the current crisis is that many buyers of digital advertising (a) haven't really understood what they've been buying, and (b) haven't really understood the metrics used by the vendors to give an account of its performance. This obviously creates the potential for some very nasty surprises when the truth belatedly dawns, whether it's the discovery that big blue-chip organizations have been buying space from racist, sexist and even terrorist organizations, or the discovery that video viewing figures involve a degree of statistical manipulation that makes them effectively meaningless.

As the world of digital media becomes ever more complex and labyrinthine, it's difficult to see how we can escape more problems like these. A few large and sophisticated companies may be able to afford to hire specialists with responsibility for monitoring actual performance, but most with have to rely on advice from third-party consultants, agencies and advisers. This, however, in itself raises a pair of potentially awkward questions: first whether these third parties fully understand what's going on, and second, even if so, whether the buyers of their services can rely on their complete integrity.

There's one more big point to make in this chapter. Every now and then a technology comes along that really does wipe out whatever went before it. We all know about the classic business-school case history about the effect of the transcontinental US railroad on the previous era's wagon trains.

And although it took a while, within a hundred years or so the printing press knocked the bottom out of the medieval manuscript-illustrating business. But on the whole, this isn't what happens. On the whole, new technologies find a new place alongside the previous versions. Cinema didn't wipe out theatre. Photography didn't mean the end of painting. Electric music co-exists with orchestral. People still wrote letters after they acquired telephones, and still make phone calls after they've acquired computers. The balance between the old and the new can vary, and is hard to predict: sometimes the new becomes dominant, sometimes the old proves amazingly resilient. (Sometimes, also, the old evolves to make room for the new. There are, for example, as many horses in the UK today as there were in the heyday or indeed hayday of horse-drawn transport, but they're not pulling carriages, buses or taxis.)

This lengthy preamble is by way of an introduction to the point that data-driven marketing seems most unlikely to replace the previous, more broadly targeted kind. In part, this is certainly because it's so fearsomely difficult to do well, but it's for other reasons, too:

1. At risk of sweeping generalization, data-driven one-to-one activity is likely to work better when managing relationships with existing customers, and less well when seeking to recruit new ones. In the absence of any existing relationship, the advantage of engaging with people individually is reduced.
2. Data-driven activity is particularly powerful when there is an important timeliness issue. If you're able to communicate with individuals at a time when you're certain, or pretty certain, that they're thinking of buying a new car, you can deliver outstandingly relevant propositions to them. But timeliness isn't always achievable: how do you know when someone is likely to need a sticking-plaster?
3. There is still a great deal of strength in that old tried and tested formulation, 'As Seen on TV'. In many markets – certainly including much of financial services – consumers are reassured to know that a particular brand has the scale and substance to spend money on making itself known. An e-mail may well be a scam. A commercial in the centre break of *Coronation Street* really can't be.
4. One of the central beliefs of the data-driven marketing community is that behavioural data is powerfully predictive, whereas other kinds of insight – attitudinal, demographic, whatever – aren't. This isn't always true. Some attitudinal insights – for example, most of the behavioural scientists' most powerful biases, such as loss aversion – are hard to pick up through behavioural data, but can provide a highly effective basis for traditionally segmented marketing activity.

5. Especially as far as marketing communication is concerned, there are a number of available options that only work at scale, or at least that only work when there is a broad-scale element to them. Take sponsorship. If a firm sponsors an arts or sports event, there will very likely be some brilliant opportunities for one-to-one hospitality. But those one-to-one opportunities would not exist without the much broader-scale opportunity arising from sponsoring the event as a whole. The need, clearly, is to integrate the two levels to get the most out of the overall budget.

6. This same point, that the most effective marketing approach will involve some kind of integrated combination of mass and one-to-one activity, is also true of a great deal of digital marketing, and it's particularly likely to be the case when there is a significant social media element. Firms will often initiate activity or specific campaigns with broadcast social media messaging, but look for opportunities to move on into one-to-one dialogues with individuals.

All of this, of course, only adds to the pressure on marketers. It isn't just a question of learning a large number of new skills: it's also a question of retaining most if not all of the existing skills, and then finding a way to bring both sets together.

On the upside, the prize for doing so successfully is a very valuable one. It may well be that it's through the gradual emergence of Peppers' and Rogers' one-to-one future that marketers finally achieve a new level of authority in their businesses.

CHAPTER 12

Do You Get the Power of Behavioural Economics?

Your authors have agreed on the very large majority of the things we're saying in this book. We've generally agreed quickly, too, with little need for difficult debate or awkward compromise.

This chapter is the exception. It's broadly about the emerging – or perhaps now largely emerged – science of behavioural economics. Anthony believes this is one of the very most important drivers of the new financial services marketing. In essence, he thinks that the insights increasingly available into consumers' wants, needs and above all behaviours open up a whole new world of marketing opportunity. Lucian believes that most of these insights have been well-understood for decades by almost everyone except classical economists. In particular, he thinks that a great many originated in the field of direct marketing, and therefore have little or nothing to teach the marketing community.

Clearly, we need to sort this out between us. But both points of view have merit. So, rather than have the argument privately and then write something we can both put our names to, we thought you might find it interesting if we have the argument publicly in this chapter. We might even finish up coming to an agreement. And if not, you can decide for yourself which of us you think is right.

LC: Let's start by pinning down what it is that we disagree about. What exactly are you saying about behavioural economics, and why do you think it's so important?

AT: Before we get to the disagreement, we'd better agree on the vocabulary. I prefer behavioural science. To me that's the big idea. The economics is just a subset.

LC: I'm okay with that, although as an abbreviation I'd have thought you might prefer BE to BS. Still, behavioural science it is. What exactly are you saying about it?

AT: I'm saying that for many years – at least since the middle of the twentieth century – the dominant idea that shaped attitudes and policies in financial services was the confidence of classical economists in the existence of the 'rational consumer'. But over the past 20 years or so, behavioural scientists have increasingly challenged this belief and have been able to demonstrate, more and more convincingly and in more and more detail, that this 'rational consumer' doesn't exist, and instead that consumers' behaviour deviates from 'rational' models in ways that are consistent, persistent and reliable. And by understanding these deviations, a whole raft of new and powerfully effective strategies become available to us.

LC: Ah, yes, the rational consumer – an oxymoron that's right up there with 'cold heat', 'German comedian' and 'Spurs defender'. (Actually, we have to rethink the last of these examples a bit these days, given my team's awesome recent impregnability.) What did economists mean by this implausible idea?

AT: By economists' standards, it's a remarkably simple concept. They say that given perfect information and a perfectly functioning market, consumers will make financial decisions that, as the economists like to express it, 'optimise their utility' – that is to say, give them the biggest available bang for their buck.

LC: And they haven't been discouraged by the fact that billions of decisions made by millions of consumers conclusively demonstrate that this absolutely isn't the case?

AT: Economics is a theoretical science, not an empirical one. But no, they would argue that when consumers make decisions that clearly don't optimise their utility, that must be because either the market is functioning imperfectly, or they have imperfect information. Unless …

LC: Unless what?

AT: Unless it's an anomaly. When classical economists find evidence that seems to contradict their theories, they declare that it must be an anomaly. That means they recognise the evidence exists, but their theory remains intact all the same.

LC: It seems to me it's no big surprise that behavioural science has come along to challenge this obvious nonsense. What happened? Where did the challenge come from?

AT: Long story short, most behavioural scientists would agree that the founding fathers of the discipline were Daniel Kahneman and Amos Tversky, two psychologists who stepped extremely bravely into the economists' lair, so to speak, and demonstrated step by step that most of what they said about consumers was wrong.

LC: Yes, I know about Kahneman and Tversky. You can tell they were important from the fact that Michael Lewis has written a book about them. Not his best, but still.

AT: True. But you didn't pick up on the most significant point about Kahneman and Tversky, which is that they were psychologists. That's important for two reasons. First because they weren't economists, and so they had never bought in to the rational consumer concept. And second because psychology, unlike economics, is an empirical science. Psychologists base their insights on evidence, not theories.

LC: And as we all know, they carried out all sorts of brilliant experiments to prove how far from rational we really are.

AT: I don't think that's quite right. What was really important wasn't so much the proof that we're irrational, but the proof that we're consistently and predictably irrational. It goes right back to the first paper they wrote together, the one about the Law of Small Numbers back in 1969. Basically, this showed how all of us, even the most rigorous academics, are prone to drawing conclusions on the basis of hopelessly small sample sizes – samples so small that the finding, whatever it may be, might very likely simply be the result of chance. There's a big thing in it about whether a coin comes up heads or tails.

LC: Not their sexiest experiment. But I take the point about being consistently irrational, or at least I think I do. 'Consistently' isn't the same thing as 'invariably' or 'always', is it?

AT: No. It means 'usually'. All of behavioural science is about 'usually'. Anyway, the Law of Small Numbers work got them going, but it was the stuff about loss aversion that really started to make their names – and that is still often quoted over 40 years later.

LC: Remind me.

AT: They did zilllons of experiments basically offering people bets. Mostly they offered people a choice between two bets, and asked which they would prefer. For example:
Which would you prefer:
a. $30,000 for sure?
b. A gamble that has a 50% chance of winning $70,000 and a 50% chance of winning nothing?
Most people took the $30,000, by the way.
From this huge programme of experiments, the chaps drew two key conclusions. First, it was indisputably clear that people's choices were being strongly influenced by their emotions, which were having the effect of driving them to strictly 'irrational' decisions. And second, the

tendency of those emotions was to try to minimise the risk of loss. The big idea that came out of it all was that our aversion to loss is roughly twice as great as our liking for gain.

LC: I can't deny that's a big idea, and obviously one that's massively relevant to financial services marketing. But it's also a sweeping generalization, isn't it?

AT: Yes it is, and fond as I am of the behavioural scientists and their works I have to admit that a lot of their written work doesn't do a brilliant job of clarifying quite how generally their findings apply. And while I'm criticizing my own team, I'd also say that they carried out almost all their experiments among people working or studying at American universities, and although I know a lot of their experiments have been replicated elsewhere I don't really know how much the findings differed. For example, it's a cliché to say that as investors, there's a kind of international hierarchy of risk aversion, with the Germans the most risk-averse, then the Brits, then the Americans and then the Chinese. I don't have any hard evidence for this, but I suspect you could substantiate it by looking at the kinds of investments most often chosen in each market. But I don't know at all whether Kahneman and Tversky would recognise this hierarchy, or reject it, or simply take an agnostic view of it and say that it's not an issue they explored in their research.

LC: But anyway, they did prove that there's a big emotional element in financial decision-making, and that one of its big consequences is risk aversion.

AT: Exactly.

LC: And this came as a surprise to those classical economists.

AT: A huge surprise. There was a legendary conference at the University of Chicago when Richard Thaler, who was one of Kahneman's and Tversky's strongest supporters, presented a behavioural science paper to an audience largely consisting of hardcore monetarists and was virtually booed off the stage. They thought he was having a laugh.

LC: Hmm. I think we're coming toward the nub of our disagreement now. Because I totally accept your story about the University of Chicago conference, and the shock and horror that greeted Thaler's paper. But I have to say that in my perception, academic monetarists are pretty much the only living beings in the universe who could be surprised by the finding that there's an emotional component in financial decision-making. This strikes me quite literally as one of the least surprising things I've ever heard.

AT: Aha. Now I see where you're coming from. But you're completely missing the point. In fact, you're missing two points. Of course you, and I, and everyone else working in financial services marketing, know perfectly well that there's an emotional component in financial decision-making. In fact, many of us would say there isn't much of a rational element. But the first point you're missing is that behavioural science goes much further than that, and says that this 'emotional component' can be mapped out as a series of specific biases and heuristics that can be recognised and taken on board, and used as the basis for our planning. And the second point you're missing is that even though no-one except a University of Chicago economist could seriously defend the concept of the rational consumer, nevertheless this mythical figure has dominated many of the thought-processes of those in and around the financial services industry for practically the whole time that you and I have been working in it.

LC: Is that really true? Give me an example.

AT: Okay, take the regulators' approach to what they like to call 'financial promotions' and you and I would call financial marketing communications. The FCA has changed its tune very recently, but for far too long the idea was basically to get as close as possible to providing consumers with what those economists call 'perfect information' – that is, all the information about all the products that rational consumers could possibly need in order to make a rational choice between them. As you and I know, the effects of this were disastrous for all concerned. Providers had to spend a ton of money putting screeds of microscopic detail in front of consumers, only for consumers to find the sheer quantity of information overwhelming and off-putting, and so to feel paralysed into indecision.

LC: You're right. And some advertising media, notably radio, became effectively no-go areas for financial services because of the amount of money and airtime you had to spend shouting meaningless gibberish at the public.

AT: Exactly.

LC: Okay, so we've now established that among the people stupid enough to accept the classical economists' view of the rational consumer were University of Chicago economists and regulators. Anyone else?

AT: Well, as far as people's financial wellbeing is concerned, you'd have to say that probably the most important were in the government, and particularly the Treasury and the Department of Work and Pensions.

LC: I think I know where you're going with this. This is about pensions and auto-enrolment, isn't it?

AT: It is. And I'm pleased to say that it's a positive story – it's too early to talk about a happy ending, but we can certainly talk about a happy beginning, if there is such a thing. You know the backstory – end of the era of defined benefit pensions, need to engage people in contributing to defined contribution schemes, horribly low level of opting in, millions facing the prospect of retiring on a diet of catfood ...

LC: ... until behavioural scientists point out the huge benefits of switching from an opt-in to an opt-out system, and around 90% of people don't choose to opt out, and future prosperity is assured for all, or nearly all, anyway. Or at least it would be if the level of contributions was set a great deal higher than the current derisory 3%. Which indeed they will be when the contributions escalator kicks in with increases in 2018 and 2019.

AT: That's it. Probably the single greatest real-world success so far for behavioural science. And remember, previous governments had tried to encourage people to put money into pensions pretty much exclusively by offering the kinds of incentives that theoretically appeal most strongly to the 'rational consumer', namely tax incentives. If we'd stayed with an opt-in system, I don't think tax incentives would have been half as effective – probably not even a quarter as effective – at persuading people to join workplace pensions.

LC: I completely accept all that.

AT: But?

LC: No but. I completely accept that an opt-out process is an amazingly effective way to achieve very high levels of take-up. There's all sorts of proof from all sorts of markets, whether it's about the effect of fluoridation on tooth decay, or moving to an opt-out system on organ donation, or – a bit closer to home – packaging dodgy PPI insurance with personal loans so that people had to opt out if they didn't want it.

AT: Yes, that was a rather less acceptable face of the opt-out principle. In hindsight.

LC: My point is that anyone who knows anything about consumers – or anyone who knows anything about marketing, which as we frequently say in this book should be more or less the same thing – already knew that opt-out systems hugely increase uptake. Maybe the great and the good in the Treasury and the DWP didn't, along with the regulator and the academics at the University of Chicago, but apart from that ...

AT: I know, apart from that what have the Romans ever done for us? So your case is basically that Kahneman and Tversky and Thaler and Halpern didn't really come up with anything much that wasn't already well known and understood by Bird, Watson, Wunderman and Barraclough.

LC: Or any other leading figures of the direct marketing industry you might like to mention. Exactly. 'Cash if you die, cash if you don't'. Perhaps the most successful of all financial services direct marketing headlines, written, I think, for Lloyd's Life by John Watson back in the seventies, although, as with several famous advertising copylines, I've heard quite a few veteran copywriters laying claim to it.

AT: Actually, it's a true marketing case study and not just an advertising one. It was the product itself, not just the copyline, that connected so strongly with that loss aversion bias we were talking about a few minutes ago.

LC: And if it did all happen back in the 1970s, then it would have been before Kahneman and Tversky's work on the subject. In the pattern of cross-fertilisation between academia and direct marketing, it's actually quite difficult to figure out who was cross-fertilising who, or rather whom: late in his life, Amos Tversky actually said that all he and Daniel Kahneman did was to take up ideas that had long been known to advertising executives, and codify and classify them in a recognizable academic format.

AT: I didn't know he said that. Where did you find that quote?

LC: Actually it was given to me in an interview with the great Rory Sutherland, vice-chairman of ad agency Ogilvy Group and one of the very few people I know who can fairly be described as a guru in the fields of both direct marketing and behavioural science.

AT: Should've invited him along to this conversation. What else does he have to say?

LC: Well, Rory has a huge amount of respect for the great gurus of behavioural science. Allow me to quote:

> We'd be doing a disservice to behavioural science if we just said, 'Hey, Herbert Simon, Nobel Prize winner, and Daniel Kahneman, Nobel Prize winner – you're just fancy direct marketers.' You would not be doing them justice by describing them as such. What I don't think we in direct marketing realized, because we didn't understand economics, is just how significant some of our findings were. And I also think we didn't realize how influential economics was everywhere else in our clients' businesses. It's not about the advertising function or the marketing director. It's to do with some of the most fundamental assumptions of the business.

AT: So he's saying it's a pecking order thing, right? That economists are higher up the food chain than direct marketers?

LC: Yes, he is saying that. Sorry about these long quotes, but here's another one:

> When Michael Walsh was chairman of our advertising agency, Ogilvy & Mather, he said to me, 'I can get my clients

interested in PR. I can get them interested in design. But I can't get them interested in direct marketing.' And working in Ogilvy's direct marketing firm, I always felt a bit resentful about that. I thought, how hard can it be. But actually, Mike was right. There is something about direct marketing. I only learnt this years later, talking to a bunch of marketing directors in the financial services industry. They said that being given the direct marketing brief is your worst career nightmare.

AT: How so?

LC: 'It's very fiddly', Rory said. 'It's a real headache. Things can go wrong. And it's not that much fun, because it involves a huge amount of detail, and checking, and legals, and all that stuff'.

AT: So what you're saying here is that direct marketing is sort of behavioural science's drearier brother.

LC: A little bit drearier maybe. But also quite a bit smarter – I'm also saying that most of those astounding Nobel Prize winning behavioural science ideas that have been winning Nobel Prizes at regular intervals ever since the 1970s have been statements of the bleedin' obvious to direct marketers for a great deal longer.

AT: I think you're going to need some more evidence for that part of your proposition.

LC: Okay, well, no question, the single best source of evidence is David Halpern's book about the activities of the behavioural science team (actually known as the Behavioural Insights Team) working within the UK Civil Service since 2010. Honestly, if you read it without knowing anything about Halpern or his team, you'd imagine you were reading a book written by a direct marketing agency, so many of the breakthroughs and discoveries are drawn from the area. His team's remit is all about improving the results of public communications and campaigns from different branches of government, and first and in a sense foremost, their fundamental test-and-learn approach is absolutely in line with good direct marketing practice. And the tests that prove the most successful are the ones that would certainly gladden the heart of Drayton Bird, John Watson (two of the founders of one of the UK's first direct marketing agencies) and indeed Rory Sutherland.

Many are to do with direct mail letter variants. Letters using recipients' names work better than letters that don't. Overprinted flashes and stamps increase response. Shorter, simpler messages outperform longer, more complicated ones. Messages that emphasise the scarcity, or urgency, or popularity of what's being offered generate

more response more quickly. Free gifts of trivial value – free pens
are the classic – can motivate big and expensive purchase decisions.
Halpern, his crew and the civil servants briefing them are delighted
by these discoveries. Readers from direct marketing backgrounds
couldn't be less surprised.

AT: How about the famous loft insulation story? That isn't about comms.

LC: True, that's a bigger story that starts with the proposition itself. But
it's still all about the kind of insight that you need in direct marketing.
It's the tale of one of Halpern's earliest and most famous successes,
to do with the not-terribly-inspiring subject of loft insulation. The
team tries various ways to engage people with this, including some
significant financial incentives, but results are mediocre. Finally they
come up with a sort of Trojan Horse approach, which offers to come
round and clear out people's lofts while, almost in passing, fitting
some insulation while they're at it. People like this and business is
brisk, which comes as no great surprise to those of us who've promoted free winter safety checks on behalf of tyre and brake centres like
Kwikfit.

AT: I may have to concede as far as Halpern and his team are concerned.
But you must admit that some of the behavioural scientists' test results
go a long way beyond the more or less incremental and obvious things
we like to test in direct marketing.

LC: Such as?

AT: I'm a big fan of Robert Cialdini – who, by the way, is absolutely a
proper academic, but makes no secret of the fact that he does a lot
of his fee-earning work for clients in sales and marketing. One of his
big things is the importance of what he calls 'priming', by which he
means the things that you do to warm up your prospect before you
try to make the sale.

LC: Yes, I get that. I remember having a road-to-Damascus moment years
and years ago, when we did some focus groups on advertising concepts
for Co-op supermarkets' own-label groceries. The researchers fed back
that the first few groups had been terrible – the respondents hated the
ads, thought they were irrelevant and pointless.
I went along to watch, and I noticed that before they showed the ads,
the researchers spent fifteen minutes or so warming up the group by
asking them about their experience of supermarket shopping – how
important was car parking, what did they like and dislike in store
layout, how many times a week did they shop, how did they judge
which checkout queue to join and so forth. Then they produced the
ads, and of course they seemed totally irrelevant. They were all about

the Co-op's own-label tea, and ice cream, and cheese, and French wine – not a word about car parks or checkouts.

So then we asked the researchers to run the warm-up differently and ask respondents about cheese and tea and ice cream before showing them the ads. They loved them, couldn't wait to get out of the research groups and head for their nearest Co-op. Well, I exaggerate slightly.

AT: Good story, but Cialdini's stories are far more extreme. My favourite is the one about the consultant whose clients tended to haggle over his fee proposals in meetings. Cialdini's strategy to tackle the problem sounds ridiculous, but he swears it worked. He told the consultant to make sure that shortly before pitching his proposed fee, he should always mention a very much larger number. It didn't really matter what this much larger number might be, or how the consultant introduced it: in Cialdini's example, the consultant simply says, 'Well, as you can tell, I'm not going to be able to charge you a million dollars for this!' The client agrees – 'You're damn right!' he says. A few moments later the consultant puts forward his actual fee, which is $75,000. The client accepts it without objection.

Or take his supermarket wine-buying story. I must admit that even I find this one quite hard to believe, but it's about a supermarket with both German and French wines on display. When they played classic German oompah-oompah brass band music over the sound system, the German wine flew off the shelves – and when they played French ooh-la-la accordion music, it was the same for the French. And when they interviewed the wine-buyers outsider the store afterwards, they had no recollection at all of having heard any music.

LC: Makes you wonder how far you can take this idea. Waltzing Matilda to sell Australian chardonnays? Moody tangos for Argentinean merlot?

AT: And would it work in financial services? If you provided suitable national soundtracks on your website, would people flock toward the appropriate investment funds?

LC: Someone should run some tests. But meanwhile, we should move on from swapping anecdotes and think a bit harder about the underlying principles involved. Where I guess the academics are somewhat more sophisticated than the direct marketers in the way that they've identified and classified the conceptual biases that result in the examples we've been quoting. In direct marketing we know that, whatever, a handwritten PS at the end of a direct mail letter increases response, but we don't really know why. The academics are better on the why.

AT: You're right, they're very good indeed on the why. In fact, they're now up to well over a hundred biases that influence our behaviour, and still going strong. I wonder whether there is actually an infinite number waiting to be discovered out there.

Some, especially those that go back to Kahneman's and Tversky's research, have become famous, despite, I have to say, the great men's habit of giving them remarkably opaque and unhelpful names. Would you know, for example, unless I reminded you, that what they call the 'endowment effect' is in fact our tendency to demand far more to give something up than we'd be willing to spend to acquire it? Or that 'hyperbolic discounting' is to do with the way we tend to choose short-term over long-term gratification?

LC: Or that one of their most famous, 'prospect theory', is all about the way that we decide whether it's worth buying insurance, and if so what price we're willing to pay for it. You'd never guess.

AT: No you wouldn't. But I'm glad that you mention buying insurance. Because now that we've hopefully figured out the nature of our disagreement, I can go on to make the point I really want to make – which is that the insights available to us from behavioural science open up a whole world of new opportunities for better and more effective financial services marketing.

Prospect theory is a perfect example. I'm going to insert a lengthy footnote from Wikipedia explaining how the theory evaluates our propensity to buy insurance in two different situations. I don't expect you to follow the maths …

LC: Thanks …

AT: … because I don't myself, but the point is that the science identifies a predictable illogicality in people's behaviour. Note the combination of those two words, predictable and illogicality. Understanding how, and why, and how often people are likely to behave illogically is absolute gold dust for marketers.

LC: Provided there's someone in the marketing department who can follow the maths.

Example

To see how Prospect Theory can be applied, consider the decision to buy insurance. Assume the probability of the insured risk is 1%, the potential loss is $1,000 and the premium is $15. If we apply prospect theory, we first need to set a reference point. This could be the current wealth or the worst case (losing $1,000).

If we set the frame to the current wealth, the decision would be to either

1. *Pay $15 for sure, which yields a prospect-utility of v(–15), OR*
2. *Enter a lottery with possible outcomes of $0 (probability 99%) or –$1,000 (probability 1%), which yields a prospect-utility of π(0.01) × v(–1,000) + π(0.99) × v(0) = π(0.01) × v(–1,000).*

According to the prospect theory,

- *π(0.01) > 0.01, because low probabilities are usually over-weighted;*
- *v(–15)/v(–1,000) > 0.015, by the convexity of value function in losses.*

The comparison between π(0.01) and v(–15)/v(–1,000) is not immediately evident. However, for typical value and weighting functions, π(0.01) > v(–15)/v(–1,000), and hence π(0.01) × v(–1,000) < v(–15). That is, a strong overweighting of small probabilities is likely to undo the effect of the convexity of v in losses, making the insurance attractive.

If we set the frame to –$1,000, we have a choice between v(985) and π(0.99) × v(1,000). In this case, the concavity of the value function in gains and the underweighting of high probabilities can also lead to a preference for buying the insurance.

The interplay of overweighting of small probabilities and concavity-convexity of the value function leads to the so-called fourfold pattern of risk attitudes: risk-averse behavior when gains have moderate probabilities or losses have small probabilities; risk-seeking behavior when losses have moderate probabilities or gains have small probabilities.

Following is an example of the fourfold pattern of risk attitudes. The first item in each quadrant shows an example prospect (e.g. 95% chance to win $10,000 is high probability and a gain). The second item in the quadrant shows the focal emotion that the prospect is likely to evoke. The third item indicates how most people would behave given each of the prospects (either Risk Averse or Risk Seeking). The fourth item states expected attitudes of a potential defendant and plaintiff in discussions of settling a civil suit.

Example	Gains	Losses
High probability (certainty effect)	95% chance to win $10,000 or 100% chance to obtain $9,499. So, 95% × $10,000 = $9,500 > $9,499. Fear of disappointment. Risk averse. Accept unfavorable settlement of 100% chance to obtain $9,499.	95% chance to lose $10,000 or 100% chance to lose $9,499. So, 95% × −$10,000 = −$9,500 < −$9,499. Hope to avoid loss. Risk seeking. Rejects favorable settlement, chooses 95% chance to lose $10,000.
Low probability (possibility effect)	5% chance to win $10,000 or 100% chance to obtain $501. So, 5% × $10,000 = $500 < $501. Hope of large gain. Risk seeking. Rejects favorable settlement, chooses 5% chance to win $10,000.	5% chance to lose $10,000 or 100% chance to lose $501. So, 5% × −$10,000 = −$500 > −$501. Fear of large loss. Risk averse. Accept unfavorable settlement of 100% chance to lose $501.

*Probability distortion is that people generally do not look at the value of probability uniformly between 0 and 1. Lower probability is said to be over-weighted (that is a person is over concerned with the outcome of the probability) while medium to high probability is under-weighted (that is a person is not concerned enough with the outcome of the probability). The exact point in which probability goes from over-weighted to under-weighted is arbitrary, however a good point to consider is probability = 0.33. A person values probability = 0.01 much more than the value of probability = 0 (probability = 0.01 is said to be over-weighted). However, a person has about the same value for probability = 0.4 and probability = 0.5. Also, the value of probability = 0.99 is much less than the value of probability = 1, a sure thing (probability = 0.99 is under-weighted). A little more in depth when looking at probability distortion is that $\pi(p) + \pi(1 - p) < 1$ (where $\pi(p)$ is probability in prospect theory).**

*From Wikipedia, https://en.wikipedia.org/wiki/Prospect_theory.

LC: Blimey. If you can get a direct marketing campaign out of that, you're a great deal cleverer than I am.

AT: I must say, I'm surprised you're being so sniffy about this. You're usually the first to say that great marketing depends on great insights, and here is the biggest and richest source of insights available. I'd have thought you'd welcome it with open arms. Particularly when you consider the principal alternative.

LC: Which is?

AT: Well, I'd say, over the years, insights drawn from consumer research, most of which focus on attitudes much more than on real behaviour.

LC: I can see a long line of qualitative researchers queuing up to argue with that statement, especially all those specialists in ethnographic research who trudge round supermarkets with consumers watching how they select items off the shelves.

AT: Fair enough, there is some qualitative behavioural research, and of course a lot of quantitative, although most of it less insightful. But on the whole, the predominant belief of the research-driven insight industry has been that if you can understand people's attitudes, you can predict or anticipate their behaviour. And in fact, the truth is that attitudes are generally very poor predictors of behaviour, and by far the best predictor of behaviour is, you guessed it, behaviour.

LC: I have an obvious problem with that, which is that behaviour only has predictive value when it comes to things that people have done before. What does behavioural science tell you about their propensity to do their banking on their phones? Or choose to increase their auto-enrolled pension contributions from 1% to 4%?

AT: You're looking at this in a very two-dimensional way. Behavioural science may not tell you exactly how many people are likely to increase their contributions, or by exactly how much. But it will tell you a great deal about how you can most effectively present the choice to them, and what biases exist in their minds that will colour their response. The answer, by the way, will very likely be something along the lines of the Save More Tomorrow programme, which was one of Richard Thaler's best ideas (and also best brand names).

LC: I know about this. It's a way of tackling people's reluctance to increase their pension savings level immediately, by giving them the option of signing up to a series of small increases over the years into the future.

AT: Thus, in behavioural science terms, offsetting their bias toward hyperbolic discounting. I could add another extract full of Greek letters at this point.

LC: No, no, you've made your point. But, forgive me if I sound like a scratched record, but once again isn't this a principle that's already familiar to direct marketers? Take the example of the legendary De Agostini partworks.

AT: The what?

LC: De Agostini partworks. You know, those collections of the Great Tank Battles of the Second World War or Complete Works of Beethoven that are available from your newsagent over the next 40 weeks. I suppose it's Spend More Tomorrow, not Save More – Part 1 is just £2.99 with Part 2 free, but after that it's £5.99 a fortnight until the other side of Christmas.

AT: It's a bit unsubtle compared to Thaler's idea, isn't it? They break you in gently for a week or two, and then whoosh, the full cost hits you.

LC: The cleverest bit is getting Part 2 free. Now that you own two parts, you're on your way to a collection and you want to carry on. If you only had Part 1 you'd be much more likely to just stop there. Did Thaler offer you the first month's contribution for just 1% of salary with the second month free?

AT: I don't think he did. But, not for the first time in this discussion, a point you've made has played into my hands. Comparing an approach to the most crucial component of people's long-term financial security devised by a professor at the University of Chicago with a partwork about Great Tank Battles devised by some Milanese direct marketing people highlights the single most important point I want to make to financial services marketers.

LC: Which is?

AT: When it comes to doing big, exciting, insight-based stuff, you need all the help you can get. We agree that one of the toughest problems in financial services marketing is our continuing lack of credibility in the boardroom ...

LC: ... the colouring-in department ...

AT: And although things have improved a little bit and they're moving in the right direction, there's still a long way to go.

So you're working on a new pensions project, and on the basis of all your marketing experience, some of which for all I know may well go back to De Agostini partworks, you're convinced that the way to max-imise contributions is by introducing the Save More Tomorrow princi-ple. Adopting this is a huge decision, with millions of people's futures and ultimately billions of pounds of contributions at stake. And now all that's standing between you and this massive new departure is the need to persuade any or all of the Treasury, the DWP, HMRC, the Financial Conduct Authority, the Association of British Insurers, the Tax-Incentivised Savings Association, the FCA's consumer panel and the cautious, conservative and risk-averse directors of the country's leading pension providers. How do you rate your chances?

LC: Could be a bit tricky.

AT: There's a big meeting coming up, and you can choose who you'd like to have on your side of the table to support your cause. Do you choose (a) the Italian marketing director of Europe's leading partwork publisher, or (b) the Ralph and Dorothy Keller Distinguished Service Professor of Behavioural Science and Economics at the University of Chicago Booth School of Business?

LC: Hmm, let me think about that for a microsecond or two.

AT: So bringing this discussion to a close, my last point is very simply that for the smart, ambitious, progressive financial services marketing professional, behavioural science – and behavioural scientists – are the very best, most powerful and most influential friends who've ever come along and offered to fight in your corner. It may or may not be true that you already know and understand much of what they have to say. Remember the words of one of America's most underrated presidents, Harry S Truman, who said: 'There is no limit to what a man can achieve in life' (he wouldn't say 'man' these days) 'provided he doesn't care who takes the credit for it.' Read David Halpern's book about the work his Behavioural Insights Team was able to do from their insider's position within the PM's office, and instead of just saying to yourself, 'Yes, yes, I know all that', think how impossibly difficult it would have been for anyone in a less privileged position to do even a fraction as much. Build links with these people. Learn from the great Rory Sutherland, who from a background in direct marketing now bestrides that world and the world of behavioural science like a rather dishevelled Welsh colossus. There is nothing else out there that offers you such potential.

LC: I think I may have to acknowledge that you may have edged this debate.

CHAPTER 13

Are You Really Any Good at Innovation?

It's more or less obligatory to begin any discussion on the subject of innovation with the famous comment of the great if very peculiar American industrialist Henry Ford: 'If I'd asked my customers what they wanted, they'd have asked for a faster horse'.

Like many well-known and often-quoted quips, his words express an important truth – in this case, that you can't expect your customers to possess the imagination and insight to do your innovating for you – but at the same time, they express two untruths as well.

The first and lesser untruth is that on closer examination, it seems Ford never actually said this – at least, no evidence has emerged to prove that he did.

The more important untruth, though, is that while experience suggests that he was half-right, it also shows that in the end he was half-wrong. If asked back in the early days, his customers would have indeed said they wanted a faster horse. Consider the consequences of his autocratic approach in the first two decades of the twentieth century, when the Ford Motor Company succeeded on a truly staggering scale and built a vast industrial empire at a speed that even today's most successful tech giants would envy, and you'd think he was right not to bother too much with what his customers might say. But fast forward 20 years and look at the near-collapse of the company in the century's third decade, and you'd find Ford's customers would have been a good deal more demanding. During the 1920s, Ford's biggest rival, General Motors, correctly perceived that Ford had left big and important consumer needs unmet – a desire for new and different models, in a range of nice bright colours (at the time, Ford's other most famous comment, that you could have a Model T in 'any colour so long as it's black', sounded less like admirable single-mindedness and more like stubborn intransigence). And General Motors scored in another way too, recognising long before Ford that there's much more to selling cars than selling cars: millions of potential motorists needed financing help before they could take to the road. By meeting this need, General Motors was able not only to outsell Ford two to one by 1925, but also to build the foundations of a financial services empire that continues to this day.

To sum up, Ford was right that you can't expect customers to envisage the unenvisaged – if all they've known is a horse and cart, the Model T sits in a space beyond most people's imaginations. But 20 years later, when the motor car had become entirely familiar, good insight into your customers' wants or needs could unquestionably have helped Ford to develop something better. In the jargon of today's innovators, you could say that Ford was right as far as *disruptive* innovation is concerned, but wrong when it comes to *incremental* innovation.

Actually, it's useful to consider these two much-used words from the innovators' vocabulary in more detail. It seems to us that they can each have two meanings – both of which happen to apply in Henry Ford's case, but one of which we find more interesting than the other.

When innovators speak of 'incremental' and 'disruptive' innovation, they're using the words principally to define the extent of the commercial success available to them. Uber, the app-based minicab company, is often described as a disruptive innovation because it has disrupted its competitive environment and become hugely valuable in an astonishingly short time. (If it has also simultaneously reduced the value of its competitors, ideally by a similar amount or more, then it could be said to have achieved peak disruption.)

To a customer-oriented marketer, this definition doesn't come naturally. We tend to think about innovation principally in terms of the effect on our customers' experience. To us, Uber is an example of an incremental innovation: there have always been minicabs, but now you can book them on an app instead of your phone, and watch on your phone's screen as they come to pick you up. (Of course, if they do succeed in introducing driverless cars we would regard that as pretty disruptive.)

To us, disruptive innovations are ones that clearly disrupt consumers' patterns of behaviour, and change the way they lead their lives. Low-cost airlines, notably EasyJet and Ryanair, were disruptive innovations because they changed the way we thought about short-haul travel: the combination of low fares and easy booking brought the weekend in Barcelona, or the stag do in Tallinn, or the football match in Munich within easy reach. The same is true of eBay, which changed the way that many people led their lives in at least two important respects. On the one hand, it's said that the recent explosion in self-storage facilities around the country has been largely driven by the large number of people now running small trading businesses on the side on eBay: alongside the day job, they're now buying and selling a small stock of vintage pinball machines, or trays of Polish jam. And on the other hand, of course, eBay has made it completely easy to find and buy unique items that you could previously have spent a lifetime pursuing. You want a signed photograph of Stanley Matthews scoring the winning goal in the 1953 cup final?

Or an obscure gasket for a long-discontinued Norton motorbike? They're no more than a minute away.

On this definition, there are quite a few borderline cases. Some innovations are incremental for some, but disruptive for others. Airbnb, for example, is arguably incremental for travellers, who have always been able to choose from hotels and B&Bs, but disruptive for property-owners who now have a genuinely new and accessible way to monetise the value of their homes. And from a user experience point of view, are app-based takeaway delivery services like Just Eat and Deliveroo incremental, on the grounds that you could always get takeaways delivered, or disruptive, on the grounds that you can choose from so many more restaurants?

Anyway, returning briefly to Henry, the Model T was disruptive in both senses. In a competitive environment sense, it wiped out huge swathes of the industry that provided and served horse-drawn transport. And in a customer experience sense, it put millions behind the wheel for the very first time and created the potential for a whole new kind (and degree) of mobility.

One last point about disruptive innovation, in either or both senses of the word. If, like Ford, you approach it with a focus on what is technologically possible and a determination to give rein to your own personal obsessions, rather than any actual insight into what customers actually want and need, you may still succeed – but your success will owe a very great deal to luck. Ford passionately believed that the Model T was precisely the radical new means of transport that America (and the rest of the world) was waiting for, and that assembly line mass production was the only way to build enough of them. In hindsight it seems obvious that he was right, but at the time it would have been easy to believe he was hopelessly wrong. (Ford himself had two previous car companies fail.) In those early days, a whole bunch of tricky problems including the cars' horrible unreliability, the almost-total lack of workshops and petrol stations and deep official suspicion of this alarming and dangerous new machine could have rapidly driven him out of business.[1]

In fact, we'd argue that the importance of luck in successful innovation is often overlooked. Consider two other examples, both to do with the initial success of giant American business empires. Forrest Mars, founder of

---

[1] And at the time, not everyone thought the Model T was all that disruptive, anyway. It had a range of about 110 miles, but a horse could go all day eating as it went whereas the car was invented before the gas station. It had a top speed of about 42 mph, but that's not so much more than a fast horse. It had more horsepower than a horse (about 20bhp as opposed to 15bhp) but if you put two (or four) horses together to pull a cart, then the horses would be much more powerful, and could traverse rough terrain that the Model T never could.

the confectionery and food empire that bears his name, was a food scientist with a passionate belief that the cocoa bean was a big part of the solution to the nutritional problems of America during the Great Depression of the late 1920s and 1930s. He may or may not have been right from a nutritional perspective, but in any event Americans couldn't get enough of the combination of 'milk, sugar, glucose and thick, thick chocolate' that went into the product he designed to prove his point, and to which he gave his name.

Three decades or so later, two brothers named McDonald, who loved hamburgers but hated that the local burger joints in their part of the Midwest were dirty and unhygienic, opened their own spotlessly clean restaurant: nothing might have come of it, were it not for the fact that an entrepreneur called Ray Kroc bought the brothers' business and expanded it somewhat.[2] The moral of both these stories: if your business career is driven by personal obsession, it helps if it's an obsession that hundreds of millions of people share.

All this may seem a rather over-detailed response to a comment that Henry Ford didn't actually make. But the fact is that lessons from past and indeed present innovations in other fields are always worth learning in financial services, because on the whole we've found it so hard to figure out how it's done.

This chapter is about innovation that's pointed directly at our customers, and pays off in the nature of the products, services and experiences we're able to offer them. Of course there's much more to innovation in a business context than this. It's possible to innovate in every aspect of a business's activities – in its financial management, in its HR strategy, in its premises and facilities, in its in-house catering arrangements. Indirectly, it's possible that all of these can have an effect on the customer experience. An innovative new phone system can make a call centre run more efficiently, and providing better information on call-centre screens will mean that customers get a more personal and responsive service. But this chapter isn't about innovation that impacts the customer indirectly – it's about innovation in the propositions we offer them.

If it's true to say that our track record in this isn't brilliant, it's also true to say that neither is anyone else's. Successful innovation is hard. It's difficult to come up with the ideas, and usually even more difficult to implement them. In the world of fast-moving consumer goods, it's commonly said

---

[2]The obsession with cleanliness remained. Many years later, one of your authors worked on the McDonald's advertising account and spent the obligatory week working behind the counter. He remembers the admonitory signs on the wall in the kitchen area, 'If There's Time to Lean, There's Time to Clean'.

that 90% of all new products fail (although this figure is probably about as reliable as Henry Ford's quote, and about as difficult to substantiate). And although there are some characteristics – we'll look at them later – that make financial services a fruitful field for innovation, there are others that make it a less-than-fertile one. These include:

1. First and undoubtedly foremost, the widespread *lack of consumer engagement* in the whole market. As this book observes at regular intervals, all consumer markets segment and generalisations are always dangerous. But while there are segments of highly engaged consumers eager to act as early adopters of new products and services, there aren't very many of them. Beyond this small group, building any kind of awareness of innovations, let alone attracting customers to them, is hard work.

2. Linked to this, but separate, is customers' *low level of understanding* of the concepts on which many new products and services are based. We argue passionately elsewhere that financial services marketers must recognise and accept consumers' low levels of understanding, and not waste time and energy whinging about how much easier things would be if only consumers understood more. We don't want to lapse into this bad habit ourselves. But it doesn't help.

3. The fact is, *most consumers use a relatively small number and arguably narrow range of financial services,* and make fairly infrequent new purchases in most sectors. This means it's hard to add a new item to the list. There's nothing unique about this: most people own only one car, one mobile phone and one cooker, for example, although at least they tend to replace the first two reasonably often. But by comparison with, say, groceries, where the average family's main weekly shop includes over 60 items, financial services innovators are fighting for a place on a very much shorter list.

4. Especially in bigger and longer-established financial services companies, *most innovators are trying to do their thing in a fairly hostile corporate climate.* (In a way this is one of the central themes of this book.) It wouldn't be right to say that most big, long-established financial services companies maintain a strong culture of innovation. In fact, it would be diametrically wrong. In most, especially in highly risk-aware times like these, the strong cultural tendency when confronted with new ideas is to analyse and articulate what's wrong with them, why they'll never work and why even if they did, it still wouldn't be appropriate to do them here.

5. Despite strenuous efforts, we still have to say that *the regulator is part of the problem, not part of the solution.* The FCA has tried quite hard and for some time to become more innovation-friendly, and it may seem

a little churlish not to give it more credit for its so-called 'sandbox' initiative, part of its overall 'Project Innovate' intended to provide 'a safe space in which businesses can test innovative products, services, business models and delivery mechanisms without immediately incurring all the normal regulatory consequences of pilot activities'. The fact remains, though, that fear of the regulator is so all-pervasive across the industry these days that even after enjoying a fun time in the sandbox, innovators find regulatory constraints – or perhaps more accurately colleagues' perceptions of regulatory constraints – nibbling away at their ideas from all angles.

One way or another, these issues combine to make innovation hard to originate, and arguably even harder to test and implement.

The question of testing and implementation is particularly important, and should be explored further. If there's one cluster of ideas about good practice in the field of innovation that more or less everyone involved would accept, it's the cluster that includes the principles of 'start small', 'test and learn' and 'fail fast'. What this means is that those aiming to introduce innovations shouldn't waste too much time on perfecting them, or too much money on big splashy national launch campaigns. Instead – especially if the products and services in question are digital, which most are – they should get beta versions out into the market as early as possible, learn from initial customer experience, respond as necessary (whether with refinement, expansion or even abandonment of the whole stupid idea) and move on.

There may be sectors of the consumer economy well suited to this kind of incremental grains-of-rice-on-a-chessboard approach, but on the whole financial services isn't one of them. To be fair, it isn't one of the worst-suited either: that title probably rests with the automotive industry, where it simply isn't possible to build a few hundred of your new family hatchback, push them out to a couple of friendly dealers and see how your market reacts to them.

But the main problem in financial services, especially those intended for relatively mainstream, disengaged consumers, is the effort and expense required to build any kind of awareness of, and engagement with, what you have to offer. Take a potentially large and significant new market sector like peer-to-peer lending. It's existed for several years, there are dozens of firms involved in it, and among a small number of financial services hobbyists its profile is high. But in the mainstream market, what kind of profile does it have?

A few business models lend themselves better than others to the start-small, test-and-learn, fast-fail approach. The previous business of one of your authors, Metro Bank, has a branch-based model that requires branch staff to take the lead in developing a customer base in their own local catchment area. This clearly lends itself well to piloting on a branch-by-branch basis, and indeed Metro Bank has expanded in precisely this way over the period since launch.

But the potential of other innovative models, especially those that require customers to seek out a new proposition amidst all the noise, distraction and vastness of the Internet, will never be known until one or more significant players, with properly developed propositions, takes the risk involved in stumping up a three-year, multi-million-pound promotional budget, and gives it a proper go. Is there, for example, a significant D2C market for a simple, accessible, low-cost life assurance proposition? Several low-key innovators have tested the waters. One of them, a brand called Beagle Street, owned by BGL, the group behind comparethemarket.com, has been piloting, testing and learning for at least three years at the time of writing – but the jury is still out on whether the proposition works or not.

Meanwhile, in the area of so-called robo advice, Nutmeg (actually a digital discretionary fund manager) has been testing and learning for at least as long, and in fact spending a moderate amount of money on a number of rather miscellaneous advertising approaches focused on the London Underground. Nutmeg has been cagey about its business performance, which is usually a bad sign, but some figures released in 2016 indicated that everything is going well except for a stratospherically high cost of customer acquisition. (This of course is a rather significant 'except for'.)

But the big question remains unanswered: are the difficulties these businesses are experiencing in recruiting customers a consequence of their inefficient, sub-optimal, test-and-learn communications strategies? Or are they a consequence of the fact that consumers can't be persuaded to show an interest in what they have to offer? Until the testing and learning answers this question, no-one is much further forward.[3]

If all of this says that it's hard to innovate in financial services, there are of course plenty of considerations pointing in the opposite direction. Here are a few:

1. *The extraordinary power of digital.* Digital has the power to change every kind of business, but it can transform financial services even more

---

[3]There's another big problem with a test-and-learn, fail fast approach in long-term sectors of the market. New propositions may be perceived to fail fast and be withdrawn from the market, but any small number of customers who have been attracted to them may need servicing for the next 40 years. The costs of doing so can add up to a very expensive failure.

completely than most. While manufacturers of physical goods and providers of physical services can use digital as much as they like but still have to make products, or run airlines, hotels or dry cleaners, or whatever it is that they do, most financial services providers are able to leave the physical world and migrate into the digital world altogether. Needless to say, in this way they can utterly transform the nature of their businesses – and the experience of their customers. And, usually, dramatically reduce their costs.

2. *Never-ending change in the market environment.* You can go all round the quadrants of the PEST analysis (recently expanded by some pundits to become a PESTLE analysis with the addition of Legislative and Environmental) and find changes calling urgently for innovation in all of them. Many of the most important opportunities for innovation are in the Legal segment in the form of new regulation, legislation and/or fiscal policy: changes in recent years around the regulatory and fiscal framework in the field of pensions could keep innovators fully occupied for many years.

3. Again it's all relative, but without underestimating the difficulties *it's easier, quicker and cheaper to innovate in financial services than in many fields*. Again, in the consumer economy, the automotive industry probably stands at one end of a spectrum: researching, conceiving, building and launching a new car cannot be anything other than difficult, time-consuming and expensive (and, therefore, extremely risky, with failure proving extremely expensive). The same is true in other very different industries and for a wide range of different reasons, including IT, aerospace and pharmaceuticals.

4. Similarly, *the competitive barriers to entry are generally low*. There are some exceptions here – the barriers would be high if you chose to challenge MasterCard and VISA in the card payments sector (although we have seen interesting new entrants like Square) – but in most sectors the sheer number of existing players tells you that the barriers to entry are low. There are well over 1,000 asset management firms in the UK, for example: that being so, it can't be impossible to become the 1,001st. Even in banking, where it was believed for many years that huge economies of scale delivered enormous advantages to the existing big players and militated against young and small firms, changing economics (and again the advent of digital) have changed the rules of the game. At the time of writing, at least a score of startup challengers are working their way through the authorisation and launch process, in the belief that they can be profitable with very small market shares.

5. *Consumers may be more or less inert, but they're not particularly loyal.* Inertia represents a big challenge to innovators, whether they

have something disruptively different to offer or simply an incremental improvement. But few consumers feel strong loyalties to existing providers and are at least open to the possibility of new relationships, new products or new providers. This is, of course, a consequence of the big point that really is the theme of this book: most existing financial services businesses aren't very good at marketing, and so are much less closely connected to their customers than they could or should be. Marketing is an area where innovators can and should aim to outperform.

Overall, when we net out the strengths and weaknesses of retail financial services as an arena for innovation, we think that the picture is generally positive and attractive, but with one large cloud in an otherwise mainly blue sky. That cloud – as we hope is clear from the above – is the widespread difficulty and cost in recruiting customers to innovative new propositions.

For innovators – and particularly for innovators in small, startup businesses with limited resources – this will tend to emerge as the last and toughest obstacle. Time and time again, in our marketing services careers, we've seen entrepreneurs set about tackling the long and daunting list of challenges involved in getting their venture off the ground. Time and time again, we've seen them (hopefully we've also often helped them) deal with these challenges, one by one, until the dashboard is showing almost all green lights and the proposition is ready for launch …

… and then, time and time again, about three months later we've found ourselves taking part in an anxious discussion round the boardroom table. On closer examination it seems there is in fact still one red light, and that's the one item on the agenda: how on earth are we going to recruit the number of customers we need, at anything like a cost we can afford?[4]

Here again, as so often in this book, there are exceptions. There are three situations in which innovators can build significant customer bases relatively quickly and at low (or at least acceptable) cost. These are:

1. When there's a good opportunity to cross-sell to an existing customer base, either the innovator firm's own customers or the customers of

---

[4]In this regard, nothing could be more misleading or unhelpful than the famous quote attributed to the American writer Ralph Waldo Emerson, and usually expressed as 'build a better mousetrap, and the world will beat a path to your door'. In fact, Emerson didn't say anything half as pithy and memorable as this. What he actually said was: 'If a man has good corn or wood, or boards, or pigs, to sell, or can make better chairs or knives, crucibles or church organs, than anybody else, you will find a broad hard-beaten road to his house, though it be in the woods'. He was still completely wrong, though.

a partner. (A 'good' opportunity is one where good data is available, allowing for tight targeting on a segment or segments of customers well-matched to the new product or service.)

2. When the innovation has a strong proposition that is intended for a target market consisting of highly engaged, hobbyist consumers. As discussed elsewhere in this book, there is a segment of exceptionally engaged financial services consumers in the UK, probably numbering somewhere either side of 1.5 million individuals and made up largely of relatively upmarket middle-aged men, who have generally acted as the early adopters of new and innovative propositions. These people are relatively easy to reach with marketing communications – being interested in personal finance, they seek out opportunities to find out about it – and they are willing to try new propositions. Unfortunately, as well as being relatively few in number, they are also much more promiscuous than average and so hard to retain, and much more price-conscious than average. And also, the expression *early adopters* is rather misleading, in that it suggests that sooner or later a whole lot of later adopters will follow their lead: however, very often they don't, and the 'early adopters' would be better described as 'only adopters'. But still, if these people make up your target market, the good news is that they're much easier, and cheaper, than average to recruit.

3. Very occasionally, neither of the above applies, but the innovator has an exceptionally strong, clear and attractive customer acquisition proposition, and a business plan that can afford to include a significant budget for communicating it. We're reluctant to mention this possibility, because most innovators, being optimists at heart, will immediately assume it applies to them: in fact, it hardly ever does. But very rare examples – the most recent being the free-credit-score company Clearscore, which claims a customer base of 3 million within a year of launch – mean that it would be wrong to dismiss it entirely.[5]

But in truth, for everyone else in the direct-to-consumer sector – even those with genuinely strong and innovative ideas – the challenge of acquiring enough customers, at low enough cost, and then going on to develop profitable relationships with them, is somewhere between difficult and impossible.

---

[5] A proposition specifically designed to acquire customers is a good and valuable thing, but it's important to have a clear and achievable plan to upsell and/or cross-sell once you've acquired them. We can think of several examples where this hasn't happened – for example, a new banking service that very successfully offered a loss-leading card that was free to use overseas, but then failed to persuade its new customers to use any other elements of the service that would make it profitable.

In some ways, it's a little easier in the intermediated sector. At least most advisers, like those hobbyist consumers, are reasonably willing to engage with firms who have a new story to tell. But, that said, most are also set in their ways and reluctant to add new propositions to their repertoire. They are often particularly cautious when confronted with big, challenging, disruptive innovations, especially when taking them on board involves any implicit criticism of what they've been doing previously. By way of example, a few years ago one of your authors was involved in branding, marketing and communications planning for an innovative startup launching an entirely new product for the pre-retirement market through the IFA channel. The management team was strong, well-known and experienced; by startup standards the first-year budget wasn't at all bad; and prelaunch research indicated a strong appetite for the product among both advisers and their clients. A year later, when the company threw in the towel, it had made a total of seven sales. Winding itself up, it did the decent thing with the last of its budget, refunding the premiums to its seven customers.

This may seem like an inappropriately downbeat anecdote for a chapter about innovation. But from our particular perspective, with so much experience of customer acquisition activity, we're sure that one of the most valuable things we can do is to get across one simple message: acquiring the customers you need will almost always be harder, slower and more expensive than you think.

So, apart from lowering your target, increasing your budget and giving yourself more time, what else can you do to increase your chances of innovation success?

We'd like to put forward a four-point formula, which we think applies equally to (significant) incremental innovation as well as to the disruptive kind. But don't get too excited. The bad news is that the four points are all completely obvious, and all require judgement calls that are very easy to get wrong.

The four boxes you need to tick are all about the likely response of your target market. We're with Henry Ford in that we think the initial responsibility for developing that innovative hypothesis rests with you, and that you can't ask your target market to do your innovating for you. But once you have a hypothesis and indeed a target market, then you should certainly challenge it by asking these four questions:

1. Does this innovation offer the target market a clear and obvious benefit?
2. Can people in the target market immediately see how it can improve their lives?
3. Is the innovation quick and easy to get hold of, and does it seem to offer good value?
4. Do the perceived benefits outweigh the perceived risk?

Let's explore these four questions a little further:

1. *Clear and obvious benefit.* Of the four, this is the most important – and also the easiest to misjudge. Given their low level of engagement and their reluctance to think about financial services too hard, most consumers look for a single, simple, immediate and obvious message about what a particular financial service can do for them. Current accounts are for managing day-to-day expenditure. Pensions are for living on when you retire. Life assurance provides money for your family if you die. Mortgages allow you to buy a home. People know why they need these products. To succeed with an innovative idea, you need to be able to express the central benefit equally clearly and irrefutably.

2. *Improving people's lives.* It's no good offering a clear benefit or being quick and easy to buy (question 3) if consumers simply can't see how the product or service will make their lives better.

   Passing this test doesn't always require a digital proposition. It's interesting to compare two new brands, launched within a year or two of each other and both initially offering a limited product range focused on savings and mortgages. The innovation in co-author Anthony Thomson's Atom Bank is focused on digital: it's the first bank in Europe to exist as an app. That makes it very different, but so far at least its products are basically conventional. A year or two earlier, Lucian was involved in the launch of the Family Building Society, where the innovation points in a completely different direction: digitally it's pretty basic, but here the big idea is to focus exclusively on 'intergenerational' product solutions – mortgages for offspring needing help from their parents, products to help older people leave money to their families with less Inheritance Tax to pay, savings plans for parents and grandparents meeting the cost of school fees and so on.

   Both of your authors would like to think that these two propositions will pass the 'improving people's lives' test – but among very different people and for very different reasons.

3. *Quick, easy and good value.* This is all about perception, and often consumers' perceptions can be very different from the industry's. What seems quick, and easy and, particularly, good value to us can seem just the opposite to our customers. For example, in recent years we've a small crop of online personal finance aggregation sites with business models requiring modest monthly fees. In the great scheme of things, to the senior team at the firm behind the product, £5 or £10 a month doesn't seem a lot of money. To a young or indeed not so young consumer who never pays anything at all for any of the online and mobile services they use all the time, including news, music, games and social media, it seems out of the question. If I pay nothing at all for the whole

world of Facebook, Spotify, the BBC and YouTube, why would I pay £10 a month for some not-very-interesting graphs?

4. *Exposing customers to risk.* This isn't just about investment risk. Risk has many different flavours. There's the risk of losing all your money. There's the risk of losing some of your money, as a result of overcharging, or underperformance, or hidden catches. There's the risk of being on the receiving end of intrusive overselling. There's the risk of not understanding, and being made to look (or feel) a fool. There's the risk of discovering that you never really needed whatever it was you thought you did. The sense that any of these – and no doubt more than a few others – might apply is enough to decide not to proceed.[6] A strong brand helps to reduce some of these perceptions of risk.

Finally in this section, it's important to emphasise that these four questions relate only to the ability to recruit a customer base, not to the success of the innovation overall. Building a customer base is, of course, a necessary but in itself insufficient part of commercial success: retaining customers and developing profitable relationships with them matter at least as much.

Or, sometimes, not. We recognise that some innovators are working to a more or less hidden agenda that doesn't actually require commercial success at all. A significant proportion of those startup robo-advisers, for example, will be delighted if, having demonstrated any kind of evidence of effective functionality, they're on the receiving end of a bid from an established player keen to acquire their process and their expertise. Such established players, faced with a buy-or-build decision and choosing the 'buy' option, tend to take the view that the startup's failure to recruit customers doesn't much matter since they'll be able to provide access to several million customers of their own. Looking at examples like LV's acquisition of the startup robo adviser Wealth Wizards, or Aviva's acquisition of Wealthify, it'll be interesting to see how successfully the services of the latter can be cross-sold to the customers of the former.

Against this background, how do innovators find a focus for their innovations? Well, there's certainly plenty for them to read: few aspects of retail financial services have attracted more attention from authors of one sort or another[7] than the question of how to innovate.

---

[6]If it simply isn't possible to avoid some perceptions of risk, then it's all the more important to create perceptions of powerful benefits.

[7]We particularly recommend the excellent book *The Innovator's Dilemma*, in which author Clayton M Christensen talks about how – in any industry – successful companies with established products will get pushed aside unless managers know how and when to abandon traditional business practices.

What's more, there's something about the landscape of innovation – perhaps its big, rather shapeless, agoraphobic emptiness – that encourages authors to try to classify or codify it with lists and categorisations breaking it up into definable, manageable chunks. An excellent and comprehensive publication on this subject, the World Economic Forum's document *The Future of Financial Services*, published in June 2015, does exactly this. First it argues that the entire financial services market can be subdivided into six 'core functions' (payments, market provisioning, investment management, insurance, deposits and lending and capital raising) and then goes on to define 11 mega-trends that, it claims, are putting pressure on traditional players and acting as the main drivers of innovation. These mega-trends are:

1. New market platforms
2. Smarter, faster machines
3. Cashless world
4. Emerging payment rails
5. Insurance disaggregation
6. Connected insurance
7. Alternative lending
8. Shifting customer preferences
9. Crowdfunding
10. Process externalisation
11. Empowered investors

It's a good list, in a good document that acts as the best overall roadmap for financial services innovation we've seen. But still, it's a matter of some concern that only two or three of these trends are actually to do with consumers, while as many as six or seven are to do with technology.

Looking across the range of successful market-facing innovations in retail financial services over a long period, we can see surprisingly few common strands. Some have been driven by technology, but some haven't; some are simple and easy to execute, but others are complex and multi-faceted; some are highly differentiated and hard to copy, but some have rapidly become generic; some address very specific needs among niche target groups, but others appeal to large, broad target audiences. But if there's one thing that the successes seem to share – and the failures don't – it's that they start with some kind of insight, or imaginative understanding, of something that customers might want to have, use or do.

In our own experience as consumers, we've been around for just about long enough to trace this pattern back to the coming of the first ATMs right at the end of the 1960s, liberating us from the need to queue in branches to withdraw cash. That was a technology story second, but a consumer insight story first, and plenty of others have taken the same path.

Sometimes, a consumer insight doesn't actually require any technology to provide the solution. Commerce Bank, the US-based predecessor of Anthony Thomson's Metro Bank, built a substantial business via a network of branches located in upmarket East Coast residential suburbs. Two of its USPs were that its branches were open at weekends, and that every customer was given the use of a safe deposit box. These two apparently disparate elements combined brilliantly to offer a powerful, insight-based benefit to women customers. Many would keep their jewellery in their safe deposit box, drop into the branch on Saturday afternoons to select the items they wanted to wear that night, and then go back on Sunday mornings to drop them off again. We can't say whether Commerce Bank also offered a discount on home contents insurance to customers who used the branch in this way, but if so that would make for an almost-perfect insight-based innovation.

On the other hand, innovations based on poor insight into consumers' needs – or, even worse, a failure to identify a clear consumer segment at all – will struggle to find customers. One of your authors was involved recently in a project to develop an online investment service for one of the UK's biggest financial services providers. The plan was fatally flawed by the intention to launch the same service across several of the group's brands, each positioned very differently and appealing to different target segments in the market. In seeking to create a one-size-fits-all service that would appeal to customers of all the group's brands, it inevitably appealed to none of them.

By chance, the same project highlighted another common theme of some unsuccessful innovation: products and services that could theoretically meet customers' needs and provide a real benefit, but which in practice simply ask too much of their ability to understand. In line with the regulator's requirements, this online investment service was built around a powerful tool enabling customers to choose investments that would be aligned with their appetite for risk – or rather, as it turned out, not enabling them to do so. The output from the tool took the form of a series of complicated graphs, showing projections of various rates of return over a 20-year period into the future. Consumers peered at it in a state of bemusement. Most decided that since they could make no sense of it, it would be better not to risk making an investment.

There is another trap in the process of insight-based innovation: identifying the insight, but declining to act on it. A good example is the provision of guarantees. In the abstract, uncertain and generally untrustworthy world of financial services, consumers love guarantees. They love all kinds of guarantees - guarantees that investments will achieve a certain level of performance; they love guarantees that bonuses, once allocated, can't be taken away; they love guarantees that payments, or anything else for that matter, will happen within a certain timeframe; they love guarantees that claims will be met, ideally in full.

The industry, on the other hand, doesn't like guarantees much. It dislikes them partly on its own account – they can be expensive to deliver, and of course on one painful occasion were responsible for virtually wiping out the large and previously highly successful pension provider Equitable Life. But actually, people in the industry dislike guarantees, at least as much if not more, on behalf of their customers. They take the view that guarantees cost money, and in one way or another the cost detracts from a product's performance; and in any case the consumer's anxiety about whatever it may be that isn't guaranteed is probably misplaced. So, on the whole, better not to offer one. Hopefully, this kind of arrogance will gradually fade as financial services becomes more genuinely customer-centric. Genuinely powerful and motivating insights that can drive successful innovation are quite rare in financial services, so declining to act on those that can be found is not wise.

Elsewhere, on the whole, we still think there's a long way to go in terms of the potential for game-changing, disruptive innovations resulting from the combination of consumer insight and digital technology. At the time of writing (although we suspect, not for much longer), it's still difficult to find many innovative, digitally based success stories that have genuinely brought about new consumer behaviours. The one big exception is price comparison sites, which have quickly become UK consumers' preferred way to buy insurance (although not yet to anything like the same extent in other sectors, like loans, mortgages, cards or savings).

It's interesting to submit these to our four-point success test from a few pages back. When customers use them to buy motor insurance, do they tick all four boxes?

1. Does this innovation offer the target market a clear and obvious benefit?
   Yes: cheaper insurance.
2. Can people in the target market immediately see how it can fit into their lives?
   Yes: I have to buy insurance.
3. Is the innovation quick, easy and good value?
   Yes. Buying insurance in this way is more or less as quick and easy as any other way, and the result gives better value.
4. Do the perceived benefits outweigh the perceived risks?
   Yes. There aren't really any perceived risks, unless you choose an obscure and unknown company simply because it offers the lowest price. And most people don't do this – the quote most people are likely to accept is the lowest from a company they've heard of.

That seems to add up to a solid four out of four, and may help to explain why price comparison sites have been so successful. But otherwise, while there are many exciting digital innovations launching into specialist or niche markets – and very significantly changing the way that intermediaries do business – mass-market consumers' financial lives seem remarkably unchanged.

This seems certain to change. The new generation of challenger banks, for example, are starting life with a recognition of the extraordinary power of data to extend their role in their customers' lives – one, for example, is not just proposing to handle payments to its customers' gas and electricity suppliers, but to use its insights into their usage patterns to choose the most suitable contracts and to switch suppliers automatically whenever necessary – even on a weekly basis.

Time will tell, and there's no doubt at all that the industry's enormous investment in innovation will continue. Only a small fraction of that huge total falls directly within our remit as marketers: most is back-office innovation, investment on innovation in processes that make businesses more efficient, manage risks and improve financial performance, but have little direct effect on our customers or on the products or services we're able to offer them. But even so, managing customer-facing innovation is a big and exciting part of the new financial services marketing. It may even be both the most important, and the most enjoyable, part of the job.

CHAPTER 14

Are You Absolutely Sure About 'Restoring Trust'?

If there's one thing that most people in financial services marketing accept – one statement that gets a near-universal show of assenting hands in the conference room – it's that 'our number-one priority as an industry is restoring trust'. Carried, with very few disagreeing.

But a few do disagree, and your authors are among them. We think this statement is wrong at so many levels that it's hard to know where to start. We'll have a go in a minute. But first we need to disentangle the meaning – or more accurately meanings – of this deceptively simple five-letter word.

A curious phenomenon highlights the need for disentangling. On the one hand, journalists and consultants frequently publish research showing just how little consumers tend to trust financial institutions. (We'll quote from some of it in this chapter.) On the other hand, the institutions themselves, especially banks, regularly publish research showing that consumers do in fact trust them a great deal. What's going on? How can both be right?

There's a simple explanation. There is no single definition of trust. Psychology tells us that there are two fundamentally different kinds. In people's attitudes toward financial services firms, we'd argue there are in fact three.

The two kinds of trust recognised by psychologists carry the kinds of opaque and mystifying names that psychologists like: they call them 'cognitive' and 'associative' trust. Cognitive trust is about *competence*. Do I trust my bank to pay my mortgage, transfer some money to my children, to ensure that my savings will still be there next week? The answer is, in most cases, yes, I do. That is the trust that the banks tend to measure and yes, unsurprisingly, their customers do trust them to make payments and not to run away with their savings.

The second form of trust is about *intention*. Associative trust asks: 'Do I trust you to have my best interests at heart?' This is the question that journalists usually ask, and it may not surprise you to hear the answer is commonly 'No I bloody don't. I think you'll find every way you can to get more money out of me, and/or to sell me things that are in your best interests but certainly not mine.'

Not being psychologists, we don't get much meaning from the terms 'cognitive' and 'associative', so for the purposes of this chapter we'll replace them, respectively, with the words 'functional' and 'emotional'. For the sake of completeness, we'll also add a third species of trust, not quite the same as either of the other two, which we'll call 'existential' trust – that is, trust that the organisation will continue to exist, and won't go bust, taking my money with it (or, in the worst case, that if it did go bust then there'd be a mechanism that would mean I'd get my money back).

In consumers' perception, different kinds of relationship with different kinds of organisation meeting different kinds of need display different profiles across these three kinds of trust. Big, established banks score well on functional and existential trust, but very badly on emotional trust. Small, little-known digital start-ups may score better on emotional trust, but not so well on functional trust and quite possibly rather badly on existential trust. In the wake of some well-publicised crises, defined benefit company pension schemes score much less well on existential trust than they used to. With different relationships displaying different profiles, it's easy to see how anyone commissioning market research into trust can devise their study so as to produce whatever result they're looking for.

At risk of generalisation, overall the level of *Existential Trust* remains high. That said, on the rare occasions when it does become an issue – as it did for Northern Rock in autumn 2007 – it's a very serious one. National news coverage of panic-stricken customers queuing round the block to get their hands on their money is an epic fail, a PR disaster, an existential vicious circle from which it's hard to see any way back.[1]

On the whole, *Functional Trust* also remains fairly – some might say surprisingly – high. Given many institutions' appalling error rates, and the constant drizzle of media coverage of customer service cock-ups, most people on the whole remain remarkably confident that most institutions will get most things right most of the time. When you ask a bank to make a payment, you expect the payment will be made, to the right person, in the specified period of time, and your account will be debited with the appropriate amount of money. Things go wrong quite often, especially if you're asking for anything special or different, and when they do it's very annoying and horribly difficult to sort out. But, nevertheless, with certain

---

[1] Even then, there remains a high level of awareness of, and confidence in, the Financial Services Compensation Scheme. While the existence of organisations can at times fall seriously into question, the continuing 'existence' of the customers' money isn't seriously doubted, at least for those with no more than £70,000 in any one account.

exceptions, we still remain reasonably confident that next time, they'll probably go right – and that if they do make a mistake, they'll correct it.

But in recent years, it's the third category of trust, associative or *Emotional Trust*, that has become the problematic one. A very large majority of consumers simply do not trust financial institutions to act in their best interests.

There's no shortage of research to substantiate this view. The major global Trust Barometer study carried out by PR giant Edelman, for example, consistently rates financial services as the least trusted of the eight industry sectors it features. In the latest study, published in 2017, there is a slight overall improvement, but a closer analysis reveals an increasingly polarised position, in which what Edelman describes as its 'informed public' respondents (drawn from the better-educated and higher-earning groups) show a much higher level of trust than what Edelman calls the 'general population', with the former showing some improvement while the latter continues to decline.

In territory like this there's no such thing as a definitive measure, and the Trust Barometer's figures across all respondents are generally higher than those published by Nottingham University Business School in its annual financial services Trust Index. This research distinguishes between 'base-level trust' (something very similar to what we're describing here as functional trust) and 'higher-level trust' (very similar to what we're describing here as emotional trust, or in other words trust that financial services providers have their customers' best interests at heart). In each of seven financial services sectors, the higher-level trust scores are consistently low: those giving low marks to each sector outnumber those giving high marks by approximately three or four to one.

What's more, the research – undertaken annually since 2003 – provides no evidence of any significant recovery in trust since the financial crisis of 2008. Scores are bumping along at a low level: according to the report, they're 'nothing special and there is an air of weary resignation about them'.

Another research study, carried out in late 2016 by Opinium Research among a nationally representative sample on behalf of consulting firm 3R Insights, looked at consumers' perceptions of the attitudes and behaviours of the chief executives of financial services firms. CEOs reading the findings must be glad of their gigantic remuneration packages to cheer them up as they come to appreciate the depths of the public's hostility toward them.

The sample – a large, nationally representative one – was asked about their level of confidence that the leaders of financial institutions would put their interests – that is, their customers' interests – first. Here is their reply:

	All		18–34		>55	
	Some/ Complete Confidence %	Little/No Confidence %	Some/ Complete Confidence %	Little/No Confidence %	Some/ Complete Confidence %	Little/No Confidence %
Insurers	21	69	23	60	22	72
Banks	22	68	29	54	21	74
Investment Firms	21	68	24	57	20	70

With a very high level of consistency, all respondents – older and younger alike – when asked the question with regard to insurance companies, banks and investment firms, responded by just under seven votes to two that they had little or no confidence.

The researchers asked whether the sample thought financial CEOs cared about the quality of service they provided. This is what respondents said:

	All		18–34		>55	
	Reasonable/ Great Extent %	Little/ Poor Extent %	Reasonable/ Great Extent %	Little/ Poor Extent %	Reasonable/ Great Extent %	Little/Poor Extent %
Insurers	26	62	29	51	25	68
Banks	30	59	37	44	26	67
Investment Firms	28	57	34	45	28	61

The good news is that the answers are slightly more positive. The bad news is that they're not more positive by much: this time those believing the CEOs didn't care much outvoted the others by just about two to one.

And then thirdly, respondents were asked whether they thought financial firms' CEOs cared about providing customers with value for money. Here's how they replied:

	All		18–34		>55	
	Reasonable/ Great Extent %	Little/ Poor Extent %	Reasonable/ Great Extent %	Little/ Poor Extent %	Reasonable/ Great Extent %	Little/ Poor Extent %
Insurers	17	70	21	60	15	76
Banks	18	70	26	57	15	78
Investment Firms	22	63	26	53	20	68

This was the most negative response to all the questions, with respondents thinking the CEOs didn't much care outnumbering the others by around four to one (although feeling slightly less negative toward the investment firms' bosses).

Looking at findings like these, it's difficult to distinguish the chicken from the egg: are the CEOs viewed so negatively because their firms are so distrusted, or are the firms so distrusted because their leaders are viewed so negatively?

There is also, of course, a bigger question about whether these findings represent a failure of perception – in other words whether consumers are wrong to hold such negative opinions, or whether they're right and their opinions more or less represent reality. It's difficult to imagine the piece of research that could tackle this question: not many CEOs would admit in an interview to caring little about customer service or value for money, or confirm that they rarely put customers' interests first. But in any case, the question is largely academic. To customers, perceptions like these *are* their reality.

And not just to customers, but often also to people in the industry. Here is an exchange between two senior Financial Services Forum members – marketers taking part in one of our Financial Services Forum focus groups:

Respondent 1:　I trust my bank to transfer my money, but not to do the best thing with my money.

Respondent 2:　I agree with that.

Respondent 1:　If you had the opportunity to rip me off, you would.

Respondent 2:　You would, yes.

Respondent 1:　If you have an opportunity to obfuscate over charges, you will do so. If you have an opportunity not to pay my claim, you will do so.

Respondent 1:　Yes – which is why, if you talk to anybody who has had or feel they're about to have, a bad experience, there is a massive amount of nervousness.

We think that the crisis of emotional trust reflected in this exchange results from a toxic combination of three main ingredients.

- There's a great deal of *personal experience*. Many millions of people have found themselves personally caught up in the big mis-selling scandals – PPI, personal pensions, mortgage endowments. Millions more have lesser but still uncomfortable tales to tell, often involving poor sales practices, unsuitable or poor value products and poor delivery at key 'moments of truth'. And millions more with no direct personal experience still have indirect experience, involving close family members or friends.
- These personal experiences are greatly amplified by an *unending media blizzard*, which provides clear evidence that individuals' personal

experiences are not isolated examples, but are part of a much bigger national picture.

- And as a backdrop, it's important to remember that for many, *the subject of money is, in itself, difficult and emotionally charged*. A Financial Services Forum focus group respondent says: 'The fact is that the primary responses at a basic human level to thinking about money are fear, uncertainty and doubt. It's almost impossible to stop people feeling those emotions. And it is much easier to blame the bank than to get your own head in order and sort it out for yourself'. There's a reluctance to take much corporate responsibility in that statement – but also more than a grain of truth.

There are of course exceptions to this bleakly distrustful picture, and some are important. For example, most customers tend to have more confidence in the behaviour of their own providers or advisers than in those of which they have no personal experience. Some sectors as a whole enjoy higher levels of emotional trust than others – financial advisers score particularly well in the Nottingham University study, which also suggests a fairly strong residual presumption of innocence toward building societies. And some individual organisations are rated more highly than others – among banks, for example, both the Co-operative Bank and First Direct are thought less likely to behave badly towards their customers than any of the biggest High Street brands.[2]

(First Direct is perhaps the most striking exception to the overall picture. In a study of 10,000 respondents on customer experience by KPMG Nunwood published in September 2016, First Direct is rated first among the 100 organisations included, ahead of such paragons as John Lewis, Amazon and M&S. 'Customer experience' isn't the same thing as trust, but this ranking certainly says something very positive about the feelings of First Direct's customers.)

But still, it's undoubtedly true that the overall picture is very negative. And that being so, it's hardly surprising to find such a high level of agreement among financial services marketing people to that soundbite, 'Our number one priority is restoring consumer trust'.

---

[2]The Co-operative Bank also provides evidence of the long-term value of brands, particularly in a low-interest category like financial services. In recent years it has suffered a seemingly unstoppable series of PR disasters, including a change of ownership that, in real terms, disconnects it from its Co-operative heritage. All the same, it has avoided any dramatic loss of customers, and maintains its comparatively virtuous image despite a track record of sometimes-less-than-virtuous behaviour. In a similar way, many people still think the Halifax is still a building society, despite the fact that it demutualised back in 1997.

At the same time, though, when we explored the issue further in our Financial Services Forum members online research, the findings showed a somewhat more nuanced picture than we expected.

A little under half of the respondents agreed that 'it's gone and we must do everything possible to get it back'. More than a third of respondents, 37%, thought that while trust might have gone generally, trust in their own organisations remained high (they can't all have been First Direct employees), and 19%, remarkably, agreed that 'people have more trust in financial services than we imagine'. More remarkably, no-one at all agreed with the statement that 'it's gone and it's not coming back'. Your authors are clearly out of line with these respondents.

So why do we take such a different view? Why do we think that there are as many as five very good reasons to reject the idea that trust could or should be restored? What could those five reasons be?

To deal with the most obvious and positive reason first, as we've already said it doesn't seem to us that there's any need to restore *existential* or *functional* trust, because we don't think there's any widespread crisis in either of these areas. When individual organisations are affected by either, then as far as possible it's certainly necessary to take action, and of course even better not to be affected in the first place. Young and financially weak organisations are wise not to draw attention to their youth or weakness. But there is currently no general crisis in existential or functional trust.

It's *emotional* trust where there is an overall and widespread crisis. But in four words, we reject the idea of making efforts to restore it across the industry, because we think that trying to do so would be:

1. Immoral
2. Impossible
3. Unnecessary, and
4. Unaffordable.

Consider these four objections in turn:

1. *Rebuilding trust in financial services would be immoral.* Once upon a time, many years ago, individuals were big on trust. In fact not just individuals – societies as a whole functioned largely on the basis of trust. People tended to trust sources of authority, and individuals and organisations to whom they believed they owed deference and respect. They trusted kings. They trusted priests. They trusted the four estates, the Parliament, legislature, law and the Press. They trusted political leaders. They trusted their elders. They trusted public figures, especially those with reputations for good works.

Quite often the people they trusted proved worthy recipients of their trust. But quite often they didn't. Sometimes those people were Adolf Hitler, or James Jones of Jonestown Massacre infamy, or Jimmy Savile.

It's difficult to say exactly when this kind of trust began to wither, but if Don Maclean is right that the date of Buddy Holly's death was 'the day the music died', then 1 July 1916, the first day of the first battle of the Somme, could be said to have done much the same for trust. Whether the Allied generals were incompetent, indifferent to their soldiers' well-being or, as some now argue, doing the best they could in impossible circumstances, the fact was that the British 4th Army lost some 20,000 dead and 40,000 wounded on that day – and the expression 'lions led by donkeys' stuck as a deeply embittered summary.

Against that kind of background, we go on to say unhesitatingly that the continuing erosion of trust over the years since has been one of the very best, healthiest and most welcome evolutions in the history of society. People who are sceptical, challenging and hard to persuade are hard to take for a ride.

Financial services provide less dramatic examples, but there have been plenty of occasions when a more suspicious or challenging attitude might have saved a lot of money heartache. How many debacles could have been avoided if more consumers had called to mind the sceptic's mantra, 'If it looks too good to be true, it probably is'? Steadily rising scepticism, and an online and social media environment in which it's so much easier than ever before to check whether that irresistible proposition is actually a scam, are gradually making the parting of fools from their money more difficult. No sensible person could want to put the clock back to a time when it was like taking candy from babies.

For the time being, though, with millions of people still too trusting to be able to resist bad products, manipulative selling, excessive charges and outright scams of all shapes and sizes, we'd prefer to see campaigning to encourage less trust in financial services, not more. If there were steps that could be taken that would encourage people to return to – or remain in – a state of trustful complacency, we'd say it would be against consumers' interests – and, yes, arguably immoral – to take them.

But it doesn't really matter that seeking to rebuild consumer trust wouldn't be in consumers' interests, because:

2. *Rebuilding trust in financial services would be impossible.* The reason should be obvious from the previous section. Financial services marketing people may not have noticed, but ever since that date in July 1916

(and arguably for a good deal longer), trust across the whole of society has been eroding at speed.

These days, we may decide to place our trust in a small number of people with whom we have close personal relationships (and even then, we may find ourselves wishing that we hadn't). But beyond that, forget it. A few minutes' thought brings to mind a long list of institutions, occupations and professions in which levels of trust are much lower than they were say 50 or 100 years ago. The list of those involved in trust crises in recent years might include, in no particular order, politicians, the media, the police, the judiciary, the medical profession, army generals, DJs and TV entertainers famous in the 1960s and 1970s, the food industry, advertising, unelected faceless bureaucrats (especially if non-British Europeans), bishops (especially male and Catholic), winners of the Tour de France, oil companies, energy companies more generally, international companies (especially American), experts (remember Michael Gove saying we've had enough of them?), white people and, especially in the workplace, men.

We recorded the following exchange in a Financial Services Forum focus group:

Respondent 1:   Do you trust the petrochemical industry?
                Do you trust the pharmaceutical industry?
Respondent 2:   No.
Respondent 1:   Do you trust the food industry?
Respondent 2:   Is there anything in this world we trust?
Respondent 1:   Do you trust big business, full stop? I don't.
Respondent 2:   No.

It's difficult to think of any group, from the list above or beyond, that has managed to restore trust after losing it. It may well be that most individuals in many of these groups are entirely blameless. But we have a strange habit of judging by the exception, rather than the rule: if, say, it becomes clear that one bishop has behaved badly, we jump to the conclusion that they all have.

Amid this general collapse in emotional trust, it's impossible to see how the financial services industry could manage to stand alone in reversing the trend, especially if we assume a continuing flow of reasons for distrust. The task would be truly Sisyphean – a boulder painfully shoved a few metres up the hill, bang, rolling down in a

Libor crisis. Start again, another few metres, then rolling down in a US multi-billion-dollar fine for mis-selling sub-prime debt. And so it goes.[3]
3. *Rebuilding emotional trust in financial services is unnecessary.* (This section gives a hint of where we're going in the later part of this chapter.)

It's very important to recognise that even with levels of emotional trust across much of the consumer economy as low as they are, commercial organisations are still able to sell a lot of stuff and make a lot of money. Customers don't trust estate agents or car salesmen much, but they still buy houses and cars. They don't trust Apple, Microsoft or Starbucks to pay their taxes, but most still buy their devices, software and beverages. And they don't trust Sir Philip Green to do the right thing by BHS pensioners, but they still shop at Top Shop.

True, low levels of trust arguably make it harder and more expensive to do business, creating situations in which many consumers approach firms with excessive caution and reluctance to engage any more than absolutely necessary. If they could easily find and buy a house without dealing with an estate agent, they would. And as they're presented with an ever-growing range of digital alternatives that mean that they don't have to deal with a traditional estate agent, or car dealer, or bank, or insurance company, a growing number are voting with their feet (or, more accurately, as mobile moves up the list of consumers' preferred digital devices, with their thumbs).

But, even so, currently it clearly isn't the case that a lack of trust makes it impossible – or even all that difficult – to do business. And, similarly, in a market where it's hard to find sources of competitive advantage, not all firms would welcome an increase in trust across the board. A Financial Services Forum focus group respondent says 'It depends whether you're looking at it from a company level, or an industry level. Do I care that other banks are mistrusted? No. If I could make people trust us more than the others, then competitively I would win'.

It's just as well that rebuilding trust across the industry is unnecessary, because . . .

---

[3] Meanwhile, of course, we're seeing a hugely important and parallel transfer of trust. As our trust in virtually all sources of traditional authority dwindles, our trust in personal and much less authoritative sources increases. In the era of social media, we trust our families, our friends, people we meet in the pub and, increasingly, more or less anyone who establishes him or herself as a non-traditional source of opinion and judgement. At its worst, this means falling hook, line and sinker for the manipulative agendas of those peddling 'fake news'. At its best, it results in the explosive growth of what we might rather clumsily call 'aggregated sources of non-authoritative trust': Trip Adviser, VouchedFor, Trust Pilot, user ratings on Amazon and in app stores.

4. *Rebuilding trust in financial services is unaffordable.* Bear in mind three things:

a. the influence of the media and social media, and the enormous difficulty in influencing what they have to say;

b. consumers' propensity, noted above, to judge by the exception rather than the rule; and

c. crucially, the fact that insofar as levels of trust can be managed either upwards or downwards, doing so depends simply and solely on managing perceptions of trustworthiness.

On this basis, it seems clear to us that if the industry is to have even the slightest chance of rebuilding consumers' emotional trust, then the industry – and that means all of it – is going to have to start behaving in a totally – and visibly – trustworthy fashion. And that's going to be very, very expensive.

Just think about a small and random selection of behaviours that currently engender distrust, and that are going to have to stop. (We're not thinking here about the big bad things, the PPI mis-selling disasters that hit the headlines – we're just thinking about the small day-to-day behaviours that people view with suspicion, which make them think that you can't have their interests at heart or else you'd do things differently. Things like:

- Producing hugely lengthy Terms & Conditions, written in incomprehensible jargon and published in unreadable 8-point type;
- Punishing customers for their loyalty by increasing their charges while making discounts available to new customers;
- Maintaining theoretically 'free' current account banking, but levying exorbitant and unexpected charges for the most minor infractions of the rules;
- Selling packaged current accounts that include breakdown insurance to customers with no car, or that include travel insurance to customers who either don't travel, or who have conditions that make them wholly or largely ineligible;
- Charging interest on uncleared storecard balances of over 29% (as, for example, Top Shop, House of Fraser and Debenhams all do) at a time when base rate is 0.5%;
- Charging up to 5% p.a., and sometimes more, to manage so-called 'active' investment funds that consistently underperform tracker funds that charge a tenth as much.

Some of these behaviours – and some of the hundreds more we could have cited – are real and current causes of actual day-to-day distrust and dissatisfaction. Others are hostages to fortune – mis-selling stories that may or may not hit the headlines at some point in the future, but with predictably disastrous effects on perceptions of trust if and when they do.

All of them are profitable – some very profitable – for the organisations that have adopted them. And if we really wanted to rebuild trust across the industry, they'd all have to stop.

Ultimately, it's much more about an attitude of mind rather than a specific list of changed practices. The attitude of mind is the one that says the only rules are (1) don't break the law, and (2) don't get found out – an attitude that's reflected in this comment made in a Financial Services Forum focus group by a respondent with a very senior role in general insurance:

> 'Year on year we know that our loyal customers are becoming better and better risks, but 10% of our customers will get a 20% price increase in year 4. Don't ask me why, it's just the benchmark figure we use. So that is just frankly raping and pillaging the back book, but it's a hard thing to unembed'.

When we discussed that 3R Insights research on perceptions of financial services firms' CEOs quoted earlier in the chapter, we asked whether consumers' cynicism just reflected their perceptions, or reflected current reality. This focus group respondent's comment strongly suggests an answer.

We have no idea what the total price tag of eliminating all these trust-harming behaviours might be, but the cost of compensating customers for just a single one of the big stories – mis-selling Purchase Protection Insurance (PPI) – is already £40 billion and will rise further. Say that the total price tag is three, four, five times that – somewhere between £100 billion and £200 billion. Would it be worth it?

We asked this last question, or a version of it, in our Financial Services Forum online members research. We asked specifically about the cost of maintaining and/or regaining trust, and the findings made us raise our eyebrows.

Only 3% of respondents said that they knew the cost of building trust and knew that it wouldn't be worth it, 15% said they didn't know the cost, 50% said they knew the cost and knew it was worth it, and 32% said it would be worth it whatever the cost – that's 82% saying creating trust is worth the cost.

Frankly, we simply don't believe this. We don't believe anyone knows the cost, and in purely commercial terms we're sure it would hardly ever be worth it. The findings show that our research respondents are good people who want their firms to be trusted, but that's about all.

These are the four reasons why we feel so sure that the financial services industry will never restore consumer trust.

At this point we should add that while we've been questioning the obviously Herculean task of rebuilding trust in financial services *as a whole*, we don't actually think it's much easier to rebuild trust in *any single, specific institution*.

This is a controversial statement, so we should explain it carefully and caveat it appropriately. First the caveats.

As we've said, there are three circumstances in which levels of distrust are lower than average. People have less distrust toward their own financial services providers – 'The banks/financial advisers/insurance companies are all as bad as each other, except that mine is better than most'. They have less distrust toward small, young, usually digital start-ups that haven't done anything bad yet. (We refer here to emotional distrust – they may well feel a higher level of existential or functional distrust.) And they have less distrust towards some types of firm than others – building societies, for example, still occupy a slightly higher rung on the ladder.

But otherwise, the biggest problem for any financial services business seeking to restore trust is that widespread perception that 'they're all as bad as each other'. Organisation A can run an exemplary business, providing consumers with no reasons at all to distrust it. But if Organisation B, or C, or D – or, even worse, all of them – is found to have been less scrupulous, then Organisation A will find it exceptionally difficult to avoid guilt by association.

This isn't the case in highly branded and strongly differentiated markets. When a packaged goods brand is found to be adulterated or contaminated in some way – as when Perrier mineral water was found to be contaminated with benzene – consumers were generally (and rightly) not concerned that the same might be true of Evian or San Pellegrino.

The situation was more finely balanced in the automotive industry when Volkswagen was found to have faked the results of emissions tests. If one other big manufacturer was shown to have done the same thing, many consumers would have assumed they were all at it, but most hadn't been found out. But for as long as the only certain malefactor was VW, consumers were willing to believe that other firms' hands were clean.[4]

In the largely undifferentiated landscape of financial services, though, consumers tend to assume that even if just one is doing it, they're probably all doing it. And the truth is, consumers are probably right.

For this reason, and bearing in mind the caveats and partial exemptions summarised above, we're very cautious about the idea that single organisations can be seen to be more trustworthy than their peers. If creating trust

---

[4]They also didn't seem to care very much about the state of VW's hands. The sales of Volkswagens fell only marginally and briefly – possibly reflecting some car buyers' somewhat narrow-minded and short-sighted view that fiddling emissions level tests is, at least as far as they're concerned, a victimless crime.

across the industry is impossible, then creating (and sustaining) trust in a single firm isn't much easier.

So where do we go from here? Are we simply content with the status quo?

Not at all. Our view is that while restoring trust is an impossible task, *managing distrust* is an entirely possible and vitally important one.

And in the second part we'll discuss how to do this – suggesting, as you'll see, a range of actions and behaviours that aren't so very different from the ones you'd choose if restoring trust was indeed your goal.

This may sound as if our phrase 'managing distrust' is something of a semantic conjuring trick, just a way of saying 'restoring trust' in different words. But that's really not the case. 'Restoring trust' is about trying to do something game-changingly permanent, something that creates a different kind of equilibrium between consumers and financial services going forward. To reiterate a phrase we used earlier, 'managing distrust' is about an attitude of mind. It's about remembering that the current distrustful equilibrium isn't going to change, and so every time we want to interact with our market we have to assume, as one of our marketing directors said in a Forum focus group, that many of the people we're wanting to engage with are already asking themselves, 'Who is this bastard and why is he lying to me?' Forgive the overdramatic analogy, but it's rather as if our customers are unexploded bombs, with their distrust on a hair trigger and ready to be set off at any moment. One false move, and the credibility of anything you want to say or do has gone.

This situation is inevitably more difficult to manage when the relationship between consumer and financial services provider is closer, longer-lasting and involves more frequent contact. Most consumers have very few of these – even when we hold a product, like a mortgage, life policy or pension, for many years the infrequency of contact means that we have no real sense of what could be called a 'relationship'. For many of us, the bank that provides our current account is the only real example. When there is a 'relationship' like this, though, trust is an essential part of it, in much the same way as it is in relationships in our private life. And that being so, the first priority is to avoid – and keep on avoiding, week by week, month by month and year by year – any false moves.

This requirement applies in all sorts of ways. Many of them are about communication, about what you say and how (and even when) you say it. If you use weasel words – this product 'can' do such-and-such, or customers 'may' receive so-and-so, then what people hear is 'will'. If you 'can' lose money on this investment, then people are inclined to believe that they will. If there 'may' be an exit penalty, many assume that there will be.

And everyone knows that when you tell them about 'new' charges, what you mean is 'higher' charges – if they were lower, you'd say so.

A similar point applies to jargon and small print. Both are assumed to hide bad news. If it isn't bad news, why would you make it so hard to read and understand?

Customers today have very sensitive lie-detection capabilities, but often very little sensitivity is needed. When your IVR system keeps them waiting 20 minutes, but a voice interrupts the hold music twice a minute to tell them their call is important to you, they know perfectly well that it isn't. Insisting otherwise is just silly and counterproductive.

Then there are all those little behaviours that we do almost without thinking, as part of our usual business practice, which still infuriate and generate suspicion. We know, for example, how much existing customers hate seeing preferential treatment and lower prices given to new customers. It's particularly upsetting when firms seem to take advantage of vulnerable customers – your authors are perfectly capable of keeping our insurance premiums low by regular rebroking, but we hate seeing our elderly parents taken for a ride. Over and above the procedures required by regulation, we hate excessively cumbersome security procedures, on the telephone and online – everyone is infuriated by the frequent need to give account number and address details three times before we can actually speak to someone.[5]

There are countless examples. Many are trivial, but remember that hair-trigger – it doesn't take much to set us off. One of your authors receives a regular e-mail from a big asset management firm. It's titled 'Essential Reading for Investors'. That heading never fails to irritate him. It's not 'Essential Reading', it's a flimsy and boring marketing newsletter. What would the firm call an email that really did contain essential reading?

New distrust detonators seem to turn up all the time. An area causing rapidly increasing agitation is the use of data, particularly online. Some of the cleverer things that big data makes possible are alarming to customers. Programmatic advertising is a case in point. How does Facebook know that we're interested in a new credit card? Why is it that as soon as we fill in an online insurance application, we're pursued all round the Internet by price comparison sites? Research shows a high level of ignorance among customers on the whole subject of what data organisations hold, and what

---

[5]The most irritating thing of all is having to come up with our security information, which we've very likely forgotten, when it's our bank that has called us. In fact, of course, this is genuinely important for security reasons and in any case is insisted on by the regulator, so our irritation is hardly fair. But an emotive issue like trust causes unfairness.

uses they make of it. From an industry perspective, the use of big data to personalise and customise is massively to customers' advantage and heralds a welcome improvement in relevance and service, but many customers find it sinister and alarming.

But if having the insight and sensitivity to see these issues, large and small, through customers' eyes is the first requirement, the second is figuring out what to do about them.

There are several options:

1. *Carry on as we are.* We can't say we love this option, but it clearly does exist. Some firms may take the view that the commercial benefits of a behaviour outweigh the lessening of trust. If a big and apparently irreplaceable part of an insurance company's profit comes from ripping off our mothers, then it may decide to carry on overcharging them and accept the reputational consequences at both micro and macro levels.

2. *Stop doing it.* On the other hand, it may be that the commercial benefits don't outweigh the negative effect on trust. It might just be best to stop.

3. *Present it better.* Customers hate the idea that the prices they're paying penalises them for their loyalty, but they do more or less understand that offering an introductory discount is a good way to recruit new customers. For an industry that's often criticised for its fondness for spin, it's strange how many of our most irritating behaviours are simply the result of bad copywriting.

4. *Find a way to offset, or counterbalance, the negative.* If offering discounts to new customers really is essential to your business model, then how about a parallel initiative to offer bonuses to existing customers – say, rewarding their loyalty after they stay for five years? One of the biggest drivers of distrust is unfairness. You have to be able to demonstrate that what you're doing is fair.

5. *Explain what you're doing, and why.* If there's a good reason why we have to key in our account number three times before you can talk to us, we'd like to know what it is. Actually, even if there's a bad reason, we'd still like to know what it is.

There are no doubt plenty of examples of these strategies, and probably some other strategies as well. This book isn't intended as a practical guide to customer experience, or customer journey management – there are plenty of good books, consultancies and agencies ready to help with that.

This, as we keep saying, is about an attitude of mind – an attitude that we think is crucially important in the emerging new era of financial services marketing, and an attitude that should be ruthlessly applied to every aspect of the customer experience you provide. It's not very complicated – it's about not treating customers like idiots, not trying to steal their money and not saying or doing things that they don't believe. If you can manage to not do these things, and carry on not doing them over time, then from day to day those explosions of distrust will remain undetonated. Maybe, if you keep it up consistently enough, and for long enough, you might just find that distrust starts to fade away a bit. And as a general principle, when all else fails, try telling the truth.

CHAPTER 15

Whatever It Is, Can You Make It Simpler?

If there's one thing that really must shine through in the new financial services marketing, it is that we must learn to express ourselves more simply – most of all in writing, although at the same time it's also true that we should use writing to express ourselves less often, and other techniques much more often.

To help make sure we practise what we preach, we're going to write all (or actually almost all) of the first section of this chapter in words of only one or two syllables.

We say 'almost all' because we're going to give ourselves a small handful of get-outs – longer words that we're going to use even though they have three syllables. Yes, you've spotted it, the first word in that small handful is indeed the word *syllable* (and also *syllables*) – it would be hard to explain what we're doing without using the word at least once. We'll allow ourselves a few other get-outs too: we can't manage without the words *financial, services* and *marketing*, already used in our first sentence; we'll be using the names of firms, people and other bodies, some of which are longer; and also we'll allow ourselves some words used in comments made by other people that we'll be quoting in what follows.[1]

To be honest, writing in this way isn't a new idea for us. A year or two ago one of your authors put it forward to a client who wanted to focus his brand promise on the idea of keeping things simple (and it wasn't a new idea then, either). The client turned the idea down straightaway. Far too tricky, he said. My people will never go for it. We're not children, and the people we're

---

[1] Also, there's room for debate about the number of syllables in some words. Are there two or three syllables in the word 'idea'? Or 'average'? Or 'general'? You may say this is a bit of a cheat, but when there's room for doubt, we're going to take the view that for the purpose of writing this chapter, it's the lower of the two numbers.

writing for aren't children either. That kind of writing wouldn't impress any of them at all.[2]

We shall see. If the first part of this chapter seems naive, childish or banal, then the client was right. If it seems plain-speaking and easy to read and absorb, then it'll help us make our point.

Over the years, people in financial services marketing have very often chosen to write in a complex, jargon-ridden and opaque style. There are many reasons for this.

1. They've often been writing mainly for business readers. Business readers are much more able to absorb jargon, and are much less likely to be put off by forms of words that others find complex or opaque. (In fact, the whole point of jargon is to make it easier and quicker to get your point across – but only, of course, when your readers know what it means.)

2. We're often told what to say, and how to say it, by bodies like the Financial Conduct Authority (and before that, the Financial Services Authority) and Trading Standards. Take the Annual Percentage Rate (APR) rules, which govern how we have to express the rate of interest people pay on their loans. No-one gets this. Very few people can even make sense of the words 'Annual Percentage Rate' in themselves, and for this they can hardly be blamed. Here's the way the term is defined in Wikipedia:

> The nominal APR is calculated as: the rate, for a payment period, multiplied by the number of payment periods in a year. However, the exact legal definition of 'effective APR', or EAR, can vary greatly in each jurisdiction, depending on the type of fees included, such as participation fees, loan origination fees, monthly service charges, or late fees. The effective APR has been called the 'mathematically true' interest rate for each year.
>
> The computation for the effective APR, as the fee + compound interest rate, can also vary depending on whether the up-front fees, such as origination or participation fees, are added to the entire amount, or treated as a short-term loan

---

[2]He might have been wrong about that. The Office for National Statistics says the UK's average reading age is just 13 – and, by the way, the average adult reads less than one book in their adult lifetime.

due in the first payment. When start-up fees are paid as first payment(s), the balance due might accrue more interest, as being delayed by the extra payment period(s).

Did you get that? Thought not.

3. Quite frankly, the truth is that we've often used language to make things hard for people to follow on purpose, rather than to make it easy. Small print, complex grammar and opaque wording combine to ensure that very few people have the patience or skills to figure out what firms are really saying. We doubt, for example, if a poor-value product like PPI (Payment Protection Insurance) could ever have sold as well as it did if people had fully grasped what they were buying.

4. It's very easy to hide behind complex language, so that people never quite know what you're saying. Vincent Franklin, of language advice firm Quiet Room, highlights the use of *passive* verbs – when you say 'the ball was kicked' rather than 'I kicked the ball', Vincent points out that the passive version ducks the issue of who did the kicking. In the same way, he says, when Gordon Brown had to report at the time of the 2008 financial crisis to the House of Commons, he used the form of words 'Mistakes were made'. By whom, that's the question – but the answer is hidden behind that passive verb.

5. A lot of financial copy has been written by people who may know a great deal about financial services, but who really can't write very well. It wouldn't be true to say that the country's best writers are queuing up to write this kind of stuff. Much financial marketing copy has been written by people who aren't really writers at all, and it shows.

Of all these four reasons, we'd say the key one is the first. Far too many of those involved in briefing, writing and vetting financial services marketing content simply aren't focused enough on whether they're making any sense to the poor sods who have to read it. Changing this lack of focus is one of the big issues that the new financial services marketing has to tackle.

We say 'has to tackle' because we're sure that it really matters. The failure to keep things simple and clear creates five big problems for our target groups:

1. Big picture, it makes them feel they want as little to do with our world as they can get away with. Money is tricky, quite nerve-wracking stuff at the best of times: there's always an instinct telling you it may be best not to open that letter. But if, along with this very real angst, you also have a strong feeling that the content is sure to be wholly baffling, that

instinct to keep well away will be all the stronger. We hate feeling stupid, and that's the way that reading bad writing makes us feel.

2. Beyond this broad sense that financial matters are too hard to bother about, there's also the very real danger that people will fail in their attempts to buy products, most of all online. Drop-out rates in digital DIY channels are often very high, and research shows that a few poorly expressed phrases often cause the problem. One online savings process lost over 50% of all users when they reached one single badly worded question: when the words were changed, the results were transformed.

   It's helpful to think of someone going through an online process as someone walking a narrow, wobbly tightrope in a strong crosswind. If all goes well, they'll make it to the other side. But any sudden jolt, or gust or kink in the rope, and they'll go crashing to the ground.

3. Then of course there's a big point about trust. Unclear, complex, jargon-ridden content adds to people's feelings of distrust – and if, as is the case in financial services, the level of distrust is high from the outset, that's an even bigger problem. (The reverse is also true. In any effort to rebuild trust, keeping things clear and simple and giving the strong signal that you have nothing to hide is a vital aspect.)

   In fact, it's a bit worse than a simple lack of trust. People faced with the over-complex don't simply react with distrust, they react with something worse: they react with fear that something bad is going to happen to them, and they're not going to know when it does. Being fearful of our world is an even bigger problem than just not trusting us.

4. Common sense says there must be a point here about brands, and the ways they're perceived and seen to differ (or not to differ) from each other – and common sense is of course right. The failure to express themselves clearly and simply is seen to be so widespread across financial services firms that it gives a message that all firms are much the same.[3] Note the contrast with many other complex markets, where tone of voice is often key to the way we perceive brands. In IT, a big part of the way people perceive the Apple brand is to do with the way that Apple keeps things simple – compared, of course, to those clunky, lumpy, hard-to-use PCs.

   The Apple brand, of course, is about a lot more than a tone of voice on screen and in writing, and indeed far beyond comms as a whole. It has become an ethos for the whole firm that is expressed in every aspect of design. We think it's odd that no financial firm seems to have learned

---

[3] One of the few very firms that stands out for its simple and clear writing is First Direct – which, of course, we have praised more than once as one of the strongest brands in financial services.

from this huge success – with the possible exception of First Direct, we can't think of a single one that has really tried to build a brand on the basis of great design.

5. And last but by no means least in this list, we come to a point that is going to require another breach of our two-syllable rule, because we need to use the three-syllable word *dialogue* (and it would help if we could use another three-syllable word, *engagement,* too. You can't have a dialogue – or at least not a good one – with someone who makes no sense to you. If people's eyes glaze over before they get to the end of your first sentence, or indeed any sentence, then the dialogue won't get far. These days, financial services marketers are almost all – and rightly – obsessed with the idea of building a dialogue. They believe that in today's online world, good dialogue is the basis of good engagement – and good engagement is the basis of good business. But they'll never succeed if they can't make a whole lot more sense to people than most manage at the moment.

But the fact is that while most of us in financial services marketing would accept most of this, when push comes to shove we just can't do it. To reverse the well-worn cliché, we may be able to walk the walk but we just can't talk that nice, simple, real, human talk.

(And, by the way, when we do sometimes manage it, we do something else almost as bad, which is to keep things simple but only by talking to people in a weirdly dull, boring, empty way. There's a new, online tone of voice starting to emerge in financial services, shared by a large number of young fintechs. It has its good points – it's more friendly, simpler, more human and relaxed. But on the downside, there are dozens if not hundreds of firms now using it – and they all sound just the same.)

So far, this chapter has focused mainly on writing – the way we engage with people with words, the way we explain things they need to know. But that's only part of the story. Behind the question of writing, there's something bigger – something about the role that we're trying to play in people's lives, about how much we demand of them in order that they can engage with what we do, about the concepts that we expect them to be able to grasp.

To discuss this underlying dimension, we're going to drop the two-syllable thing, which might start to get a bit wearying for both you and us as we move into this more conceptual subject (although we hope you'll agree that it hasn't worked too badly in the chapter up to now).

The key point is that the limitations in consumers' level of financial engagement, and along with that their level of financial capability, aren't just – or indeed aren't mainly – about language, and the problem can't be solved either by using simpler words ourselves, or indeed teaching them some of our more complicated ones. There's a whole backstory of conceptual ideas that sit behind the language, and without understanding at least something of that story and those ideas the language can't be meaningful.

Take, for example, a little-known and not-at-all-financial word like, to choose at random, *crepuscular.* And then choose an unfamiliar financial expression, like, equally randomly, *absolute return.* You could prove easily enough that both are understood by only a very small minority of people.

But the lack of understanding is of two very different kinds. People may not know the meaning of the word *crepuscular.* But as soon as you tell them that it's a way of describing twilight, there are immediately a whole lot of things that they understand perfectly well. They understand what twilight is, and why it happens. They understand that it happens at, or just before, dawn, and, particularly, at dusk. They understand at least something about why it happens – that the sun is low in the sky and so doesn't cast much light. And many will have a sense of some of the science that lies behind that – the earth rotating on its axis so that night and day alternate, and twilight occuring in the period between the two.

If you explain that an *absolute return* fund is one that aims to achieve a positive return in all market conditions, then for a great majority of customers, none of this background understanding exists. The first problem is that you've simply replaced one unfamiliar word with several others – what is a fund? What is a return? What are market conditions? But even if you get past that with some more explanations and definitions, you still aren't really anywhere. Don't all of these funds try to make a positive return in all market conditions? How is this remotely special or different? How do you mean, most funds aim for a relative return, one that will be positive when measured against a benchmark? What is a benchmark? If it's based on an index, where do you find this index? (Most people find them at the back of a book.) And what will this absolute return be, anyway? And is it guaranteed? And if not, what's the point of it?

We could go on, but you get the message. To understand what the words *absolute return* mean, you don't simply need a definition from a dictionary – you need a beginner's course in asset management.

Of course, to make a point that seems to come up in virtually every chapter of this book, all consumer markets segment. There is, as we acknowledge in several places, a small segment of knowledgeable consumers who know all about absolute return funds, and about modern portfolio theory, and could even explain the concept of the efficient frontier.[4] These people,

---

[4]Which, as we all know, is of course the graphical depiction of the Markowitz efficient set of portfolios representing the boundary of the set of feasible portfolios that have the maximum return for a given level of risk. Any portfolios above the frontier cannot be achieved. Any below the frontier are dominated by Markowitz efficient portfolios.

although private individuals, have attitudes, expertise and in many ways behaviours in common with the business target groups who are much more familiar to many financial marketers. Everyone recognises the existence of this segment, including the FCA, which is happy to see them served, and addressed, in a manner that reflects their sophistication.

The problem is what to do about everyone else. Is it just a question of producing simpler marketing collateral, with a glossary giving a brief definition of Absolute Return? Although that would probably satisfy the regulator, we don't really believe it solves the problem. If an unsophisticated investor can't understand a proposition quickly and easily, we don't really think it makes much sense to offer that proposition to that investor at all. Not all financial propositions that work for professionals or for sophisticated consumers can be presented in ways that make them work for all consumers. Recipes and ingredients that work well for professional chefs and keen domestic followers of Jamie and Nigella can be too difficult, no matter how simply presented, for most of the rest of us.

And of course by the time less-expert readers even think of turning to the glossary – if indeed they ever do – a misunderstanding may have already taken root, and may be extremely difficult to correct. At the time this was researched, for example, there's an investment poster in the London Underground, where it will be seen by a number of more experienced investors but also a great many more inexperienced ones. The headline says: 'Your Route to Spreading Risk Across Many Investments'.

Experienced investors probably read this rather clunky form of words as it was intended, as a positive idea about diversification. Inexperienced ones may misunderstand it completely. 'Risk' is a bad thing, isn't it? We don't want risk. We're better off without it, or at least with as little of it as possible. Yet this fund, or thing, or whatever it is, says it's 'spreading risk across many investments'. Not just a few, but many. Sounds terrible. I'm going to stay well away.

Again, this isn't just a point about language. It's a point about the concepts in the investment world of risk, and of diversification. If the baffled tube-travelling inexperienced investor decides to turn to that glossary, or more like to Google or Wikipedia, to try to decode this message, they'll have a fair bit of reading to do.

None of this means that financial propositions should be withheld from the consumer market. They all have their place. Absolute return funds should be there, on the market, available to anyone who wants to work their way through the Hargreaves Lansdown website, in just the same way that titanium flanged exhaust inlet valves should be advertised in *Practical Mechanics*. But the propositions we present to consumers should be designed *from the ground up* to meet the level of sophistication and understanding of those consumers, which means that they can't be – as they so often are at the moment – propositions designed for professionals but offered in dumbed-down versions in the direct-to-consumer marketplace.

This is a point that clearly presents a very significant challenge to the industry. In most financial services categories, standard operating procedure – refined over many years – is, precisely, to design products and processes for professionals, and then to go on to develop dumbed-down consumer versions ('dumbed-down' in this context means simplified either in terms of product design, or in communication or, very likely, both).

Sometimes, the implications of this line of thought can raise eyebrows – especially when they mean limiting the availability of appealing and effective products and services. We mention offset mortgages elsewhere as examples of excellent and beneficial products that are just too complicated to explain to most borrowers. Most of those choosing their mortgage on a DIY basis don't choose offset mortgages because, try as the copywriter might, they sound complex and intimidating; and even among those who do finish up with an offset mortgage, usually on the basis of an intermediary's advice, very few use the product to anything like its full potential.

Even in categories that are now very largely direct-to-consumer, and where the role of professionals has been dramatically reduced over time – like, for example, general insurance – the dumbing-down approach still largely prevails, and still causes plenty of discomfort. Consumers are generally content to buy general insurance direct, but it's disturbing to realise how little they understand about what they're buying. Motor, travel, home and pet policies are still built around hugely lengthy and detailed terms and conditions, stuffed full of traps for the unwary and little-understood ground rules: this basic approach was developed in an era when brokers dominated the market, and has never changed even though their market shares are now down to single-figure percentages.

The new financial services marketing is already starting to move on. In many categories – insurance, investment, banking, peer-to-peer lending – start-up pure-play digital propositions are beginning to reject old-style complexity and simplify propositions to the bare minimum, often using data to achieve 'simplified relevance' that makes it possible to offer no more, but also no less, than each individual customer needs.

But this evolution still has a long way to go. It's very, very difficult for people working in financial services to completely clear their minds of assumptions carried over from the old world. Traditional tools and processes – even if in much more modern, much more accessible presentations – have a habit of surviving. Insurance underwriting may now happen on the phone, but it's still underwriting.

Again, we have to make the point that the regulator often doesn't help. It's regulation, for example, acting on the mistaken belief that more information makes for more empowered consumers, that insists that the marketing of lending products has to focus around the communication of APRs (Annual Percentage Rates), which no direct borrower understands.

And in attempting to satisfy the regulator's requirements, many new-generation investment propositions still give themselves a mountain to climb by basing their processes around attitude-to-risk (ATR) questionnaires originally designed to work in a financial adviser's office, but horribly difficult and intimidating for younger people with little investment experience who are going through the process on their tablets or phones. (At the end of this chapter, we run through a real and frequently used ATR questionnaire, the 10-question version developed by Oxford Risk, adding in some of the kind of responses and anxieties we would expect it to trigger from a typical inexperienced customer.)

The same problem arises in countless other tools and processes originated for the adviser, professional or sophisticated investor market, and then subsequently simplified a bit and presented in D2C environments. From the name alone, for example, you might imagine that an unsophisticated DIY investor would be likely to struggle with something called Stochastic Modelling, and you'd be right. One of your authors has sat in research focus groups where people were exposed to the kind of 'fan charts' that show the potential range of investment outcomes over a range of periods of time: for all the sense they could make of them, the charts might as well have been written in Sanskrit.

And let's not forget completely about doubts and uncertainties that are triggered by language, even though – as we argued earlier – language problems often reveal underlying problems with financial principles and concepts. New-generation online life insurer Beagle Street, for example, claims to offer a quick, easy, online quote-generation process. But at the time of writing, as soon as it's asked you your name, gender and age, the next question in its online application process as at spring 2017 is whether you want Level Term or Decreasing Term insurance. Most people won't know. There is a little video to watch, but we found it rushed and quite confusing. And the three-screen written explanation is very strange, the third of the three screens saying only:

What's Not a Type of Life Insurance Policy?
The two main types of Life Insurance are covered above; it's a common misconception that Critical Illness and 'life assurance' are classified as types of life insurance policy.

Even with our combined 60 years of financial services marketing experience, we have no idea what that means.[5]

After that, the process asks a series of simple questions – how much cover you want, how long you want the cover to last, whether or not you also want Critical Illness. The explanatory notes are notably short, but not notably explanatory. The Critical Illness explanatory box, for example, states:

Why You Might Need Critical Illness Cover
You can set the level of Critical Illness Cover that's right for you, providing extra security just in case you need it. If you were to become critically ill you may find your costs increase, for medical appointments, equipment, lifestyle changes, even a carer. A lump-sum pay-out could help cover these additional expenses.

This is, to say the least, a pretty sketchy sales pitch for what is effectively a second level of cover that will usually more than double the cost. We think it's an unhelpful distraction from the main business of the site, which is selling life assurance – but at the same time an insufficient argument to make a persuasive case for CI.

By the way, while Beagle Street is undoubtedly an online business looking to make sales directly from its website, there are others with rather murkier aims. Particularly in life assurance, but in other sectors too, there are players which use a seemingly online process to generate leads for a telesales operation. At some point in the online process you'll be asked for a telephone number, and fairly shortly thereafter you'll start receiving calls from remarkably persistent callers. These firms operate on the basis that good telesales people can achieve much higher conversion rates than 'pure' online services, and also that they're likely to be able to walk customers up to more expensive and profitable options. For the firms concerned, it can be an effective model and one that can overcome the problem of unviably high acquisition costs. But from the customers' perspective, it's a manipulative and misleading tactic that has little to do with the new financial services marketing.

To sum up, it's obviously true to say that if the new financial services marketing has to engage more effectively with consumers, and help build their confidence and understanding to the point that they're able to find their

---

[5] The Beagle Street team may have felt the same way. The current online process is a good deal easier, quicker and clearer.

way through our processes, choose good products and services and make effective use of them, we have to get better at communicating with them.

The most obvious requirements are to do with how we express ourselves in writing. On the whole, our writing is still far too complex and opaque – and, no less important, it's also far too boring and unrewarding to read. We seem to have reached a point where we've eliminated some of our very worst habits, at least from our marketing communications, and then slumped back exhausted, failing to build on these limited achievements.

At the next level, we've been making a bit more progress recently in finding other ways to communicate that get us beyond reams of text. Very large amounts of time, money and effort have been ploughed into so-called infographics, for example, although it has to be said that results have been mixed. And fairly large amounts of time, money and effort have gone into the use of video (including, obviously, a lot of animated infographics), but the results have been rather more mixed. Too many of these have a patronising air, which is insulting to customers.

But it's the third level that presents the real challenge, specifically to marketers but actually to the industry as a whole. The third level says we will never become good at engaging with consumers if our default assumption is that we will offer them dumbed-down versions of products, propositions and processes originally designed for professionals. We have to start again, with blank sheets of paper, and think about what our customers really want from us, and how they want to buy and use it.

There are of course a few parts of the industry with a lot more experience than others when it comes to this kind of thinking. Many retail banking services, for example, have only ever been intended for individual consumers, so rebuilding propositions originally intended for professionals doesn't arise. But that's no reason for complacency – as a new wave of challenger banks are demonstrating, there are still plenty of ways to make basic banking services a whole lot more meaningful and relevant to consumers.

And amid all this room for a great deal of improvement, there are now some examples of firms that have developed genuinely customer-centric propositions, which are now clearly setting the pace. It's not the most original or popular example, but it is hard to imagine how you could improve on the core of payday lender Wonga's wonderfully simple online application process, with its two questions – how much cash do you want, and how long do you want it for? – and its two simple slider controls to use for your answers. It's very difficult to imagine why anyone would drop out rather than answer these (although of course those incomprehensible APR details, if they register with people, might create some alarm).

'ATTITUDE TO RISK' QUESTIONNAIRES

Finally in this section, we turn our attention to an element which, thanks largely to the enthusiasm of the FCA, has become a ubiquitous part of online investment processes: the Attitude To Risk questionnaire. There are several currently in use, but there's little difference between them and the aim is always the same: to identify how much risk the respondent is comfortable to take in pursuit of investment returns.

We're well aware that a great deal of science has gone into all of them, and that they've been designed to provide good, reliable outcomes even when – or arguably especially when – people complete them quickly and without thinking too hard. We're by no means expert enough to cast any doubt over the outcomes they generate: it may well be that their questions, although seemingly ambiguous and repetitive, give genuinely robust results.

(Actually, behind the admirably mature and balanced perspective of that previous paragraph, we can't help secretly thinking that the whole idea of people having an 'attitude to risk' that is (a) one single thing and (b) pretty much unchanging over time is a lot of old tosh. Behavioural scientists quoted in Chapter 12 who are a great deal cleverer than us make it very clear that we all have different attitudes toward the risk that we're willing to take with different lumps of our money – for example, we're much happier to take risks with money we won on a horse than money for which we worked hours of overtime. And equally, although we can't produce any Nobel laureates to support our view, we know from personal experience that we're a whole lot more bullish about making risky investments when the TV news every evening is about the FTSE hitting record highs, and a whole lot more bearish when the headlines say it's plunging like a weighted sack. But what do we know?)

Anyway, these aren't the doubts we want to focus on here. Our concern, as demonstrated in what follows, is that when consumers complete these questionnaires for themselves,without the presence of an adviser to guide them, the process of answering the questions creates a growing level of uncertainty or anxiety – so much so that a significant number will drop out before they get to the end.

This isn't a minor problem. Like many digital direct-to-consumer financial propositions, the kinds of online investment service we're discussing here are, at best, very marginally profitable. Many are hopelessly unprofitable. Given the horrendous cost-per-response and cost-per-customer figures that most are experiencing, they certainly can't afford to frighten off perfectly good prospects: it may well be that for some, an unnecessarily high drop-out rate on this questionnaire, in itself, will make the difference between a viable and an unviable business.

In what follows, we've created a hybrid questionnaire which combines elements typical of the main offerings currently in use. And having created it, your authors decided to have a go at answering it...

Please indicate your response to the following statements on a five-point scale, where 5 means that you agree strongly, 4 means you agree slightly, 3 that you neither agree nor disagree, 2 that you disagree slightly and 1 that you disagree strongly. Got that? OK.

1. *My family and friends think of me as a person who doesn't like to take risks.*

LC: Well, what kind of risks? They'd say I'm quite careful with money, but the last time we went out for a meal I chose a white wine from Hungary. Which was delicious, actually. Do they mean financially, or in real life? Not too sure about that one. Perhaps I'll come back to it.

AT: I suppose it depends which ones you ask, and about what. I don't think the ones who've been around a motor-racing track with me probably would say that.

2. *I'm happier when I know my money is safe from risk.*

LC: Of course I'm happier. If I could choose between putting my money in a safe, or balanced on the edge of a glowing red-hot barbecue, I'd choose the safe. Who wouldn't? Is that what they mean?

AT: Who's going to say they're happier when their money is unsafe? Of course I prefer it to be safe.

3. *I feel comfortable investing in the stock market.*

LC: Honestly, that's such a generalisation. Comfortable investing what? Every penny I own? A modest flutter? Pity there isn't an answer saying 'It depends...'

AT: Not sure if I ever feel completely comfortable investing. You're never 100% sure what you're getting yourself into.

4. *I'm usually slow to make decisions on investment matters.*

LC: Now, you see, that's another 'It depends.' I make decisions not to invest in things all the time, and usually in seconds. It's the few I go for that take some pondering. Is that a yes?

AT: Define 'slow.'

5. *I've made extremely risky financial investments in the past.*

LC: This is getting really difficult. Yes and no. It depends.
AT: I don't think so, but to be honest I'm not really sure.

6. *I want high investment growth for my money. I am willing to accept the possibility of greater losses to achieve this.*

LC: That's another tricky one. What do you mean by 'my money'. All of it, well, yes, definitely. A bit of it, well, I don't mind a flutter. I might be overthinking this.
AT: Some of my money? All of my money? Not sure what this means...

7. *I would never make a high-risk investment*

LC: Haven't we done this one? Never say never is what I'd say. Probably not, but you never know. A definite maybe.
AT: You've already asked me this.

8. *Maximising long-term investments is my goal, and I would be willing to accept dramatic, short-term falls to achieve it.*

LC: Is it guaranteed,this maximising angle? And when are these short-term drops going to occur? Depends. Again.
AT: But how would I know? And anyway, the first rule of research questionnaires is to ask only one question at a time.This is actually two questions. Which one am I meant to answer?

9. *I would prefer small certain gains to large uncertain ones.*

LC: Well, obviously I'd prefer large certain ones. How small? How large? How certain? How uncertain? As you may have guessed, I'm a Libran – it's all 'on the one hand...on the other hand' with me.
AT: Have we nearly finished yet? I'm losing my patience with this.

10. *How much risk do you feel you've taken with your past financial decisions?*

LC: This time I'm sure I've done this one. Or one very like it.
AT: Sorry, no, I'm out.

As we said, our main worry about all this is not whether the science is robust and a sensible and reasonably reliable score can be derived from respondents' answers. Our main worry is whether the experience of dealing with this kind of ambiguous, seemingly repetitive and frankly rather irritating questionnaire sits comfortably with the inexperienced, anxious, time-poor DIY investor – and, therefore, whether he or she is likely to have the confidence and motivation to persevere through to the end. (The same is true, though obviously rather more so, of the longer versions which sometimes include up to 20 questions.)

These questionnaires were originally envisaged, like so much in retail financial services, for use in the face-to-face intermediated channel. No doubt with guidance, reassurance and interpretation from a good adviser, they work perfectly well in that environment. Beyond that channel, like so much in retail financial services, they're nowhere near simple enough.

CHAPTER 16

Are You Just a Little Bit Boring?

Considering how long it is since either of your authors could be said to have had young children, the memories are remarkably fresh: those distant days when we were actually better at football than our sons; when if you wanted to talk about something that wasn't for their ears all you had to do was spell, not say, the key words; when £1 a week was more than enough pocket money.

Not many of our memories of our children in those days are to do with brands and marketing, and even fewer are to do with financial services. But some are. For people with our particular professional interests, one unexpectedly fascinating and thought-provoking experience, back in those early years, was to see awareness and perceptions of brands form in their minds – and not just brands intended for young children like Haribo and Nickelodeon, but a lot of remarkably grownup brands too.

Of course the brands that made the biggest impact soonest were the ones that, in one way or another, were personally relevant to them. We'd like to make it clear for the record that neither of our families were frequent visitors to McDonald's, but Chloe, Sarah, Felix, James and Oliver could all spot those golden arches at a range of half a mile or more by the age of three. But there were others where, even though the relevance was marginal, awareness was still strong. By the time they were a little older – maybe 5 – they could have recognised airline liveries, particularly BA and easyJet. And they could probably have distinguished between the main automotive brands appealing to middle-class marketers' families like ours (BMW, Audi, Mercedes and more or less anything else German) by the same age too.

It wasn't simply a question of basic brand recognition. While still very young – maybe not five, but not a lot more – they could have expressed some remarkably sophisticated brand perceptions. They'd have understood, for example, that BA and easyJet occupied different spaces in the airline market. Or that Waitrose is posher than Asda. Or that Apple is cooler than Microsoft. Or (probably) that *The Guardian*, the *Daily Telegraph* and *The Sun* are intended for different readers.

A lot of these perceptions were simply copied from their parents, of course. Others were copied from their peer group, and to some extent from advertising and other marketing communications. Many resulted from a combination of these influences.

But whatever the inputs, it seemed pretty clear to us then – and we've seen no reason to change our view since – that very large chunks of their own individual brand landscapes had formed in their minds by the time they were 7 or 8 or so, and the whole brand atlas was largely laid out before them by the time they reached their teens.

With the exception – yes, there is some kind of point to these reminiscences – of one dark continent, one land-mass that remained still very largely cloud-covered and undefined. This was of course the territory headed 'financial services'. By the age of, say, 12 or 13, they still knew next to nothing about this.

To be fair, it was 'next to' rather than 'nothing'. The occasional stretch of visible shoreline could be glimpsed through the clouds. Heaven knows why, for example, but Lucian's children Chloe and Oliver paid fascinated attention to a truly terrible TV commercial for direct lender Lombard Direct, whose media strategy seemed to skew heavily toward children's cable channels presumably much watched by cash-strapped parents. As a result, twenty years later, Chloe and Oliver can still recite every word of the voiceover: 'Want a low-cost loan at your convenience? Call Lombard Direct on 0800 2 15000. Our rates reflect your circumstances, and our typical APR is just 7.4% ...'

Of course they didn't have the faintest idea what any of this meant, and still don't now ('Our rates reflect your circumstances'?). But that's not unusual when it comes to things that children learn by heart – an APR of 7.4% is probably no more obscure than a quinquireme of Nineveh. And even today, 20 years later, if they did want a low-cost loan at their convenience, it's more than likely that Lombard Direct would get the call.

Several points arise from these reminiscences:

1. First and foremost, of course, they tell us that perceptions of financial services and financial services brands are late to form in children's minds. They're not unique in this, of course: at the same ages, the children probably knew little about professional services firms, the chateaux of Bordeaux or manufacturers of gardening tools. But on the basis of Aristotle's famous 'Give me a child until he is 7, and I will give you the man', you wonder whether financial services, coming so late into the picture, ever really catch up.[1]

---

[1] We wonder to what extent MetLife, in the United States at least, would be an exception to this pattern, having for many years licensed the Peanuts cartoon characters as its advertising property. The main intention, no doubt, would have been to resonate with adults who had grown up with Snoopy, Lucy, Linus and friends – but would there be a resonance with the current generation of children, too?

2. They say something about the sheer lack of salience of financial services in day-to-day life. Many of the sectors that the children did learn about made themselves known in random and happenstance ways – they chanced frequently on ads, or passed particular retailers on the way to school. In financial services, this doesn't happen often (how many ads for asset managers do you chance upon?) and when it does, it's simply not interesting enough to be memorable (is there anything more boring to look at than the outside of a bank branch, except perhaps the inside?).

3. Similarly, they tell us that parents don't talk much about financial matters, or financial brands – at least, not in front of the children. Maybe some parents do. But even though both fathers were running financial services marketing agencies at the time, we didn't.

4. And finally they tell us that few if any financial services providers have much interest in building initial awareness among children. Some years before our children were born, NatWest was something of an exception, at least for a while: people older than our children have hazy memories of a collectible series of NatWest piggy banks (even today, you occasionally see faded examples at car boot sales). But they're long gone now.

In short, by the time they had reached their teens, the implicit message that Chloe, Sarah, Felix, James and Ollie had received, at some level, was that financial services is a boring, recessive, not-very-relevant part of life, offering very little in the way of interest to them (except for that stupid blue Lombard Direct telephone). We can't prove the extent to which these early perceptions have shaped the way they think and feel on the subject today. But, let's be honest, although they have built up a bit more knowledge, understanding and of course engagement over the years, their current perceptions of the financial world aren't so very different.

All of which goes to introduce the topic of this chapter: that in the light of most people's low level of engagement with financial services marketing and brands, by far the biggest challenge for most financial services marketers is winning from their target markets any or all of their attention, interest, desire or action (the famous 'AIDA' mnemonic that's been said ever since the late 19th century to summarise how people engage with brands).

Or to put it another, simpler way, by far the greatest danger is the danger of being ignored.

That is of course a huge generalisation, and there are at least two important caveats. For one thing, the scale of the danger varies greatly depending on your target market. We must again remember the existence of that small segment of highly-engaged consumers – we tend to refer to them as 'hobbyists' – who come to your marketing activities with a hugely much higher level of engagement from the outset. These people present their own problems – they are often price-sensitive, challenging and disloyal – but they are very much less likely to ignore you.

And for another thing, the scale of the danger also depends on the extent to which firms are able to deliver relevant propositions at relevant moments in time. An individual who cares nothing about motor insurance for 364 days a year may feel very differently on the day that he or she receives a renewal notice.

But even so, there are a bunch of reasons why a great many people are strongly predisposed to ignore a great many financial services marketing initiatives. The six more important reasons are:

1. They don't have strong connections with financial services brands. There are very few financial services providers people feel positively predisposed toward. People queue up overnight outside Apple stores waiting for new iPhones to be launched: it's difficult to imagine even loyal customers doing the same for new HSBC ISAs.
2. This lack of predisposition also reflects the extraordinarily overcrowding that still exists in many sectors. There are literally hundreds of asset managers, thousands of advice firms, scores of motor insurers. It's difficult for any but the most engaged consumers to identify any particular presence amidst such a dense throng.
3. Whatever it is that we're saying or doing, many consumers will tend to assume on the basis of their past experience that it's likely to be hard to understand and not very relevant.[2]
4. Especially when it comes to communications, the requirements of the compliance process don't help. Consumers recognise that most activity pointed toward them is sure to be so hedged around with small print, warnings and generic messages required by the regulator that it's bound to be heavy going.
5. If it's a communication from one of our own providers, it is of course quite likely to be bad news. It could be very bad news, for example that we've done something bad and got into serious trouble – or just slightly bad news, for example that savings rates have gone down again.

---

[2]The track record of some organisations as the junkiest of junk mailers doesn't help here. The second that one of your authors sees yet another dreary-looking envelope on the doormat with second-class postage and a return address in Saffron Road, Leicester, he knows it's the 837th useless balance transfer offer he's received from Barclaycard. Even if the envelope in fact contained a cheque for a million pounds, it would unquestionably end up unopened in the bin just like all the others.

6. And then of course last but absolutely by no means least, it's almost certain to be very boring. Can you think of a single financial services provider we can reasonably expect to approach us in any kind of interesting, enjoyable, rewarding or distinctive way?

What we're saying, in short, is that people have quite a number of very good reasons for ignoring things that we want to say to them, or show them, or ask them. And whatever it is that we're wanting to do, if they ignore us then we can't succeed in any of our aims.

And yet it seems to us that very few marketers in the industry worry anything like as much as they should about this danger. They worry about lots of other things – first and foremost about arousing the ire of the regulator, and to some extent about expressing themselves clearly, and to a considerable extent about managing the customer journey in which this activity, whatever it is, plays a part – but hardly ever about falling at the first fence and simply failing to earn any attention.

Which is odd, because when you look at the available metrics that measure attention, they're generally dire. Open rates for e-mails are sinking steadily down toward response levels for conventional mail. Most measurable forms of content marketing deliver pitiful results (check out the average asset manager's YouTube views). Awareness of print advertising is miserably low. Organisations spending fortunes on awareness-building are delighted if awareness improves by a handful of percentage points. In a long-established syndicated tracking study among so-called active private investors, asset management brands outside the top half-dozen or so achieve between 1% and 0% (spontaneous) awareness.

And of course if we take a step back from individual brands and specific campaigns and activities, we find that average levels of comprehension and involvement remain as low as ever. When you consider how much consumers have learned over 10 or 20 years in a field like IT – where 20 years ago most of us knew nothing at all – it's quite startling how little they've learned about financial services.

In our list of reasons for most consumers' lack of engagement with financial services marketing, there's one notable omission: we don't say anything about a lack of involvement in, or concern about, the subject of money itself. That's for the obvious reason that it would be completely wrong to do so. Money is a huge thing for people. Along with health and relationships, it's one of the three biggest things there is. Every year, the Office of National Statistics (ONS) carries out research among a large and nationally representative sample, to see what's on the minds of people in the UK. Some topics come and go. But there are three that, year in year out, come top of the list. They are, unsurprisingly, money, health and relationships.

One of your authors remembers a conversation with a client who was a marketing manager at a health insurer specialising in family health plans. The client grumbled about the tedium of his job. People don't care about family health plans, he said. If only he could get a job marketing something interesting – a food brand, maybe, or a drink, or even something in toiletries. Since he was a client, your author probably politely resisted the temptation to tell him about the ONS research. But the fact is, contrary to his perception, the client quite literally couldn't be marketing anything more interesting to people.

But, as ever, perception matters more than reality. The client believed he was dealing with something dreadfully boring. And of course, as soon as you believe that, you are. The comms we produced for his company were as dull as anything we ever did. He wouldn't have it any other way.

Which is exactly why this curious paradox persists: that consumers who think of money as one of the most important and involving things in their lives think of our marketing activities as one of the least important and involving. It's not money that bores them witless, it's us.[3]

To be fair, it's not just us. There are others in the financial services world who are no better than marketers at connecting with all those concerns, and fears, and hopes, and dreams, and passions that money arouses in people. With a few honourable exceptions, another group who've done at least as badly, and maybe even a bit worse, are the journalists who are responsible for all that dreary personal finance coverage in the media (which, research tells us, is typically ignored by over 90% of the paper's readers).

Again, that small group of highly-engaged hobbyists are wonderfully well served. In print and online, there are almost infinite amounts of content to feed their interest and slake their thirst for news and novelty. But for the other 40-odd million of us, it's a different story. Personal finance sections, on the whole, are still predicated on the principle of providing an environment in which asset managers can be persuaded to advertise their investment funds, and as a result most of the editorial is narrow, dull and repetitive – endless features on choosing an ISA, and which investment sectors offer the best prospect of growth.

---

[3]We have heard people in the industry defend this state of affairs, on the grounds that what we do isn't supposed to be exciting and consumers would be alarmed if we gave the impression that it was. People who say things like this also tend to quote the words of pioneer adman Claude Hopkins, who dismissed the use of humour in advertising over a hundred years ago with the words 'People don't buy from clowns'. We think this is all rubbish, and even though we're not big fans of Ronald McDonald, we'd like to point out that so does he.

Reading this tedious stuff, you'd never guess that money, the ultimate subject matter of these pages, arguably arouses stronger emotions, more anxiety, more excitement, more argument and more drama than anything else in life. Personal finance journalism sucks all the life and interest out of it, and presents it in copy that's little more than one level up from the terms and conditions in a unit trust brochure. You could hardly make money seem duller.

There is a small handful of livelier options. The BBC's long-running Radio 4 personal finance programme, Moneybox, is stodgy and old-fashioned, but it still manages to convey a slight sense that it's dealing with a subject people actually care about. And coming at money from a very different angle, Martin Lewis's online Money Saving Expert brand recognises that everyone likes a deal, and therefore that pointing us at wherever the best deals are to be found right now is a helpful thing to do.

As for our most powerful medium, still television, it has never managed to rise to the challenge. Half-baked shows trying and failing to make personal finance accessible turn up on Channel 5 every couple of years, but few last longer than one series. It is literally impossible to remember anything good about money on television.[4]

As with so many other weaker aspects of financial services marketing, it wasn't so long ago that none of this mattered very much. There were few editorial environments beyond personal finance sections of newspapers and a few specialist personal finance magazines, and all of these were no more and no less than a marketplace where hobbyist investors could respond to ads for unit trusts. No-one else was really expected to read them, and since their main purpose was to provide an environment for the advertising it didn't really matter what the editorial said (although if it said positive things about the funds being advertised, that was useful from the fund managers' perspective).

---

[4]There is one big and difficult reason why so much media coverage of personal finance is so hopeless, of course: it's damagingly torn between commercial and public interest agendas. There could clearly be room for a great deal of crusading and investigative coverage of the industry's worst behaviours: the industry, it seems, can be relied upon to provide a steady supply, and there are a few journalists – notably the admirable Jeff Prestridge – with the skills to do justice (no pun intended) to such stories of misbehaviour. But this, of course, doesn't make for editorial environments that are popular with advertisers, who would much rather that their ads appeared in an atmosphere of positive puffery about things that have gone spectacularly right. The conflict between the two styles of coverage creates a muddled and uncertain tone.

Things have changed. That traditional coupon-clipping unit trust investor segment has largely gone away, moving to online services like Hargreaves Lansdown and Interactive Investor, and in any case the regulator has tightened the rules on off-the-page advertising to the extent that even if the audience was still there, it's scarcely a cost-effective media approach any more.

But as 'traditional' personal finance media lost their established raison d'êetre, it seems to us that they failed to appreciate the emergence of a new one. The new marketing challenge that forms the subject of this book applies to media just as much as to any other marketing arena: in an era in which responsibility for financial security rests far more heavily upon individuals' shoulders than ever before, those individuals desperately need good, engaging, relevant marketing initiatives to help them discharge that responsibility.

This is not an easy challenge, but it's an important one. We still live in hope that online, offline and, in a perfect world, on mainstream television, a new kind of personal finance journalism will start to emerge that will connect in completely new ways with millions of people who've avoided the subject like the plague hitherto.

Meanwhile, the lack of attractive options helps to explain why, in recent years, financial services advertising and direct marketing spends have been falling. But in parallel to the budget cuts among established players, there's another trend that may turn out to be more significant (and that's 'significant' in the sense of 'problematic') – the number of new players, spread across a number of emerging financial categories, that are aiming to succeed with little or no advertising at all.

We're thinking here of the crowd of young, startup digital players, in fields including investment, protection, aggregation, banking, peer-to-peer lending, insurance and others. Altogether, with some judicious Googling and reference back to the slides from recent conference presentations, we could easily come up with 100 names of young businesses eager to recruit customers (200 wouldn't be hard). And if we commissioned a big piece of awareness research across a nice big nationally representative sample, we're quite sure that no more than a handful of people would have ever heard of more than a handful of them.

At a certain level, anyone who ever launches anything and seeks to recruit new customers has to be an optimist. Somewhere in their minds, they have a picture of the front door of their offices the day after the launch announcement, where a queue of excited consumers is tailing back into the distance, as far as the eye can see, waiting eagerly for the opportunity to buy. If you didn't believe, at least at some level, that your new product or service was good enough to generate that kind of enthusiasm, you wouldn't really have any business launching it.

But at the moment, we have to say that nothing – absolutely nothing – is holding back the dramatic evolution of the retail financial services industry more than the belief, on the part of many of its most exciting and dynamic innovators, that they'll be able to recruit a customer base without spending any money. They won't. They'll just stumble along, serving customer bases of dozens or hundreds of people, until the Phase 2 funding runs out.

It must be a matter for regret that many brilliant and innovative ideas will never achieve what they might have achieved, even if cynics might say that the inability of many of these startup businesses to recruit more than a handful of customers isn't really a problem because it was never their intention to do so. The plan was always to demonstrate proof of concept, on the way to selling the startup business at a very large profit to a large, established player that would rather buy its innovations than build them for itself.

This cynical view is probably about half right (or, as the cynic would, say, half wrong). But the fact is, fame does still matter. John Duffield, founder and leader first of Jupiter's mutual fund business and then of his independent New Star business, spent more money on advertising than other asset managers 20 times his firms' size. He explained simply that if you want your firm to be disproportionately famous, which he did, you have to spend disproportionately more money to make it so.

Duffield was a hard taskmaster – his marketing and external agency people used to dread the lengthy coach tours in which they would join him on interminable inspections of his firms' outdoor advertising sites, and heaven help them if a poster was badly hung or not posted where it ought to be. But the high-cost, high-profile strategy worked, and New Star's brand awareness and fund sales among both private investors and intermediaries increased at a startling rate.

Perhaps a better-known hero among marketers is the veteran adman Dave Trott, who, while never particularly renowned for financial services campaigns, held a distinctly Duffield-like view about fame. Advertising, he said, is very expensive, and only a tiny fraction of it – say 1% – is noticed sufficiently to become the subject of conversation among people in pubs. It therefore follows that when you develop advertising, the only objective worth bothering with is making sure than your campaign falls into that 1%. If it doesn't, you're sure to be wasting a great deal of money. This is such a simple argument that you imagine there must be something wrong with it, but if so it's hard to pin down what it is.

Having considered various parts of the industry and drawn fairly downbeat conclusions, it's important to recognise that these are by no means the whole story. Arguably some of the things that we're castigating established and new players alike for doing (or indeed not doing) are practices of the old financial services marketing, now being visibly and happily overtaken by the new.

Of these, the most important and encouraging is the huge technology-driven shift in the basis of financial services marketing that's currently in progress, and which we discuss in several places in this book (and particularly in the chapter on data and data-driven marketing). As it becomes possible to interact effectively with individual customers on a one-to-one basis, much of this noisy broadcast activity starts to feel seriously out of date. If we can talk with 10 million customers individually for about the same cost that we can shout at them all at once, isn't it much better to do so?

Without repeating too much of that previous chapter, we think it's both/and rather than either/or. It is a wonderful thing to be able to base the marketing mix on real, detailed knowledge of the individual, rather than just generalised insight into a segment. If that means that the particular patterns of interactions between individuals and providers are, cumulatively, unique – if no one customer's journey, over time, is exactly the same as any other's – we will truly have moved into a very different world.

But of course, the huge majority of the components of those unique journeys won't be unique at all – or, even if they are, they'll only be unique in terms of superficial personalisation. It's great if your educational ISA video addresses you by name, and focuses on an investment that matches your known risk profile. Being addressed by name may attract and retain your interest for a few moments, at least until the novelty of such things wears off. But if the video is boring and incomprehensible, we won't be much further forward.

In short, we're unconvinced by the current belief that data-driven personalisation will, in itself, solve the problem of engagement. It can certainly help. But personalised content isn't automatically engaging, and particularly not when it falls under the influence of managers with quite different agendas in mind. We've seen examples of highly personalised new pension statements, for example, which have been developed with the single-minded intention of encouraging customers to increase their level of contributions. The graphs and charts are all about the individual recipient. But the overall effect is far from engaging: we strongly suspect that most customers will recoil from such transparently manipulative communications.

And of course returning for a moment to that swarm of wannabe disruptive digital startups, it's important to recognise that for as long as they don't have any customers, their ability to personalise their activities is limited. Some show signs of understanding the weakness of their position, and spend time, effort and even in some cases money on building a prospect database that includes some real insights into individual circumstances, wants and needs: the challenger bank Monzo, for example, had built a prospect base of over 150,000 people before it opened its doors. But with so many newcomers heading for different segments of the market, it's simply not possible for all of them to follow this example.

No, even making every allowance for the still-emerging power of digital to interact with consumers in new ways, we can see no alternative: getting better at financial services marketing has to involve getting much, much better at being interesting.

Most of us have, somewhere around the intersection of our conscious and unconscious minds, a brutally simple test for interestingness: within seconds of encountering a thing, from a leaflet to a TV programme to a website to a phone call, we can decide whether it's interesting enough to keep our attention. It's true that there are lots of different ways it can be interesting. YouTube cat videos are interesting in a very different way from a bank statement showing that we have rather more (or indeed rather less) money than we thought we had. There is no single way to achieve interestingness.[5]

But, even so, the essential point is that most of the ways that we try to interest people in financial services are miserable failures. At the moment, for example, a direct marketing communication of any sort that generates a sale from two out of a hundred people is hailed as a great success. This is massively wasteful for the industry, and bad for consumers too. Moving the whole question of engagement right up to the top of our agenda, and using every single technique we can think of to address it, we have to start doing much better.

---

[5]That said, there are several techniques that are well-tried and tested. You'll never go too far wrong, for example, if you're able to give people a sense of how their behaviour, or circumstances, or wealth, or whatever, benchmark against their peers. For some reason the financial services industry is remarkably reluctant to do this, even though it would be useful as well as interesting. There aren't many parallels between people's financial lives and their sex lives, but there is one – most people mostly keep them private, so it's very difficult to know how what you're doing compares to anyone else.

CHAPTER 17

Call That a Brand?

Of all the subjects that have baffled and bamboozled the financial services marketing community over the years, none has created bafflement remotely to compare with the issue of brands and how you build them.

To put the simplest of financial measures on the scale of the problem, over the past 20 years retail financial services firms in the UK have spent at least £5 billion, and arguably a great deal more, on activities specifically intended to help them build strong brands in their marketplace. Yet 20 years on, if we look at all the biggest firms in all the biggest sectors of the market, we find that consumers are almost completely unable to distinguish between them – and when they can, it's usually for reasons that had nothing at all to do with the branding efforts. Often, in fact, the perceptions they have are precisely the perceptions the expenditure was intended to overcome.

Of all the money that the financial services industry has spent over that kind of period, it's extremely difficult to think of an equivalent sum that has achieved so spectacularly little. You could hardly believe that such a lot of money could deliver such meagre results, and you can only conclude that there must be something – or more likely quite a few things – horribly wrong in the thinking that has shaped the spending of it.

This is bad for the industry, but it's also bad for consumers. Especially in markets that they don't understand well – and where levels of engagement are low – brands act as very important signposts, or heuristics (shortcuts), for consumers, enabling them to make decisions quickly and with reasonably high levels of confidence in achieving at least a satisfactory outcome. (For example, among users of price comparison sites, it's often said that one of the commonest behaviours is to choose the cheapest brand with a name they know.)

A Financial Services Forum focus group participant says:

> At the point of sale when you're offered three different products doing the same thing, you're generally going to go to the brand you've heard of.

One of the biggest problems is that so much bullshit is spoken and written about brands that most people tackling the subject quickly find themselves horribly confused. This chapter aims to cast some light on what is and what isn't possible in brand development, and how what's possible can be achieved. First, we feel the need to try to clean up some of the bullshit, debunking some of the myths and delusions that permeate the subject.

SOME BRAND MYTHS DEBUNKED

We said much earlier in this book that 'marketing' is a slippery term, and that no generally agreed meaning can be taken for granted. The position is even worse with the words 'brand' and 'branding'. Defining the term is the least of your problems. Almost every idea about brands, brand strategy and brand development is either contentious, or incomprehensible, or just plain wrong.

You might think, in such an uncertain area, that your best starting-point might be a dose of academic rigour. There are many books that can provide you with an introduction to the subject, including some from authors with impeccable academic credentials. The inestimable Professor Leslie de Chernatony has written two, *Creating Powerful Brands* and *From Brand Vision to Brand Evaluation*. Both are well worth reading. But we think Leslie would certainly accept that both are based on academic research and literature, which doesn't always reflect real-world issues and experiences. This chapter, on the other hand, reflects our own views as practitioners on the key issues and challenges that we see.

The first of these arises right at the outset. The moment you start to engage with the subject, you have to overcome the fundamental problem that the word *brand* has (at least) two meanings, which you might call a small one (brand with a lower-case b) and a big one (Brand with an upper-case B).

Lower-case brand means the identifying mark, or marks, which enable people to recognise something as what it is. (By the way, for the avoidance of doubt, this lower-case/upper-case thing is metaphorical. We don't really spell the two meanings like that, although it might be helpful if we did.)

As everyone knows, this meaning arose from the world of livestock farming. A farmer's brand was the mark he used to identify his sheep or cattle. In a commercial context, these identifying marks are usually an entity's name and/or logo. The brand Barclays enables you to recognise the bank of that name. When you see a can carrying the Coca-Cola logo, you know what drink will be inside it. When a television interview features Donald Trump you know what to expect – or rather who to expect – if you tune in.

Upper-case Brand means something much bigger – the totality of what that thing stands for in your mind, and in the minds of other people encountering it. If the brand perceptions in people's minds are clear, consistent, positive and serve to distinguish the thing from other things, then the brand is a good or strong one. If they're unclear, and/or inconsistent, and/or negative, and/or give the impression that the thing is the same as one or more other things, then the brand is a bad or weak one.

Any thing that has created any level of shared perceptions in people's minds can be seen as a brand (although not necessarily a strong or positively perceived one). The M25 motorway is a brand. The golden retriever is a brand. The game of chess is a brand. You are a brand.

From now on, in this chapter, we're talking only about this second, bigger, upper-case meaning of the word.

In a marketing context, brands have two key characteristics that the M25 and the game of chess don't. First, there are people who take responsibility for them, and who are aiming to build the brand's perceptions in the minds of a defined target market or markets. This target market could be very big and loosely defined, like 'everyone', or very small and precise, for example, 'people who want a great Chinese meal in Taunton'.

And second, obviously (but nothing is completely obvious in the strange and slippery world of brands), those responsible must have decided what perceptions they're trying to build. Marketing calls for a purposeful approach. You have to decide on the perceptions you want, and make and execute a plan to go about achieving them. This, in turn, is part of a bigger set of decisions about your business, starting with the definition of its purpose discussed back in Chapter 11.

To be honest, once you've mastered the two-meanings issue (which, it has to be said, a lot of non-marketers never do), so far none of this is sounding very confusing or difficult. How do things start going wrong?

One of the early-stage problems is that all sorts of people who ought to know better, many of them consultants, have come up with stupid and unhelpful definitions of the word that serve only to put people off the scent. Here are a few examples.

- The author is unknown, but one of the best-known definitions says that 'a brand is a promise that is kept'. What the hell does that mean? If you tell a friend you'll see her in the pub next Tuesday at 6, and then on the day you're there on time, does that make you a brand? Of course not. (Although, at risk of overthinking this, if your personal brand happened to stand for meticulous punctuality, then arguably being there on the stroke of 6 would reinforce your friend's brand perceptions.)

- There's an equally ridiculous thing about single-mindedness, which someone called Al Ries expresses as 'a singular idea or concept that you own inside the mind of the prospect'. Why does it have to be singular? You can usually boil the richness and multi-facetedness of most great brands down to a single idea, but in doing so you'll risk losing much of its value and distinctiveness. Single-mindedness is a good thing in a 30-second TV commercial (and an even better thing in a 20-second commercial) but it has nothing to do with brands.
- At the moment, *stories* are in. Every brand has to be able to tell its unique story. This is quite good news for copywriters, because there's good money in brand story jobs, but it doesn't really mean anything. Richard Cordiner, planning director at ad agency Leo Burnett, says: 'A brand is nothing more than a story wrapped around a product or service'. What does he mean? You tell us.
- It's often said that, whatever brands are, they're about added value and emphatically not about low prices. Someone called Waqar Riaz says: 'In today's world, differentiating a brand on technology is very similar to playing purely on price – there's always an end to it'. This isn't right either. Many strong brands stand in large part for low prices, and continue to do so indefinitely. Try telling Ryanair, Aldi or Walmart that their strategy's going to run out of road (or indeed air).

But it's not just sayings about brands, or definitions of brands, that are unhelpful and untrue. The same can be said of many other ideas or beliefs about brands and brand building.

For example, it's often said that you can't build a brand without a very large advertising budget. Completely untrue. It depends entirely on your target audience, and what opportunities you have to influence their perceptions by other means. Some of the strongest brands in financial services – the Queen's bankers, Coutts, to name but one – have scarcely advertised at all.

Vice versa, these days (perhaps even more dangerously), people make the exact opposite point – that in these digital times, and with an unlimited amount of social media available at no charge, it's now possible to build a brand at zero cost. Again depending on your target audience, and on the interest and distinctiveness of what your brand aims to stand for, this may be theoretically possible. But in a low-interest category like financial services, we wouldn't bet on it. For every brand that achieves a degree of fame and distinctiveness by blogging, tweeting and using Facebook, there are at least a hundred that will sink without a trace. The cruel truth is revealed by many of the analytics readily available on the Internet. One particularly depressing statistic is the number of views achieved by the videos on financial services firms' YouTube channels: while Kim Kardashian or an amusing cat video can easily clock up 20 million or more, the average asset manager speaking to a camera rarely reaches 500. (Perhaps the average asset manager should appear with a cat. Or with Kim Kardashian.)

As far as measurement is concerned, sadly one of the less helpful and least defensible parts of the entire brand industry is the so-called science of brand valuation. A few firms specialise in this dark art, and have developed complex statistical methodologies to come up with their numbers. It has to be said, though, that on a simple commonsense basis, a glance at their findings tells you in seconds that these methodologies don't work. One of the leading proponents publishes a list of the world's most valuable brands every year. In the 2016 listing, a firm called Brookfield Asset Management, for example, occupies a place some distance ahead of Rolls-Royce, and niche US insurer Aflac is some way ahead of Volvo, Southwest Airlines, Ralph Lauren and Prada. As the editor of Private Eye once said in a very different context, 'If that's justice, I'm a banana'. There probably is a science to be developed in the area of brand valuation, and when it's properly developed it would be extremely valuable to marketers who, for the first time, would be able to put a hard commercial value on this aspect of what they do. But to say that it's currently in its infancy is an insult to infants.

Even one of the most commonly repeated and apparently least controversial observations about brands and how to build them doesn't stand up to much scrutiny. Few people will disagree with the statement that in service businesses like financial services, brands are built experientially – in other words, it's what brands do, not what they say they do or say they are, that forms brand perceptions.

A member of a Financial Services Forum focus group says: 'Your brand is your reputation, and that's delivered by what people see and what you do, and how you behave'.

It's an idea explicitly acknowledged in a major brand development initiative on the part of NatWest, launched in 2016, around the strapline 'We are what we do'.

There's obviously a lot of truth in this, especially for organisations like NatWest whose huge existing customer base makes up their most important target market. But clearly, by definition, experiential marketing can only work among those who have experience, and therefore it doesn't help much when you're trying to reach out beyond your customer base. To do this, it's necessary to go beyond experience into allegation, usually by means of some kind of advertising.

There's also the considerable problem that for many people, both their actual customer experience and their perceptions of customer experience have not been positive. In an interview in *Marketing Week,* NatWest's Chief Marketing Officer David Wheldon says: 'Over the last nine years, I cannot think of a single financial brand that has even nodded at the fact there were serious problems in the past. It annoys people'.

He's right about that – financial services companies have managed to find a remarkably large and diverse range of ways to annoy us over a very long period. As an obscure example, one of your authors remembers logging on to the websites of the UK's top 10 High Street financial institutions at the height of the 2008 crisis looking for help, for reassurance, for some kind of counterbalance to the frantic media headlines of that period. He searched the terms *mortgage crisis, credit crunch* and one or two others then appearing in every news broadcast and on every paper's front page. Without exception, every single one came back with a code 404, 'credit crunch not found'. It was hard to believe that not a single institution had heard of a single one of the terms he searched.

In short, it's certainly true that especially among large organisations with many customers, managing customers' experience is an absolutely central and critical part of the marketing mix and the brand-building effort. But it makes no sense to think of it as the whole story.

So amid such a lot of disinformation, confusion and misunderstanding about brands and how you build them, what are we saying? What we're saying is this:

1. A strong brand (that is, a brand that is well known and is perceived clearly, consistently, positively and differently among a target audience) is a hugely valuable asset. When all other things are more or less equal – and in service sectors like financial services all other things are very often more or less equal – people tend to make choices on the basis of their awareness and perceptions of brands.
2. The essential requirement for building a brand is a clear, simple and credible differentiating idea. This doesn't necessarily need to be objectively unique, but it doesn't half help if no-one else owns it yet. (Having worked in packaged goods marketing, we have little time for financial services marketers who bemoan the lack of 'hard' differentiation between their firms and others. In some of the most strongly branded FMCG markets – lager, washing powder, toothpaste – consumers are hard put to make any kind of 'hard' distinctions between one product and another.)
3. Especially in service businesses that offer a large number of different touch-points and customer experiences, it's important to layer some distinctive secondary characteristics onto this central core idea. A brand

built on only one idea will be somewhat two-dimensional (or indeed one-dimensional).[1]

4. It is important that people find the truth of the central idea, and indeed the secondary or supporting ideas, confirmed to a greater or lesser extent, and certainly never contradicted, whenever they encounter the brand. (This is one of the few clichés of financial services brand building that is actually true.)

5. If you want perceptions of your brand to extend beyond your customer base, you're going to need to spend some money on building those perceptions. This is likely, although not certain, to involve advertising. Whatever it is, there must be enough of it, and it must be engaging enough, to become well-known among your target group.

Of these five simple ideas, by far the most important – and the one with the biggest implications – is the second. It's worth repeating: 'The essential requirement for building a brand is a clear, simple and credible differentiating idea'. If you can identify one of these, you're in with a chance. If you can't, you aren't. You're just creating name awareness. That might be what you want to do, and on the whole it's a good thing to do – having name awareness is generally better than not having name awareness. But don't kid yourself, you aren't building a brand.

And quite frankly, if yours is a big, long-established, complex, multi-line, multi-site financial services business that has evolved over time without any such idea having informed its development, we don't think you'll be able to do it.

Of all the myths about brand-building, probably the most unhelpful has been the idea that it's possible to back-fit a brand into a big, complicated, long-established business that has previously displayed no trace of the idea that's now claimed to lie at the heart of it. People aren't stupid. They can see that it's just something that's been made up by an ad agency or a brand consultancy, that it could just as well have been applied to any of the organisation's major competitors, and that within a year or two a new marketing

---

[1] The First Direct brand, for example, a brand frequently praised in this book, stands first and foremost for accessibility – for the arguably counterintuitive idea that a bank with no branches can be more accessible and more responsive than a bank with branches everywhere. But First Direct isn't only about accessibility. It's also about frankness and simplicity of communication, and about a simplicity and modernity in its look and feel, and about a willingness to surprise and say things in ways they haven't been said before, and even about style points, such as the way it doesn't use capital letters and communicates in black and white, not in colour. There is much more to the First Direct brand than just that central, core idea about accessibility.

director will be launching a new strategy and saying that in hindsight the old one was all wrong.

Some say that things are different when an organisation has a CEO – or, even better, an entire management team – genuinely committed to delivering on the new brand promise, and ready to make big changes in the organisation in order to do so. We can't see it. We can't think of a single large, long-established, complex financial services firm – and only a very small handful of firms outside financial services – that have deliberately achieved rapid and significant change in brand perceptions as a result of management actions. If you can, please let us know – we'll change this section in the next edition.

This is not to say that no large, complex, long-established firms have the makings of a differentiated brand idea. A few do.

As the last big building society, Nationwide is different, and should be immune from consumers' fierce hatred of fat-cat bankers and their grotesquely large bonuses. (However, Nationwide has played the mutuality card so feebly over a long period that this strength is very much less well known and understood than it could be by now.) The same can be said of Royal London as the last large mutual in insurance, although again it's a card the firm rarely chooses to play.

It's very strange that these two large mutuals, as well as other medium sized and smaller ones, have chosen over such a long period to make little or nothing of this fundamental difference in their structure and ownership. We know many have carried out consumer research that tells them that *in itself*, the fact that an organisation is owned by its customers doesn't mean much or make much difference to people. But as Nationwide's recent *Building society, nationwide* initiaitive has shown, it isn't beyond the wit of good marketing people to express mutual ownership in ways that make it meaningful, and to link the principle of mutual ownership to hard points of difference that people do value. Especially in the world since the 2007–2008 global financial crash, it seems to us that a huge opportunity has existed for a mutual organisation to demonstrate the benefits of its difference: we think it's extraordinary that so few have chosen to do so.

A notch or two down from the real, substantive difference of mutuality, a couple of large firms have what you might think of as the next-best thing – namely, a carried-over heritage from past times that somehow makes them *feel* a bit different, especially among older consumers who remember them as they were. Prudential and Halifax come into this category, the Pru thanks to its long-disbanded bike-riding 'home service' sales force, and the Halifax thanks to its building-society past. Organisations with a lot of heritage are typically unsure about what to do with it, and such is the case with these two: over the years both have alternated between embracing and trying to modernise their heritage, and discarding it in search of something new.

What else? HSBC seems a shade more international than other big UK banks, so maybe its brand proposition *The World's Local Bank* has a bit of credibility, although it's difficult to explain precisely why it's good for people. (To a small audience segment of international travellers it may mean something, but to the huge majority of its retail customers around the world it's hard to see a real benefit.)

And talking of internationalness, organisations operating outside their home market always have the option of building a brand around consumer perceptions of their country of origin. Conceivably, for example, Santander could be Spanish, Allianz could be German and AXA could be French. Oddly, it's difficult to think of a financial services brand that takes this option, even though for many the home market these days accounts for only a small percentage of their overall business. In other sectors of the consumer economy many do, either as a core brand positioning or as an important secondary attribute. It's not difficult to think of examples – Audi and *Vorsprung Durch Technik* bringing German-ness to automotive; any number of wine brands, Kronenbourg and, oddly, Grey Goose vodka bringing French-ness to alcoholic drinks; Levis spending decades bringing American-ness to apparel, and so on.

As the saying mysteriously has it, you can't make bricks without straw, and beyond these few exceptions it's difficult to see anything much for most large, complex, long-established organisations to build on. As a focus group respondent says:

> If you're trying to combine this idea of reaching a very wide audience with a consistent sense of differentiation, that becomes a massively difficult challenge – especially retrofitting into an organisation that wasn't previously known for this or that, or that had lost its way over decades from where its roots were.

We'd agree, except only that we'd go one step further than 'massively difficult'. We think it's virtually impossible.

If that's right, then inevitably the question arises: what does it mean, first for those big, complex, long-established organisations, and second for everyone else?

For the big, complex, long-established organisations, it means that they face a clear choice.

a. The first option is to forget about building a distinct brand, and go for the lesser but still worthwhile objective of developing and maintaining a well-known name. Name awareness is, so to speak, semi-skimmed milk compared to the full-fat of distinctive brand awareness, but it still has value. The old marketing proverb 'familiarity breeds favourability' has much truth in it (and in case you doubt it, clever behavioural economists like Richard Thaler have recently provided confirmation). It's particularly true in markets where consumers are lacking in confidence and worried about the implications of making a mistake. We may not particularly need the reassurance of a well-known name when we buy a box of matches, a litre of screenwash or a 5-amp fuse, but it's a bit different when our long-term savings are at stake.

Financial Services Forum members, it must be said, are not so convinced that a well-known name is an acceptable alternative to full-fat brand awareness. In our online research, we asked whether they thought a strong consumer brand was important for their businesses. Even though over half of them told us that less than 50% of their customers bought from them direct, 93% said that a strong consumer brand was either 'important' or 'increasingly important', and 52% thought their organisations currently have a strong consumer brand, which as we said back in Chapter 2 shows either touching faith or perhaps just a lack of reliable metrics.

Two participants in one of our marketing director focus groups shared the following thought-provoking exchange:

Participant 1: *I'm not saying brands aren't important, I'm saying a lot of people think they have them and they don't.*

Participant 2: *Exactly, I'd agree with that – but in fact, is our definition of a brand wrong? Is a brand something with which you have a deep and meaningful relationship, while what we have is something else – just well-known names?*

The second comment introduces a new dimension to the subject, to do with the importance of relationships between customers and brands. 'Relationship' is another of those slippery marketing words that means very different things to different people. At one extreme it can simply describe any kind of sense of emotional connection more or less regardless of the level of actual contact between brand and customer, whereas at the opposite extreme it's defined specifically by the amount of interaction that actually takes place. (In between, of course, many would argue that the measure of a strong relationship requires some kind of combination of the two.)

Another participant says:

Name recognition is infinitely much more important than a brand that doesn't have a depth of experience associated with it.

A third spells out the point even more clearly:

Everyone says they're in the business of brand-building, and I say no, 90% of you are in the business of name awareness building, because you don't have a brand. You don't have anything that differentiates you from anyone else.

b. There is a second option available to big, complex organisations, although it's one that has become increasingly unfashionable in recent years. If you can't build a genuinely strong and distinctive single master-brand out of a fragmented, disparate collection of businesses with nothing that really holds them together, the alternative is to break them up into a deliberately separate, segmented, strategically managed portfolio of brands – a 'house of brands', as this approach is generally known.

Among the largest UK financial services providers, Lloyds Banking Group has for many years stood out as the main proponent of the 'house of brands' approach, with a portfolio that currently includes Lloyds Bank, Bank of Scotland, Halifax, Scottish Widows, Black Horse, Lex Autolease, LDC, AMC, Colleys and Birmingham Midshires.

On the other side of the argument, another very large institution, HSBC, favours the single master brand – in the UK, its only distinct sub-brand is its remote banking business First Direct.

It's notable that both Lloyds Banking Group and HSBC, and indeed most other large financial services groups, have grown very largely by acquisition, and acquisition forces brand strategy issues on firms whether they care about them and have a strong philosophy on the subject or not. As usual, actions give a better indication of firms' strategies than words. Lloyds has generally tended to retain brands that it has acquired, at least when it has been able to do so. HSBC, on the other hand, as a strong proponent of the master brand approach, has dropped virtually every acquired brand and applied its own identity to the acquired businesses.

For many years in financial services, proponents of these two approaches jockeyed for position, with both groups proclaiming the superiority of their approach. (The same struggle has continued in other parts of the marketing world, for example between a confectionery firm such as Cadbury, which believes in a strong Cadbury master-brand prominently applied to all its confectionery products, and a rival like Mars, whose house of brands includes Snickers, Bounty, Milky Way, Twix and all the others.)

Recently, though – arguably since the 2008 crash – it seems that a winner has emerged, at least in financial services. We're not suggesting that brand strategy had any effect on the unfolding of the meltdown or its aftermath, but the fact is that among the big UK banks the two that had more or less adopted a master-brand strategy – HSBC and Barclays – were widely agreed to have had a relatively good crisis, while the two on the house of brands side – Lloyds and RBS – were badly damaged.

This may well have been a coincidence. But as we emerged from the depths of the crisis into the ongoing Age of Austerity, the fact that maintaining a single master-brand is a lot cheaper than maintaining a portfolio of separate brands loomed large in marketers' minds. Even if for this reason alone, it seemed that the long struggle was over, and the master branders had won.

This point about cost isn't by any means just to do with brand communication, and how many brand advertising budgets you need. It's a much more fundamental point about organisational structure, and the major trend in recent years toward centralisation of resource. Back in the pre-crash era, if you'd looked below the surface of many, if not most, groups operating a House of Brands model, you'd have found a large number of functions deployed separately and therefore duplicated across the range of business units. Many of these groups ran an essentially federal model, with some central controls especially in risk, compliance and finance, but a very high level of autonomy at business unit level. Clipping business units' wings and centralising functions offers big cost savings, and also arguably much better control and risk management: could the catastrophic pre-crash corporate lending decisions made within Halifax, which nearly destroyed the bank, have been prevented in a group with strong central controls?

In the past decade, almost every large organisation has been involved in this process of centralisation at least to some extent. And the more aggressively an organisation moves in this direction, the more likely it is that the new structure will be reflected in its brand strategy. It's no coincidence, for example, that a group like Royal London, which under the leadership of a new CEO moved in a short period from a federal model to a highly centralised model, moved at the same time from a house of brands that included Ascentric, Bright Grey, Caledonian Life, RLAM, Scottish Life and Scottish Provident (and, in the recent past, a host of others including Co-operative, Royal Liver, United Assurance and Scottish Mutual) to a single Royal London master brand.[2]

---

[2]Actually, not quite 'single' – the group's investment platform brand Ascentric lives on. For reasons too boring and complicated to explain, some believe it's unhelpful for investment platforms to be positioned too closely to large parent groups. Even in a business with such a strong drive toward centralisation and a master brand, this kind of consideration at business unit level still carries weight.

Anyway, while these kinds of cost and organisational pressures have been driving a clear move toward master brands and away from houses of brands, going forward we wonder whether the victory of the master brands has been quite as decisive as it may appear.

The key point, we believe, is that so few proponents of the house of brands had ever made very much of the opportunity available to them. Far too often, far too many of the 'brands' in their house aren't really brands at all: they're just well-known names. Consider that list of Lloyds Banking Group 'brands'. Lloyds Bank has a horse. Halifax, as we've said, has a faint echo of its building society past. Bank of Scotland is, well, Scottish. Scottish Widows has a funny name and advertising featuring an attractive woman. But apart from the connotations of these names and logos, how do we really understand them to be different? What do you expect from Scottish Widows that you wouldn't expect from a major competitor?

Vice versa, as noted above, HSBC maintains a 'house' with only one brand in it, First Direct. But First Direct is a proper brand, with its own young and affluent target market and its own distinct idea that a remote bank can be more accessible and responsive than a bank with thousands of branches. And HSBC has said that it intends to take another step along the house of brands road in the near future, rebranding its UK retail branch network (possibly reverting to the Midland name, dropped when they adopted HSBC in 1999. This will happen at the insistence of the regulator, requiring this UK retail part of the bank to be ring-fenced from the rest. But then that's what brands are good at, creating a sense of things that are separate from other things.

As marketers, your authors are instinctively drawn to the house-of-brands model. We like the way that it's possible to create focused, coherent, distinctive brands out of focused, coherent, distinctive business units. We think that master brands backfitted to large, complex, unfocused, incoherent business will almost always become an exercise in lowest-common-denominatorism, and will never mean as much to consumers or be worth as much to their owners.

We accept that elsewhere in the marketing economy there can be exceptions, when large, long-established, complex businesses do in fact possess a strand of DNA that runs through everything they do. Returning to our Cadbury example, Cadbury stands for chocolate. Cadbury can provide a wide range of products that fit within its master brand, provided they're made with chocolate. We struggle with Cadbury's chewing gum, or orange juice.

A Financial Services Forum focus group participant puts the case to revisit the house of brands in this way:

> In insurance, brand differentiation is driven by price points. I don't think we've ever gone beyond demographics and price points and really gone into goals, motivations and behaviours. There's a lot of opportunity there – it would take a multi-brand approach to do that.

To sum up, at the time of writing the house-of-brands approach is at something of a low ebb in financial services, and master brands like HSBC, Barclays, Aviva or AXA[3] seem to represent the preferred option for large organisations. But a bit like supporters of communism who believe the trouble with its track record to date is that it's never properly been tried, your authors believe that the same is true of the house of brands. The occasional flicker of positive evidence suggests that it may get a second wind.

None of these complications arise for small, focused, young businesses (whether genuinely independent or spun out from larger groups). Many of these, especially the independent ones, may lack the resources to make their brands famous, but apart from that everything else is in their favour. When one of your authors was closely involved in the early stages of developing the MORE TH>N brand, representing the direct insurance activities of its parent company Royal SunAlliance (now RSA), extensive research was in place to measure how perceptions of this fledgling brand compared and contrasted with its parent, founded nearly three hundred years earlier. On a range of a dozen or so measures, from simple awareness to a number of image attributes, the newcomer overtook the parent on every one within four years.

It's no coincidence that the strongest and most distinctive brands in financial services are to be found among smaller, simpler, more focused and generally (though not always) younger businesses. Bearing in mind that the important thing is the strength of the brand among their most important target audiences (almost always including customers who could do more business with the brand more often), a list of examples would certainly include:

---

[3] Although AXA still hasn't been quite brave enough to kill the PPP healthcare brand, which has some value in the healthcare market even if a great deal less than BUPA. It's still visible, although in the awkward hybrid AXA PPP healthcare.

Brand	Target Audience	Brand Proposition (Roughly …)
Hargreaves Lansdown	Self-directed investors	The natural home for self-directed investors
St. James's Place	Affluent but financially unengaged people	Becoming a St. James's Place client makes you feel you've made it
Coutts	Affluent people	Becoming a Coutts client makes you and everyone around you feel you've made it
Wonga	Very poor people prone to short-term running-out-of-money crises	Wonga will get you some cash when no-one else will
First Direct	Young(ish) urbanites	Banking made more accessible and easier
Co-operative Bank	Socially responsible people	Banking with a conscience
Hiscox	Various, but with an emphasis on small business owners	The insurance company that gets how it feels to be a small business owner

The important thing about this list is the way that all the organisations included deliver a brand proposition to their target markets that they can only offer because of their focus on those target markets. No big, multi-faceted master brand could credibly follow any of these examples. It's the focus that makes them possible.

A focus group participant says:

> You know, I think it's incredibly much easier with smaller and more focused businesses. If you look at banking, you know, no question, First Direct is a brand.

Financial services is an industry that offers big players huge economies of scale, which work enormously to their advantage and to the disadvantage of small and young players. We strongly believe that brand is one of the most important business attributes – perhaps the most important – where the balance of advantage swings the other way.

BRAND ARCHITECTURE AND PRODUCT BRANDING

Having discussed the subject of corporate branding at some length, we now move on to the next level down. This is to do with building brands at specific product or proposition level, and it's a subject on which there is much less to say - for the simple reason that in financial services, remarkably little of it goes on. Whether master brand or house of brands, in financial services the very large majority of efforts, and budgets, are deployed at corporate or business unit level, and as a result the very large majority of products and propositions at lower levels in the brand hierarchy carry simple generic and descriptive names – Instant Access Account, UK Equity Fund, Buy-To-Let Mortgage, Guaranteed Income Plan, Personal Loan.

This is obviously in sharp contrast to the marketing of consumer goods, and to a lot of the marketing of services, too. Although emphasis is quite often placed on corporate brands (as in our Cadbury example), in consumer goods the main brand focus is usually at the product or category level. Even when a master brand is as strong as Cadbury, individual brands like Bournville, Dairy Milk, Wispa, Fudge and Flake are still important, embodying different propositions and targeting different sectors in the confectionery market. And among competitors like Mars, the investment is almost entirely at product level: the eponymous Mars Bar arguably bestrides corporate and product categories, but most consumers are unaware which firm actually makes Twix, Snickers, Bounty, Milky Way and the rest.

Corporate brands are generally more important in services – customers are never in any doubt that they're flying on a British Airways plane (although of course these days there are other brands, including Iberia, Aer Lingus and the truly dreadful Vueling within the group). But at the same time BA has made great efforts for years to develop Club and First as lower-level sub-brands, representing particular propositions and indeed price points, and targeting particular consumer groups. And the fact that some people – mainly business travellers – are willing to pay up to 20 times more for seats in these parts of the plane indicates they've been reasonably successful.

The same is also true in hospitality, where the large French-owned group Accor lays claim to a truly enormous collection of brands. The list currently includes Raffles, Fairmont, Banyan Tree, Sofitel Legend, Rixos, So Sofitel, Sofitel, Onefinestay, MGallery, Dhawa, Cassia, Pullman, Swissôtel, Angsana, 25hours, Grand Mercure, The Sebel, Novotel, Mercure, Mama Shelter, Adagio, ibis, ibis Styles, ibis budget, JO&JOE, hotelF1 and Thalassa sea & spa - a list long enough to make you wonder whether any hotel where you might choose to stay doesn't in fact belong to this extremely extended family.

Against this background, it's odd that more financial services providers haven't tried harder to develop sub-brands enabling them to tailor propositions to particular market sectors (and, equally, that when they've acquired businesses that could provide sub-brands they've tended, as we've seen, to fold them into the parent brand).

There are exceptions. One of the brands listed in the previous section, Coutts (acquired by NatWest which was then acquired in turn by RBS) is used in exactly this way to represent its proposition in the high net worth private banking sector.

But there are plenty of other financial services sectors that seem on the face of it to be crying out for product- or proposition-level branding. Investment funds stand out as an example. There are over 3,000 investment funds domiciled in the UK, but as far as branding is concerned the brand of the fund manager dominates almost all of them, with the individual funds carrying generic descriptive names shared with most of their competitors – US Equity Fund, Emerging Markets Fund, High Income Fund and so on. It's notoriously difficult to find any kind of corporate positioning or brand identity that can make any sense or provide any coherent differentiation across what will often be a range of fifty or more funds, investing across a wide range of investment markets and with enormously varied investment processes, risk profiles and performance objectives.

To go to the opposite extreme and seek to establish clear sub-brand identities for every individual fund would be equally problematic (and prohibitively expensive). But surely it must be possible to establish groupings that make sense as a brand, in much the same way that an automotive firm like BMW creates groupings of vehicles around sub-brand identities like the 3-series, 5-series, 6-series and 7-series. It's inconceivable that firms in this industry would adopt the same generic approach as fund managers, all naming their vehicles Family Hatchback, Five-Door Family Hatchback, Faster Family Hatchback, Large Estate Car and so on.

There is no single right approach to brand architecture, and the right solution for any firm will depend on the way it is structured and organised, its target market or markets and the range of propositions it intends to offer. At the moment, though, despite huge expenditure on brand consultancy and brand promotion, the situation across UK financial services is a shambles, with only a very small minority of providers having brand strategies which are (a) fit for purpose and (b) successfully executed.

This, like so many other instances of poor marketing in financial services, is bad for companies but bad for consumers too. For companies, it represents probably the biggest and most widespread failure to build value. Most consumer goods companies think of building brand value as their principal purpose: few financial services companies recognise it as an objective at all. And for consumers seeking to find an appropriate path through complex and crowded markets, brands are one of the most important navigational aids available. Brands help consumers to find their way, and to recognise what might be relevant to them, and what probably isn't. Brands don't tell consumers what to do or buy, but they certainly play a big role in pointing them in the right direction.

As we move further into an era in which consumers are going to need to get better at this, brands and brand strategies could, and should, be doing a great deal more to help them.

CHAPTER 18

Yes, But Can You Prove It's Working?

A man hears the sound of an air rifle being fired. He follows the sound. He finds a small boy with a hopelessly dilapidated weapon, barrel bent, sight broken. There are some hand-drawn targets on a wall, and all the boy's shots are right in the middle of the bull's-eyes. 'That's amazing', says the man. 'How do you shoot so well, with such a useless gun?' 'Easy', says the boy. 'Doesn't look easy', says the man. 'It is', says the boy. 'I draw the targets after I've taken the shots'.

Hopefully the financial services marketing moral is obvious: hitting your targets isn't difficult if you don't decide what they are until afterwards.

But who would do such a thing, we hear you cry. Wouldn't that be a tad unprofessional? Well, yes … but that doesn't mean it doesn't happen.

In researching this chapter about marketing measurement, your authors have access to a unique and invaluable source of material: 16 years'-worth of entries to the Financial Services Forum Marketing Effectiveness Awards. Each year since 2002, firms have been selecting their best and most effective marketing activities and writing them up as entries for the awards, following the instructions in the entry pack which guide them on how the scoring system works. Altogether, over 300 firms have submitted a total of over 1500 entries. And though there have been hundreds of winners, many of them genuinely outstanding, it also has to be said that overall, if these are the marketing activities that firms have picked out for their very most impressive and demonstrable records of effectiveness, we'd hate to see what the rest of their activities look like.

This chapter draws extensively on the experience of running and judging these awards, because it provides such clear insight into some of the industry's best and worst habits when it comes to effectiveness. Let's begin with the scheme itself – revised and refined somewhat in its early years, but for several years now sticking to a set of largely fixed and consistent benchmarks for measuring effectiveness.

To be clear, the scheme's judging process is designed simply and single-mindedly to award marketing effectiveness, no more and no less. (Unlike most communications awards, the judges are under instruction not to take any account of creative excellence or originality.) The categories have varied a little over the years but at the core are:

- Advertising
- Content Marketing
- Customer Experience
- Customer Loyalty & Retention
- Digital Marketing
- Direct Marketing
- Integrated
- Internal Communications
- New Product, Service or Innovation
- Public Relations
- Social Media

There are also three Judges' Special Awards, for Best Consumer Insight, for Marketing Learning and for Marketing Excellence.

As in most awards schemes, the winners are chosen by a panel of judges – typically about a dozen financial services marketing luminaries of taste and discernment, plus both your authors (joke). But, again unlike most awards schemes, the judges aren't there just to express opinions and prejudices. We're there to assess, as accurately as we can, the extent to which entries deliver against the marking system – a marking system that is applied consistently across all the categories, and that has been designed specifically to measure what the activity actually achieved.

There are 400 marks available altogether, allocated unequally across seven sections, each headed with a question. These seven questions, together with the number of marks available for each, are:

1. What was the issue or challenge facing the business?	(50 marks)
2. What was the insight that underpinned your strategy and tactics?	(50 marks)
3. What was your proposed strategy to address the issue or challenge?	(25 marks)
4. How did you execute the strategy?	(50 marks)
5. What metrics did you put in place to track the effectiveness of your solution?	(25 marks)
6. How can you prove that your strategy met its objectives?	(100 marks)
7. What value was added to your business as a result of the strategy?	(100 marks)

You'll notice that half the marks – 200 out of 400 – are available for the measures of achievement, and in fact it's a little over half – 225 out of 400 – if you include question 5, which asks entrants to itemise the measurement techniques used. What's more, the earlier questions – as well as carrying fewer marks – are really there mainly as scene-setting, to provide the basis on which the answers to the last two questions can be assessed. Entrants are given a paragraph of guidance on how to tackle each question, as follows:

1. **What was the issue or challenge facing your business?**

   Articulate the problem, challenge, project or opportunity. Describe the business environment in which the marketing activity was completed. Only by giving a clear, well-articulated and quantified description of the issues at outset will the judges be able to determine the overall effectiveness of your marketing activity. It never ceases to amaze the judges how few entries quantify their objectives.

2. **What was the insight that underpinned your strategy and tactics?**

   How and why did you establish your approach to solve the original issue? What drove the decision to focus your resources on this marketing activity? Maybe it was insight from external research, or a collection of comments from your colleagues. Provide a clear explanation of the insight and how it was developing your strategic thinking.

3. **What was your proposed strategy to address the issue or challenge?**

   Provide an explanation of the overall marketing strategy being used. The strategy might encompass a number of marketing campaigns for a brand (maybe not specific to the category being entered) but your description here will hopefully clarify why certain activities were performed in question 4.

4. **How did you execute the strategy?**

   Describe in detail, using images if necessary, the marketing activity completed. Whether an innovative approach, or just doing the basics well, showcase the tactics or elements of the campaign that you feel delivered the greatest impact.

5. **What metrics did you put in place to track the effectiveness of your solution?**

   Give a clear description of the controls used to measure the effectiveness of your marketing activity. Were metrics and objectives set at the start of the campaign, giving a clear definition of effectiveness over a set period? How well do these metrics complement the category being entered?

6. **How can you prove that your campaign strategy met its objectives?**
Tell us how your marketing activity met, or exceeded, the original objectives. Where possible, provide the data related to all the metrics you had in place to measure effectiveness. How well does this go toward resolving the issue – or meeting the opportunity – set out in question 1? Can you match the marketing activity specifically to the results being achieved? Is there clear evidence that the activity was cost-effective, with greater revenue than cost?

7. **What value was added to your business as a result of your strategy?**
As well as the short-term cost-effective benefits of the marketing activity provided in question 6, the judges are looking for evidence of long-term value-add to the business. The very best entries go beyond the results of the marketing activity, to explain the additional benefits achieved for the organisation as a whole. What long-term impact will this activity have on your business or the industry sector? Give a complete definition of the value to the business, with quantification where possible.

We reproduce this questionnaire firstly in the context of our discussion of the awards, but also with a broader purpose in mind. It seems to us that any team setting off on any kind of marketing initiative would do well to tackle the task with these seven questions in mind, knowing that when the task is completed they'll need to be able to answer them.

In the awards judging, though, the performance of the entries against them can only be described as mixed. Across all the entries, the average mark out of 400 is a little over 200. The lowest scores are typically around 120 (although one 2016 entry managed a truly remarkable 85), and the highest are between 300 and 350: an entry scoring 350 will almost certainly be a winner, and an entry scoring 300 has an excellent chance.

The average number of marks varies a good deal between categories. In general, the highest averages are to be found in the categories where either gathering detailed performance measures is intrinsic to the activity (for example Direct Marketing and Digital Marketing), or budgets are big enough to justify significant expenditure on measurement techniques such as econometrics (for example Advertising and Integrated). Vice versa, the lowest average scores are to be found in the categories where, how can we put this, the least marketing rigour tends to go into planning the activity in the first place: Sponsorship and Corporate Social Responsibility stand out, with Content Marketing not far behind.

Overwhelmingly, the principal weaknesses of the poorer entries are vagueness and lack of detail. Many start vague and imprecise, and end the same way. A few include absolutely no hard measures of effectiveness at all.

Here are some short verbatim quotes from the 2016 entries showing what this means in practice.

> (From an answer to Q1 on the challenge facing the business):
> Our primary objective was to maintain our presence in the IFA [Independent Financial Adviser] sector.
> (From an answer to Q7)
> Across the IFA market, sentiment toward the range as a whole has improved.
> (No details)
> (from an answer to Q6)
> [The product] has been highly praised by advisers and … clients like the simplicity of the approach
> (No details)
> (From an answer to Q1)
> We wanted to build our reputation among professional and consumer audiences
> (No details)
> (From an answer to Q7)
> We were delighted with the overall result, which answered our objective of raising our profile.
> (No details)
> (From an answer to Q2)
> Engagement – Distributing relevant content to our audience and engaging them was paramount

There are literally hundreds of examples of vague, imprecise statements of objectives and summaries of results like these across the entry forms.

It should also be said, though, that there's a similar number of well-researched, well-documented and well-written entries, most if not all of which find their way onto the judges' shortlists and the best of which will eventually win the awards. By way of examples, we include three of the winning entries from the 2016 Awards as an Appendix.

While the biggest problem afflicting the weaker entries is, quite simply, a lack of available data to define their objectives or to substantiate their effectiveness, it's sometimes apparent that entrants have encountered more particular problems in attempting to answer the questions. The biggest of these is confidentiality. Entrants are allowed to use indexed, or percentaged scores – 'sales increased by 63%' or 'call volumes were 135% of target'. But we know from our experience as awards entrants, as well as judges, that clients can be very sensitive about even semi-disguised results like these.

The other most frequently-occurring problem is the difficulty in attributing performance to particular elements of the marketing activity. If sales did increase by 63%, and call volumes were indeed 135% of target, was this the effect of a brilliant direct marketing campaign, or was it more because the entrants had slashed the price by 50%? Or a combination of the two, and if so in what proportions?

Your authors, neither of whom is an expert in more advanced measurement techniques, suspect that statistical methodologies with challenging names such as regression analysis and econometric modelling may well be able to cast light on such complex questions. But such techniques, if indeed they do have a role to play, seem to be beyond the capabilities of most of those writing the awards entries.

More often than not the two broader problems that shine through the least satisfactory entries are easy enough to identify:

1. Few, if any, objectives were set for the activity in the first place (or, similarly, those that appear in the entry have the same distinctly post-rationalised flavour as the targets drawn by the boy with the air-rifle).
2. Very few, if any, specific and tailored metrics were put in place to measure the performance of the activity. If the entry reports on any metrics at all, they're often either largely irrelevant ones that have the advantage of being available free of charge, like Google Analytics, or completely irrelevant ones that the firm happens to have commissioned anyway for some quite different purpose, as for example when internal staff surveys are pressed into service to measure the performance of external communications campaigns.

It is of course possible to sympathise with both these problems, which are by no means always easy to solve or avoid.

The challenge with objective-setting is coming up with any plausible way to determine what the objectives ought to be, or what good objectives might look like. In sales-oriented campaigns, it's sometimes possible to do something based around the calculation of ROI – if we're spending £100,000 on an activity, we want a result that delivers an acceptable return on that investment, like say at least £110,000-worth of business. But on closer examination even this is often thin, and usually raises at least as many questions as it answers: is £110,000-worth of business a good result? What was the opportunity cost - could we have spent that £100,000 more effectively? Is it a real figure when you factor in less visible costs, like the time of the people involved?

And of course many, if not most, marketing activities are either not directly sales-related, or only partially sales-related, or only partially responsible for the sales that may be achieved. We are resolutely unconvinced, for example, by methodologies that claim to attach an ROI to less tangible objectives such as brand awareness. And we can think of at least a dozen reasons to explain how a firm was able to generate sales of £110,000, 11 of which have nothing to do with the £100,000-worth of marketing activity.

Surprisingly, these objective-setting problems are particularly tricky when it comes to digital activities. This is for two contrasting – you might almost say opposing – reasons. The first is that so much of the available performance data is horribly unreliable. Some of the figures on digital advertising performance, for example, are really almost entirely fictional. There is little point in targeting a million views if the viewers in question are Chinese schoolchildren paid 50 cents a hundred. But conversely, when reliable and detailed digital performance data are available, it's horribly difficult to know what they mean or what value should be ascribed to them. How important are email open rates? Or unique visitors? Or page impressions? Or dwell rates? They may be indicators of good and valuable behaviours. Or, quite likely, not. On a number of occasions in PR entries, we were proudly told that a particular piece of trade press promotion resulted in opportunities to see (OTS) in excess of the adult population of the UK...

The challenge with relevant measures is a combination of our old friends (or old enemies?): time and money. It's almost always – maybe even always – possible to put relevant metrics in place, and obviously doing so is hugely important and beneficial for your objective-setting. If you're able to frame your objectives very precisely against totally relevant measures, then framing them becomes immensely much easier. But measuring things takes time and costs money, and when both are already in scarce supply for the marketing activity you have in mind, diverting a chunk of the little that's available into measurement is painful. It's no coincidence that in general, the biggest, most tailored and most robust measurement programmes are usually attached to the most expensive marketing activities: the best example is big-ticket consumer brand advertising. There are three complementary reasons why firms spending many millions year after year on a heavyweight media campaign will almost always put in place a brand tracking study to measure its performance:

1. In relative terms, it feels affordable. If you're spending £20 million a year on television, diverting less than 5% of that amount into a classic Hall & Partners tracking study doesn't seem unreasonable.

2. The firm can be reasonably confident that the measurement will be worthwhile, and will show that the campaign is having at least some measurable effect. (By contrast, the authors know of a syndicated study in the asset management world that reports, at six-monthly intervals, that the advertising awareness of some syndicate members remains, as it's always been, in a range between 0% and 1%. It's difficult to understand the value of this information, or why participants in the study would keep stumping up their share of the research cost twice a year.)

3. If we need an annual sign-off from the Board for a recurring £20 million budget cost line, we're going to need to present some kind of evidence that we're producing something for our money.

None of these points applies with anything like the same force to lower-budget, less visible or more tactical activity. In the worst case, the cost of putting robust metrics in place can be as much as the cost of the activity itself, especially when addressing business audiences: reducing a budget for an activity by 50% in order to channel the other 50% into measuring the proportionately reduced effects would be a decision reflecting a level of rigour alien to pretty much all marketers. Similarly, going to a lot of trouble and expense to measure the performance of short-term, ad hoc activities that probably made little impact anyway feels more than a little pointless.

Against that, the only sure way that a firm can build up norms and benchmarks of its own, against which it can direct and relatively easily measure its future activities over time, is by measuring the things it's doing now. Of course you have to draw the line somewhere – but where? Spending half the total budget on measurement is silly. But how about a quarter? Or an eighth?

While we think about measurement principally from the perspective of cost, there's another dimension to take into account. We've focused so far very specifically on the cost of using research to measure the effectiveness of a marketing activity. But many would argue that using research and measurement tools only at this stage is foolish, unprofessional and indeed downright risky: that if you're intending to submit the performance of the activity to robust measurement, it's imperative to take an equally robust, research-driven approach to the development of the activity in the first place.

Take a simple example, such as a lead-generation direct marketing campaign. As a starting-point, the obvious performance metric, which will (probably) be readily available, will be the number of leads actually generated.[1] If we're looking to do a particularly thorough job, there are other elements we could add. It would be extremely valuable to know how many of those leads actually do convert to sales, of course, to make sure that we haven't just generated response from numbers of tyre-kickers. We could usefully profile and analyse the respondents to find out more about them, and to what extent they match our intended target market. And down the track, we could look at these buyers' stickiness: do they stay with us and make further purchases, or have they moved on within months?

But long before we get to any of this, those responsible for this and subsequent campaigns are likely to ask what insight is available to help them develop a more effective approach next time. This is a fair question, not least in the context of assessing the performance of those individuals in producing whatever they produce. In our creative agency days, both of your authors felt thoroughly uncomfortable when placed in a situation where our work would be judged entirely on results, but we had no research or insight available to inform the work we were producing. If we were relying on guesswork all the way through the development process, we felt, it seemed unreasonable to fire up a whole dashboard of quantitative measures to assess the quality of our guesses. Or to put it in the language of that boy with the air rifle, if we're just taking shots in the dark it's hardly fair to turn the lights on afterwards to see how close we've come to the target.

Of course in this particular example – a lead generation campaign – it may well be that the direct marketing methodology itself is designed to provide the insight that's needed. Rather than carry out initial consumer research, it may well be that the team develops a best-guess solution that it takes into live testing, very likely against a control version that has achieved the best results previously. If the campaign is a digital one, it will usually be possible to learn from a wider range of test executions and variables. In such cases, it's understood that the project is in itself designed at least in part as a learning experience, and those responsible know they have permission to fail – although in our experience of the agency side, it's not a good idea to take advantage of this permission too often.

---

[1] Actually, this is more than a little simplistic, and the number of leads may not be available at all or, if it is, may be so unreliably as to be almost worthless. The main problem arises because of the complexity of capturing multi-channel data – it's easy enough to count the number of people responding by calling the number in the ad, but what about those using the website, or social media, or visiting a branch, or doing nothing but keeping the ad and making contact a year later? There are of course some techniques for looking at bigger-picture levels of overall consumer response, but these are likely to be affected by other activities and variables. It's very rarely clear or simple, this measurement business.

Still, the general point about adopting a research-and-measurement-based approach stands. If those responsible for any marketing activity know that rigorous measurements will be made of the effectiveness of the activity, they're right to insist, as far as they're able, that equally rigorous research should go into the planning of the activity. And much more often than not, that'll have implications for timetables and budgets too.

So far in this chapter, we've focused almost entirely on the issue of measurement of marketing activity, by marketing people, for the benefit of marketing people – the sorts of metrics we need to help us to do our jobs well. Arguably, though, there are at least two other levels where measurement matters.

One is to do with overall, big-picture, ideally single-number research intended to track customers' general level of satisfaction with their experience of the firm. Of these, the long-standing favourite has been the CSAT (Customer Satisfaction) score, while more recently we've seen NPS (Net Promoter Score) become extraordinarily popular and fashionable, but, we'd say, start to decline in popularity over the last year or two.

CSAT doesn't actually refer to any single research approach, but in fact is an umbrella term used to describe a variety of (quantitative) methodologies used to measure, fairly obviously, how satisfied your customers are. NPS is a more singular thing, referring to research specifically providing a single number – the percentage of customers saying they're willing to recommend your product or service to a family member or friends, minus the number saying they're not willing to do so.

As relative measures that can be tracked over time we have nothing against these methodologies, or indeed against a growing number of less well established approaches jockeying for position. (Very recently, for example, we've seen a cluster of firms adopting the CES technique, which apparently measures the Customer Effort Score.)

However, while useful as relative measures, we'd warn strongly against thinking of techniques like these as providing any kind of objective reality. Using such blunt instruments to explore the subtleties of the workings of the human mind will always lead to unreliable outcomes. One of your authors, for example, no matter how delighted he may be with a financial service, will always tick the box on the NPS questionnaire that says he will 'definitely' not recommend it to a family member or friend. This is an entirely truthful answer, but only reflects the fact that he doesn't think of himself as the kind of person who goes round recommending financial services to people.

Anyway, simple research measures like these, especially those which lead to a single-number key finding, are often intended to address the second additional measurement need that exists in many firms. This is the need for marketing people to demonstrate the effectiveness of their activities to colleagues outside the marketing department, and, most importantly, to their firms' senior management and Boards. This is a problematic area, and an important one. We think this is one of the very most important and necessary areas for improvement in the new financial services marketing.

A recurring theme of this book is the continuing low status of marketing within many, if not most, financial services businesses – a low status perfectly expressed in that over-used phrase, the colouring-in department. We've argued that the single most important reason for this perception is simply that on the whole marketing really hasn't been as central to the success of most financial services firms as it has been in so many other parts of the consumer economy – just try describing the marketers at Nike, Procter & Gamble or Amazon as the 'colouring-in department'.

But it seems equally clear to us that the second most important factor that depresses the perceived status of marketing, not far behind the first, has been the continuing failure of marketers to express the commercial value of what they do in terms that are meaningful to non-marketing colleagues – and, perhaps most of all, to colleagues in functions that are typically most remote from marketing, like risk, actuarial, finance and IT.

Improving our performance in these areas isn't easy. Not many directors of finance or IT will want to sit through all the 90 slides in the quarterly brand tracking presentation, and even if they did they'd retain a fair amount of scepticism when it came to more abstract and highly qualitative measures like Brand Salience and Emotional Temperature. At the opposite extreme, though, reducing all the complexity down to a monthly email to the Exec, announcing that this month our NPS has improved from minus 16 to minus 14, is if anything even less useful. What do these figures mean? Are they good? Why have they moved? Without a good deal of supporting insight, we're very little further forward.

Of course there is huge variation in the quality and quantity of marketing measurement tools used by marketers to give an account of their effectiveness to their senior management colleagues, and some do a superb job of presenting meaningful, hard and compelling business metrics to their colleagues. But especially in light of the fact that marketing expenditure is often one of the largest budget items needing Board approval, it's remarkable how thin, anecdotal and generally unfit for purpose a great many firms' measures can be.

For all these reasons, we put measurement very near the top of the list of areas for improvement in the new financial services marketing.

CHAPTER 19

Must Planning Your Comms Be So Horribly Complicated?

If you're one of that significant minority who still thinks that 'marketing' is the same thing as 'marketing communications', then this is the chapter you've been waiting for. This chapter discusses some aspects of what marketing communications will look like in the new financial marketing era.

In three bullet points, the answer is that overall, compared to how things have been previously, they will be a whole lot more:

- Measurable (and measured);
- Multilayered;
- Concerned with engagement.

Or in one bullet point, having responsibility for them will be a whole lot more:

- Complicated.

The short answer to the question in the chapter's headline is 'Yes.'

Like much in this book, these are of course generalisations. Some financial services marketing communications (do you mind if for the purposes of this chapter we call them FS marcomms?) have been measurable, and/or multilayered, and/or concerned with engagement for many years. If we pick out the firm that, in our view, would walk away with the FS Marcomms 30-Year Consistent Excellence Award, the direct-to-consumer insurer Direct Line, we'd argue that give or take the odd lapse in the middle of the period, it has fairly consistently been all three:

1. As a 'brand response' communicator dependent on direct-to-consumer marcomms for the great majority of its business, all of its comms activities have always been measurable (and measured);
2. By the same token, as a very large player in its sector with a large existing customer base and steep annual acquisition targets, Direct Line

has always integrated a complex, multilayered programme extending from heavy TV advertising at the broadest, acquisition-driven end of the spectrum through to well-integrated customer comms by mail and increasingly digitally at the other;

3. In an increasingly crowded category, and dealing with a low-interest purchase, Direct Line has always placed at least a reasonable amount of emphasis on the need for communications to engage. The red telephone became a highly successful (and, in the industry, much-envied) brand icon: how many times, in their agency days, were your authors briefed to come up with 'a property like Direct Line's red telephone'?[1]

But if Direct Line ticks all three of our boxes, there are plenty of examples of firms that ticked two, one or indeed none at all.

In hindsight, as financial advertising levels increased steadily in the pre-internet years up to the turn of the millennium, the lack of integration was a particular weakness. A number of organisations explicitly adopted a dis-integrated approach, with entirely separate strands of advertising intended to build corporate brands and to promote products (the two often shorthanded mysteriously as 'theme' and 'scheme' advertising). Insofar as these separate streams were measured, they were measured separately too, typically with a tracking study to monitor brand perceptions and a separate, much harder set of direct marketing measures to monitor the performance of the product advertising.

In many organisations this bifurcation went even further, with separate external agencies and even separate internal teams responsible for the two strands, At worst, this could lead to a good deal of negativity and hostility between the two - the direct marketing team perceiving their brand colleagues as fluffy, irresponsible wastrels spending huge amounts of the available budget on achieving small shifts in brand perception of dubious value, and the brand team thinking of their direct marketing colleagues as vandals and hooligans doing lasting damage to brand perceptions with tacky free-gift offers intended to achieve tiny improvements in cost-per-response rates.

Sadly, it's probably fair to say that some of that era's most admired and most fondly remembered brand campaigns, usually on television, were created in circumstances like these. Examples include Allied Dunbar's memorable 'For The Life You Don't Yet Know' campaign, Barclays' 'Blade Runner'

---

[1] One other direct FS provider, the lender Lombard Direct, so well-remembered by Lucian's children, actually went so far as to come up with a blue telephone, which did rather call to mind that old saying about 'the sincerest form of flattery'.

films (directed by the great Ridley Scott shortly before he completed his journey from making commercials in the UK to making blockbusters in Hollywood), and even the most highly regarded of all financial services brand campaigns, Prudential's 'Wannabe' commercials.

These certainly didn't lack engagement, and as you can see if you search for them on You Tube are still charming and watchable today. It may very well be that the tracking studies showed improvements in perceptions of all the brands involved. But as largely unsupported TV advertising vehicles, not reflected in other advertising or communications in any other media – and long before the days of digital, so not possible to reflect on a website or other online comms – the TV campaigns stood alone, failing to cast much of a spell over any of the firms' other activities.

The rationale for this kind of activity was particularly difficult tom understand in the case of businesses which were wholly, or largely, intermediated, as for example Prudential was at that time. It's a matter of great regret to advertising agencies, including those managed by your authors in their time, that it has never been easy to demonstrate that consumer-facing brand advertising is an effective way to affect intermediated business levels. For every case study showing a correlation between heavy advertising and strong intermediated sales, there is another case study showing strong intermediated sales without any brand advertising at all.[2]

It's a pity that we can't look back on the era of the big unsupported brand campaigns with more enthusiasm, not only because some were very enjoyable to watch but also because they were a lot of fun to produce. Writing 60-second TV commercials and paying Ridley Scott a large amount of money to shoot them was an agreeable way to make a living, especially when you needed little more evidence to prove the success of what you were doing than, say, a 10% increase in a somewhat ill-defined consumer 'brand salience' score.

But these days, right across the whole of retail financial services, there are very, very few unsupported, stand-alone, big-budget, TV-based brand awareness advertising campaigns. In a sense, their disappearance reflects the macro-trend that forms the underlying theme of this book: financial

---

[2] Over many years, one of the most successful of all life, pensions and investment businesses distributing entirely through financial advisers is one which, as well as never building any kind of awareness, has also traded consecutively under two remarkably unhelpful names. Today the company does business under the name Old Mutual Wealth, despite the fact that it's not old, isn't a mutual and doesn't by any means seek to exclude the less-than-wealthy. And previously its name was Skandia Life, completely unknown to consumers as a financial services business but widely – and wrongly – thought to make crispbread and/or heavy trucks.

services marketing today increasingly has far too much real work to do, far too many ways in which it needs to deliver real value to the consumer, to be able to afford such a very large chunk of the available budget on fun but not hugely meaningful ways of raising brand awareness.

As we shall see, this is certainly not to say that broadcast advertising addressing brand objectives is, or should be, a thing of the past. On the contrary, as we'll explain, we think there should be a good deal more of it. It's just that most financial services marketers would now agree that it's part of a story, part of a strategy, and despite its cost arguably a fairly small part. It's certainly not the whole bloody thing.

This chapter isn't intended as a practical guide to planning or producing marketing communications. That's a subject for a whole book in itself, and plenty already exist. Instead, it's more of a checklist of practices and principles, based on your authors' experience on client and agency side alike, which can help achieve good marcomms outcomes. Or, to put the same point the other way round, which can help avoid bad ones.

In no particular order, the following section presents our thoughts on the ways in which tomorrow's FS marcomms will be different from those of the past.

IT'S BROADCAST *AND* NARROWCAST, NOT *OR*

We certainly don't challenge the big idea – discussed in more detail in Chapter 13 – that the most important difference between the old financial services marketing and the new is today's focus on marketing to *individuals* rather than to *groups*.

We acknowledge that this huge change has been driven primarily by the growing power of technology, and its increasing ability to manage and manipulate the stupendous quantities of data that are required.

And we recognise that this change in focus has transformational consequences, requiring organisations – and not just marketers – to see their world fundamentally from a customer-centric perspective, rather than one that is based around products, services and channels.

But in Chapter 13 we do express one caveat that we want to revisit here. We think there are a whole bunch of reasons why it would be wrong to believe this development represents a binary change, in which after a transitional period an old way of doing business is replaced with a new one. On the contrary, we think:

- Individualised marketing and mass marketing aren't in any way binary opposites, but rather are points on a spectrum;

- Individualised marketing absolutely isn't new, and has represented a very significant part of all marketing activity for many years;
- Mass marketing, and its close relative niche marketing, aren't going away and will continue indefinitely to account for a large proportion of all marketing activity.

Let's consider some of the reasons for these points of view.

- To see how mass marketing and individual marketing are points on a spectrum, it's helpful to realise how comfortably – and how frequently – they combine. Say that a financial services provider develops a packaged, or bundled, product that individual customers can tailor to their own requirements, and which will engage with customers on an individualised basis. It might well make perfect sense to launch the product to the market via a single, mass-marketing, product-led campaign – and to present it in detail through a single, though customisable, website. And even when the product is successfully launched and has developed its own customer base, it might very likely still make sense to promote it on a broadcast basis.
- This is part of a bigger picture in which it's clearly necessary to maintain both customer-centric *and* product-centric views of the world, and to be able to switch seamlessly between the two. For startups, or young organisations with few customers, a customer-centric approach that relies on external data is likely to be an expensive way to acquire a customer base, and broadcast activity is likely to play a big role. Once an organisation has a number of customers (and, of course, a way of capturing and manipulating the necessary data), the balance shifts the other way.
- Although the quantity of data now available to us is far greater than ever before, as is our ability to slice it and dice it, we'd argue that ultimately the change is incremental, not fundamental. Individual customer and prospect data has been available in quantity for decades. Large parts of the direct marketing industry have taken an individual, customer-led approach, focusing on share of customer, cross-selling and upselling, for as long as we can remember.
- This isn't just about marketing. A surprisingly large number of other functions and disciplines in financial services have always taken a customer-centric view. What is underwriting, for example, if not a process designed to individualise a customer's insurance cover and premium? Or portfolio management, if not a process of personalising a customer's investments?
- Vice versa, at the same time the opposite is also true: especially for large organisations crippled by legacy systems and outdated organisational

structures, the challenges involved in overlaying a new customer-centric approach are absolutely immense. For large, long-established, complex firms, moving to a position where they can take a customer-centric view of *some* customers *some* of the time isn't impossibly difficult. Moving to a situation when they can take this kind of view of all their customers all of the time is mind-blowingly hard.

- Although it's true that digital communications dramatically reduce some of the costs of communication with customers at an individual level (and ever-advancing machine learning capabilities will reduce costs a lot further), they often don't. Overall it will frequently be a lot more expensive (and a lot more complicated) to manage a business in this way: in ROI terms, taking both costs and outcomes into account, we're not at all convinced that a more individual approach will deliver better results.

- This may sound heretical, but we're genuinely not convinced that customers are always hugely impressed or delighted by a highly personalised approach, especially if the personalising requires any significant amount of extra effort on their part. Certainly there are aspects that will pretty much always be welcome, perhaps most of all in the ability to manage customer relationships with a much higher level of relevance and timeliness. But if personalisation generally means bells, whistles and complexity – even beneficial bells, whistles and complexity – a lot of people will decide they can't be arsed. (We appreciate the counter to this point, which is that good data should ultimately be able to highlight which customers will feel this way, and make sure they get nice simple stripped-down services that don't try their patience.)

- It would be wrong to underestimate the potential problems of what the industry tends to call creepiness, at least for some years yet. It may be that future generations won't worry about being followed around the Internet for months by insurers offering discounts off cover on the exact model of Jaguar they just checked out on a used car site but at the moment a lot of us find it a bit weird. And this kind of experience highlights an important new problem, in the emergence of a new category of 'highly personalised junk'. If I decide against the Jaguar after that used car site visit then all that retargeting just becomes a tiresome intrusion.

- And finally, there is the cluster of perceptual issues around a group of words that includes fame, credibility, trust, confidence and awareness. Like the previous point, this may change over time. But as things stand today, it's not for nothing that many point-of-sale advertisers still make use of that old expression, 'As Seen On TV' – the fact of this kind of prominence does act as a reassurance to many.[3] It's often said that for smaller organisations with shallower pockets, one of the great advantages of the digital world is that it enables every firm to appear the same size. From the perspective of smaller firms, that may well be a great advantage, but for many consumers it's uncomfortable. Many will seek indications of size, scale, stability and credibility – reassurances that giving their business (and money) to an unknown firm wouldn't be a stupid thing to do. Being seen to have a ton of money to spend on mass marketing (or half a ton, anyway) is one of the easiest, most visible and least fakeable ways that firms can do so.

On the whole, the steadily increasing ability to deliver what might be called 'mass personalisation' – that is, to personalise at scale, and at low cost – is one of the most significant developments in the consumer economy since the Industrial Revolution of 150 years ago.

While that revolution made it easy and affordable for us all to own the same things and have the same experiences, this new information revolution makes it possible for us all to own different, or personalised things and have different or personalised experiences. This, in turn, imposes huge challenges on companies dealing with consumers, requiring them to be able to adopt a consumer-centric view of the world so that they can understand, manage and optimise what those consumer experiences actually are. On the whole that's a very good thing, although also a very big and demanding thing.

But as is so often the case with brave new worlds, the old world isn't going away any time soon. For large, complex, long-established organisations, and in different ways for new, young, small ones, the real challenge is to plant one foot firmly in the new world – while keeping the other foot no less firmly in the old.

WORRY MOST ABOUT BEING IGNORED

We've written a whole chapter about this, so in this one we'll keep it brief. People responsible for developing marketing communications, and equally people responsible for approving them, worry about all sorts of things that might go wrong. Risk avoidance can be taken to amazing lengths. One of your authors remembers developing an ad for a banking client, with a visual that showed a photograph of a cliff-top path. There were no people in the shot, but the client worried that the path looked dangerous. At considerable

---

[3] Indeed, the name of the leading digital fashion retailer ASOS is said to be an acronym standing for the expression 'As Seen On Screen.'

expense, we had to retouch in a fence between the path and the cliff-edge before the ad could appear.

But while worrying to a preposterous degree about things that are never, ever going to happen, most people don't seem to worry at all about the thing that happens almost all the time: that your marketing communications activity will be ignored.

This is true of almost all activity, in all formats, addressing all target groups. It's just as true of mass advertising as it is of social media campaigns, YouTube films and individually addressed emails. Most consumers, whether customers or not, have horribly low expectations of marketing communication in financial services, and are willing to make virtually no effort at all to seek it out or engage with it.

And the fact is, they're not wrong. Much is, quite simply, dreadfully boring, and in some media there is literally little or nothing to relieve the tedium. Before writing this paragraph your authors have wracked their brains to try to find an exception, but when we think about financial services marketing material we can remember having received through our letterboxes, neither of us can recall a single example that made it worth the bother of opening the envelope. (Vast forests must have been reduced to barren tundra to meet the insatiable demands of Barclaycard's balance transfer mailings. But as soon as you see that logo on the envelope, you know it can go straight in the bin.) And don't get us started on those campaigns that mislead us by stamping the words 'Private and Confidential' on the envelope of a promotional pack...

Our message is simple. In the new financial services marketing, we deeply hope that everyone can manage to stop worrying about the danger of the clifftop path, and start worrying about the infinitely greater danger of the waste paper bin.

THE RULES OF DIRECT MARKETING STILL APPLY

This is a point that arguably shouldn't need making, and no doubt for some of our readers it doesn't. (Direct marketing gurus like John Watson, Steve Harrison, Rory Sutherland and others, if you're reading this feel free to skip on to the next bit.) It's a point that arises mainly, we think, for a single reason – a lot of the ways you can communicate on the Internet, particularly those to do with social media, don't cost anything.

As a result, a troublingly large number of financial services marketers, especially less experienced ones in smaller, younger, digitally driven firms, seem to believe that the economics of first acquiring customers, and then going on to build relationships with them over time, aren't a problem. Many of these firms apparently pay little attention to the basic economics and disciplines of consumer marketing, and in some cases seem to be pursuing business models that stand no chance at all of commercial success.

The fact is, amidst all the complexities, the basic business-plan numbers for a consumer-facing financial services business are simple. Fundamentally, you need to know:

- How much it costs to acquire a customer;
- How much it costs to deliver your products and services to that customer;
- How much revenue you can generate from that customer, either initially or over their lifetime.

Everyone knows these are the figures that matter. What they often don't know, though, is what these numbers are going to be in their specific case. And not least because everyone who starts up a new business has to be an optimist, many expect the numbers will work out a lot more favourably than they actually do. The fact is, customer acquisition in particular is almost always harder, slower and more expensive than those responsible for the business plan imagine. In particular, those lovely free social media turn out to be less-than-ideally suited for the task, and often not really free given the amount of time and money that need to be spent to make use of them. Social media are great for engaging with people you know, and have a relationship with. They're usually not so great for engaging with complete strangers.

In 2015, Lucian made a speech at a conference on the then-very-hot topic of robo advice (digital investment services) that attracted a lot of attention. It was on the subject of the first of those three numbers in the bullet-points above, the cost of acquiring customers. He said that as a universal average – so universal and so average as to have fairly minimal predictive value – on the basis of his 30 years' financial services direct marketing experience, across all product categories and all channels, he would tend to start off any plan with an initial assumption that it would be possible to generate a lead for £30, and a customer for £200. This, he said, would probably be reasonably accurate plus or minus, say, about 500%. Okay, he admitted, that's not very impressive – but at least it's a starting-point. Start there, and then go on to refine your own numbers in the light of your actual experience.

On the day, he felt embarrassed that these numbers were so vague and tentative. But to his surprise, they were seized upon eagerly, both on the day and subsequently – they've been re-quoted frequently, time after time, in a variety of reports and publications ever since. The reason was simple: for many of the people trying to make a success of direct-to-consumer investment businesses, these were the only figures they'd ever seen. For all their vagueness and tentativity, they were still better than nothing.

This is extraordinary, particularly since there is so much direct marketing material readily available – books, papers, awards submissions and agency case studies – that seem to be so widely ignored.

It's true that today, many of this industry's achievements seem more typical of yesterday's bad old days of financial services marketing than today's or tomorrow's. Too much of it was, and too often still is, characterised by overpriced, poor-quality products, sold on the basis of propositions that were often misleading and manipulative. But that doesn't mean that there isn't a great deal of valuable learning to be had from a vast amount of well-documented experience. And after all, it really isn't rocket science. If it is really true, for example, as widely believed, that some of today's digital direct businesses are paying £1000 to acquire a customer, but then going on to generate first-year revenue from those customers of less than £50, it does look as if there's a lot of good direct marketing practice that they need to learn – and quickly, too, before the funding runs out.

NOTHING MATTERS MORE THAN THE BRIEF

While we're on the subject of client/agency relationships, let us tell you about the single thing that goes most wrong most often (at least, from an agency point of view – if you have a view about what goes most wrong most often from a client point of view, please let us know at our website www.nosmallchange.co.uk).

Before we get into the detail of this, let's just pause to agree that in any piece of work that an agency is doing with, or for, a client, the brief is the only thing that really matters. Assuming (perhaps rashly) that everyone is reasonably competent at their job, then the finished product, whatever it is, is likely to be more or less as good as the brief. Excellent brief should lead to excellent outcome, terrible brief to terrible outcome and all points in between. Agree? Good.

So here's what would happen on virtually every job when one of your authors worked on direct marketing for a large, well-known High Street organisation – one which, like many, was organised by product team, savings, loans, mortgages, current accounts and so on, and with a centralised marketing function that acted as a service provider to all the product teams. Here's how more or less all those projects would go.

- Someone quite important in a product team (say, mortgages) decides that some kind of direct marketing activity to promote a particular product is required.

- This person calls a briefing meeting with someone from the marketing team. This marketing person is much younger, much less senior and knows little or nothing about mortgages.
- The quite important person hasn't thought about it very hard before the meeting, and so gives a vague, rambling and confusing account of what's needed. The marketing person doesn't understand much of this, but doesn't want to admit it.
- The marketing person might write up an agency brief, and if so a copy might be sent to the product person. If so, the product person doesn't read it.
- The marketing person arranges a briefing meeting with the agency. There are various things that the agency doesn't understand and which the marketing person can't explain, so the agency requests a meeting with the product person. The marketing person isn't keen on this because it's a threat to their authority, so it probably won't happen.
- The agency works on the brief, using up much of the available time, and comes up with some pretty good ideas. These are presented to the marketing person, who seems quite positive, if a little unsure.
- There's then a presentation to the product person, which the agency might or might not attend. Either way, the product person is bewildered and usually incensed by what's being shown. What the hell is this, the product person asks. Wasn't anyone listening to a word I said? This is completely wrong. What I want is ... (the product person now gives a much clearer brief than at the first attempt.) Now please go away and do what I asked for.
- Either in this meeting (if the agency is present) or subsequently (if not), the marketing person makes it clear that what has gone wrong here is entirely the agency's fault.
- Of the two weeks originally available for the job, there's now one day left. The agency will now go with any stupid idea it can think of that more or less meets the brief, because there isn't time to do anything else. This will be grudgingly approved, again because there isn't time to do anything else. The activity will go ahead.
- At the so-called washup meeting, when it's all over, the agency will be bitterly criticised for its poor listening skills and inability to follow a clear and simple brief.
- A few days later, another quite important person in another product team (say, savings) will decide that some direct marketing is needed.

We went round this pointless and depressing loop what seemed like dozens of times, the only significant difference being the identities of the product and marketing people, and the specific nature of the many different products we'd evidently so consistently failed to understand.

You might think that, learning from this experience, we'd insist on some kind of process improvement to solve the problem. Let the agency be in the briefing meeting with the product person, for example. Or insist that the marketing person does write an agency brief and the product person does read it, comment on it as necessary and sign it.

But proposals like these were never popular with the marketing people, because they created difficulties for them in their relationships with the product people (who, as the budget holders, were by far the dominant of the two groups). If the product people start dealing directly with the agency, or getting involved with agency briefs, why does the client need a centralised marketing function at all?

Even writing this brief account brings on a painfully vivid flashback of a miserable and frustrating time. Let's move on.

FOR HEAVEN'S SAKE, TRY TO BE A GOOD CLIENT

If you work with external agencies, what do they really think of you? Not you personally, although if you're involved in the relationship that's kind of interesting, too, but your organisation as a whole? Are you a favourite client? A mediocre client? Or the one that everyone avoids like the plague?

There are two points to understand here. First, agencies do an incredibly much better job for their favourite clients than for their least favourite clients. This is partly for hard, quantifiable reasons (they put in far more hours, they allocate their very best people to the account, they see you as a flagship account for whom they can win creative awards), but it's more for qualitative, emotional reasons. They care more. They want to do well for you. They're proud of what they're doing. They're enjoying themselves.

And second, assuming that we're talking about a generalist agency here, you start with a major disadvantage – namely, that you're a financial services business. Many years ago, when Lucian was launching his first agency specialising in financial services, he commissioned what in hindsight was a remarkably large-scale and robust piece of market research among agency people to find out how they felt about working on accounts in different sectors. The research covered 10 sectors in all, including food, drink, automotive, travel, retail, technology and financial. Among a sample of 250 agency account handlers, creatives and planners, the picture could hardly have been clearer: in terms of both personal preference, and perceived quality of their own agency's output, financial came bottom by a distance.

It's true that this was a very long time ago, but we'd be surprised if the situation was very different today. Certainly the verbatim comments on why financial services performed so poorly still ring true today – too much regulation, too boring and complicated, conservative and risk-averse clients, generic and uninspiring propositions, no real intention of doing anything different. ...

This doesn't sound good, but of course it's perfectly possible to buck the trend. While most creative teams tend to hide under their desks when colleagues are approaching with a financial brief, there are a few accounts that have consistently inspired. (There are also a few that have occasionally inspired, which can be almost as good – imagine the surprise and delight when comparethemarket.com actually bought the meerkat campaign).

What's curious is that, in our experience, so few clients have – or even seem to care about – any clear sense of where they stand in their agency's favourite-account pecking order. If you want great work and great service, we strongly recommend making it a key metric. It's very measurable.

Before we move on, we should mention an obvious tactic to overcome the handicap of being a financial services business. If you appoint one of the fairly small number of agencies that specialise in the sector, the problem goes away.

Many clients believe that in doing so, they simply swap one weakness for another – that while a specialist financial agency may be more enthusiastic about their business, its standards will be generally lower than a good generalist agency and its output won't be as good. We'd say that it's difficult to generalise, and it all depends. Some generalist agencies have performed brilliantly for financial clients, especially when those clients do fairly mainstream things like motor insurance and want to advertise a lot on television. But expecting a generalist agency with a centre of gravity tilted towards mainstream, mass-media, consumer products and services to do a great job on communicating an absolute return fund proposition to a target group of financial advisers is clearly absurd. No-one in the agency knows the first thing about it, and, worse, no-one cares: the client's best hope is that the job will be freelanced to a team from a specialist agency, whose costs will be marked up to a level several times higher than the client would have paid by going direct.

BETTER TO BE CONSISTENTLY (A BIT) WRONG THAN INCONSISTENTLY RIGHT

The era in which a football manager like Sir Alex Ferguson can do the same job for 27 years has now very nearly come to an end. (As we write, Arsene

Wenger is still in charge at Arsenal after 20 years, but we'd be surprised if he's still there for more than, say, a year after this book is published. And no-one will ever manage a football club for as long as that again.) No confectionery advertising strapline will ever last as long as 'A Mars a day helps you work, rest and play' (which first appeared in 1959 and went on working, with occasional periods of rest, for well over 50 years) or 'Bounty gives you the taste of paradise', which was launched even earlier. And no small car will ever retain the same basic shape for as long as the original Mini (41 years) or the original VW Beetle (a startling 65 years).

It's a truism to say that life-cycles of almost all sorts have become faster (with the obvious exception of ourselves, since the life-cycles of human beings have become, on average, considerably slower or longer).

In marketing, we think very differently about the life-cycles of products and services, and even more so of communications campaigns. The old masters of brand-building in consumer goods – the Procters, the Unilevers, and the Marses responsible for the two straplines quoted above – believed that the task of deeply embedding a strong brand in the national consciousness took decades. It was a water-dripping-on-a-rock kind of business, year by year taking a slightly firmer hold on a little corner of the target market's brain.

Today, we can't understand what took them so long. The world is full of pretty well-established brands that haven't been around for one single decade, let alone several. Some of the digital brands provide the most obvious examples: which would you say is the stronger brand, Twitter (introduced in 2006) or another Mars confectionery brand like Topic (introduced over 40 years earlier, back in 1962).

And by the way, while you may think the comparison is hardly a fair one, it's worth pointing out that the Mars product has been supported by many times as much awareness-building TV advertising over that very much longer lifetime.

But.

This section is actually heading in the opposite direction to the previous few paragraphs.

As far as brand-building is concerned, even in this sped-up world of shortened life-cycles it's still important to give consumers a bit of time to get their heads round what you're saying. If you keep changing everything – moving on from one brand positioning to another, one organising idea to another, one look and feel, one tone of voice, on what seems like an annual basis – you'll simply never build a clear space in consumers' minds.

It's a curious paradox that financial services providers, and particularly those involved in long-term business like pensions, investments and insurance, chop and change everything to do with their brands and their communications so bewilderingly often.

It's not difficult to think of large, high-profile institutions which change their brand positionings with extraordinary frequency. Some – perhaps Barclays is the first to come to mind – seem scarcely able to sustain an idea for more than two years.

This kind of inconsistency must represent a gigantic waste of money. We say in our chapter on brands that the financial services industry has spent billions of pounds on brand communications over the years, and has only a small handful of genuinely differentiated brands to show for it. This ruinous and extravagant short-termism is one of the biggest reasons why.

We need to keep things moving in marketing these days. There's a pressing and unending need for innovation, for novelty, for something new that can capture attention and keep our customers engaged with us. But we need to innovate and originate within a longer-term framework, within a distinctive sense of what our brand stands for that isn't junked and restarted from scratch every year or two. A brand that's repositioned every couple of years simply isn't a brand at all.

MAKE SURE YOUR ORGANISING IDEA REALLY ORGANISES

This point follows on from the previous one. If we're going to wrap up a whole range of activity, addressing a whole range of consumers and consumer segments, relating to a whole bunch of propositions, over a long period of time, within a single overarching brand idea, then that brand idea is going to have to be fit for a very challenging and demanding range of purposes.

In our experience, far too often, especially in bigger and more complicated organisations, it just isn't. Typically, what happens is that the marketers embark on a quest for an 'organising idea', often with the help of an external agency – but, as they set off, have failed to appreciate the full range of situations in which this idea will have to be applied. The result is that before long, it becomes clear that it isn't fit for purpose – and before much longer, it's history and the next quest begins.

There's no shortage of examples. When it comes to short-lived brand strategies, Barclays is usually a reliable source of for-instances, and it doesn't let us down here. Some years ago Barclays introduced a brand strategy that focused on an approach to photography that it described as the 'gallery of life' – a real, vivid, human style of photography that showed their target groups living their daily lives, as they really were.

Unfortunately the plan failed to cope with the fact that Barclays then operated, and needed to promote itself, in many dozens of countries around the world, targeting people of many dozens of different ethnicities. This added enormously to the scale and cost of the approach. Worse, in some individual countries, populations were made up of several different ethnicities, not all of which reacted positively to real, vivid, human photographs of members of the others. The gallery of life quickly closed its doors.

But Barclays' most famously ill-fitting brand idea appeared a year or two later, this time with a verbal property rather than a visual one. The big idea was, quite literally, bigness – as the strapline put it, *A big world needs a big bank.* Unfortunately, as a result of not-untypically poor internal co-ordination, the TV advertising around this theme launched in the week that elsewhere in the bank, the PR team announced a programme of 200 branch closures, which obviously would have the effect of making Barclays a rather smaller bank. The strapline staggered on for a short while, but it was a dead copyline walking. A year or so later, the quest for a replacement began.

Barclays doesn't have a monopoly on this sort of thing. NatWest ran into a slightly different problem when launching an organising idea with a television campaign based around a fictional family, the Cannings, played by a bunch of well-known character actors. The problem here was a purely practical one – that the image rights to most of these actors had only been acquired for use in TV advertising. When other agencies on the NatWest roster – including the one led by one of your authors – tried to extend this property into other media, such as in-branch, print and mail, it emerged that only two of the most minor family members – from memory, the grandmother and the young son – were available. This was fine for retirement income and children's savings propositions, but unfortunately NatWest's range is rather wider than that.

Finally, though, it's worth adding that sometimes a remarkably inflexible-looking idea turns out to offer a lot more flexibility than you might imagine. An extremely simple play on words based on the fact that the word 'market' sounds quite like the word 'meerkat' didn't seem likely to last long as an organising idea for a big-spending, high-profile brand with a proposition that's pretty much all about saving money. Over the years the advertising for comparethemarket.com, it has to be said, has shown increasing signs of strain as a result of the need to express this kind of proposition within this organising idea – but, eight years later, the meerkats are still going strong.

APPROACH CONTENT MARKETING WITH GREAT SUSPICION.

Recently, we've all heard an extraordinary amount about content marketing. The phrase generates 25 million results on Google – which, for what it's worth, is not far short of half the number generated by that hottest of all recent topics, Big Data. The large majority of financial services firms claim to do at least some of it. Digital channels – especially social – are crammed full of it. Every freelance copywriter in the world has rebranded as a content creator (and wisely, too – 'creating content' pays about 50% better than 'writing copy').

These practical developments reflect a strong theoretical case. Arguably, as far as communications are concerned, a move into content marketing is the natural consequence of adopting a customer-centric approach. If we're focusing on our customers and their needs, it makes logical sense to engage with communications that they want to receive, rather than communications that we want to transmit.

So against this strong momentum in both practice and theory, it feels quite brave for us to say that in our view, most of it is complete tosh and a total waste of time, effort and money.

If that's true of most of it – and we'll make that case in a moment – what about the tiny proportion of which it isn't?

The tiny proportion that we would call worthwhile is the material that genuinely engages with the people you want to engage with, *in a way that predisposes them at least to some extent to do business with you.*

There's a story about how the peer and barrister Lord Birkenhead, way back in the period between the wars, would walk across St James's Park on his way to the House of Lords. On his way along Whitehall, he would invariably stop off to use the lavatories at the National Liberal Club. One day, exasperated, the doorman said to him, 'You use our facilities so regularly, Lord Birkenhead, why don't you become a member of the club?' The peer reacted with genuine surprise. 'Good heavens', he said, 'I had no idea it was a club as well'.

Somehow there's an analogy here with even the most engaging content marketing: people may enjoy it, but do they have any real idea that it has a commercial purpose as well? (And in focusing on 'the most engaging' content marketing, we're limiting ourselves to a tiny proportion of the total – the overwhelming majority really isn't engaging at all.)

And beyond this, there's another big point: does your firm's content marketing have any effect at all in terms of differentiating and reinforcing your brand? And if not, why not? This is a slightly unfair example, but can you guess which general insurer's online magazine features articles with the following headlines?

- What Is Insurance Premium Tax?
- Infographic: What Is Condensation?
- Looking After Your Car Tyres
- Reviewed Your Insurance Lately?

Yes, it's a trick question – you can't possibly tell. These headlines are all absolutely generic to the world of insurance, and the magazine could come from anyone.

In fact, though, it come from Direct Line, currently we'd say the general insurer with the strongest, clearest and most distinctive brand positioning – as fixers and problem-solvers, as reflected in the Winston Wolf TV campaign. Why is there no trace of that positioning in this customer magazine?

We don't think that any content marketing is worth the time and cost unless it can pass three tests:

1. Does it really engage the target market?
2. Does it engage them in a way that, at least to some extent, draws them closer to doing business with us? (This is a very tough one to call.)
3. Does it help to differentiate our brand?

We don't think very much of the mountain of stuff that exists out there would survive all three of these tests.

TIME TO CLOSE UP THE FRONT OFFICE/BACK OFFICE DIVIDE

If you are indeed a financial services marketer, you may not like this much. It's all about taking on a stack of extra work, with very little extra money available: what's more, most of it is boring to do, and there's no glory in it.

Taken together, these are probably the main reasons why most marketing people have generally wanted as little as possible to do with that large raft of communication of one sort or another that is broadly said to come out of the back office – and also, rather mysteriously in our view, out of something called the 'middle office', that we would generally struggle to locate.

The fact is, though, that our widespread failure to get a grip on this stuff is absolutely indefensible. If it's true (which it is) that financial services brands are overwhelmingly experiential, and if it's true that from a customer perspective the large majority of experiences, over time, are encounters with back-office communications, then it clearly makes absolutely no sense for these to remain as a marketing-free zone left largely in the hands of Ops people.

The failings here are of two main kinds, and both kinds are serious. The first are what you might call sins of commission: much of the material that's sent out is horribly badly written, badly conceived, badly designed, and badly produced. The second are the sins of omission – the communications that don't happen at all, but really could or should.

As a case in point, one of your authors has a 25-year term insurance policy, arranged by an adviser and provided by a household name insurer. The policy is now into its last year, and over that period he has paid a large five-figure sum in premiums. In that time, he has never heard a single word from either adviser or provider.

Many marketing people have had depressing experiences on forays into this back-office area. At one time or another, for example, most of us have become excited about the possibility of developing our firms' statements of one kind or another so that they can do double duty as a marketing tool. We arrange a few meetings to investigate. It quickly becomes apparent that we're facing a toxic combination of horrendous IT problems, and deeply entrenched silo positions. After a short while, we withdraw and get on with something nice and easy like redesigning the website.

But really we can't go on like this. Being responsible for the customer experience except what comes out of the back office is a bit like running a restaurant and closely managing every aspect of the customer's experience except the food.

SPEND MORE MONEY ON INTERNAL COMMUNICATIONS

Our final discussion is the companion-piece to the previous item, and makes basically exactly the same argument. If it's true (which it is) that financial services brands are overwhelmingly experiential, and if it's true that from a customer perspective the large majority of experiences, over time, are encounters with your organisation's people, then it clearly makes absolutely no sense for these to remain as a marketing-free zone left large in the hands of the HR department.

You may be on top of this one. In our experience, rather more marketing teams have got a grip of internal comms than of communications from the back office. But even so, there are a great many that haven't.

Sometimes there are some major structural problems in the way. The trickiest is probably the growing enthusiasm for outsourcing, even of front-line customer service functions. When one of your authors, together with his client, visited the outsourced customer service team of one large life and pensions company, we were told we were not just the first marketing people, but in fact the very first people of any description from the client company, to actually spend time in the call centre.

It's not just a question of doing stuff, and keeping an eye on how it's going with an annual staff survey. It's a question of treating the internal audience like any other key target audience, developing and executing a proper plan, complete with objectives, budget and timetable, and running a tailored programme of relevant metrics to understand what you're achieving. If you're doing all this already, congratulations. The great majority of your competitors aren't.

We began this list by saying it would represent some of the ways in which the marcomms of the future would differ from the marcomms of the past. Looking back over it, and appreciating that several of the points it makes look a) difficult to implement, and b) not always enormously appealing to marketers, perhaps we might have said '*should* differ', not '*would*'.

CHAPTER 20

How Far Can You See Beyond Financial Services?

In recent years, we've been pleased to see the gap slowly narrow between the world of financial services marketing, and the broader consumer marketing economy.

Once upon a time, the financial service world was not far from literally a different planet, populated by a different species and governed by different rules. As we mentioned a couple of hundred pages back, for example, some 50 years or so ago the advertising accounts of all the country's biggest banks were handled by the same agency (an agency, by the way, that handled financial accounts only), and by gentlemen's agreement the banks declined to make use of expensive television advertising as a form of competition. More recently, though, perhaps over 20 years or so, this other planet has been moving steadily closer to planet earth – a process clearly visible in the evolving career paths of many of the marketing professionals involved.

In the first stage of these journeys, a view spread across the financial services industry that it had much to learn from people involved in marketing fast-moving consumer goods (FMCG).[1] There was a time when anyone with a few years' brand management experience at Procters, Unilever or Diageo could expect to double their salary by moving into FS. This first surge of incomers didn't achieve very much, except to get approval for huge uplifts in advertising budgets that contributed enormously to ad agencies' income, profits and bonus pools.

You could write a book (well, a short one) about why most of these FMCG specialists failed in financial services, probably the single most important reason being that service businesses are so much more complex and multi-dimensional than products in packets, cans and bottles. But the key take-out is that few of them lasted long.

---

[1] It may seem artificial to talk of a view 'spreading' across an industry, but financial services was and still is remarkably prone to herd behaviour. Beliefs like this one really do spread across the sector at extraordinary speed, almost like an epidemic.

The next wave of incomers had more relevant qualifications, because they came from other sectors of the service economy. Around the turn of the millennium, the industry view changed: now the idea was that on second thoughts it didn't have all that much to learn from FMCG marketing, but it did have a great deal to learn from other service-sector businesses and especially from retailing. Anyone with a few years' brand management experience at an airline, a telecoms firm or, even better, a major supermarket could expect to double their salary by moving into FS. (They might well be able to make the move without actually moving, of course. At about the same time, most major supermarket firms and a lot of other service-sector businesses started to take steps, with varying degrees of ambition, into financial services.)

The people arriving in this wave were generally a lot more effective than the FMCG people had been, and they introduced many of the service marketing concepts that are still central in financial services today. Perhaps foremost among these is the crucial – although still difficult – idea of *managing the customer experience,* which connects directly to the idea that service brands are principally *experiential* and depend more than anything on the distinctive and coherent management of what is usually a large number and wide range of touch points between firms and their customers.

Some service marketing principles proved harder to import than others. Severe limitations in data and IT, for example, often resulted in insuperable difficulties in introducing expensive and elaborate Customer Relationship Management (CRM) systems. At the time when spending on these was at its peak, few large institutions even knew how many customers they had or what combinations of products they held, so the idea of managing the relationship with them was, in hindsight, absurdly ambitious, and vast amounts of money were wasted. It's also arguable that some of the individuals who joined from other service sectors failed to recognise how retailing financial services is different from retailing groceries: many believe that some of the more extreme risks run by certain institutions in the run-up to the 2008 crisis resulted from rash decisions taken by executives promoted into general management from backgrounds in retail marketing, with little experience or understanding of how catastrophically the climate can change in the financial world. But be that as it may, on the whole the service sector incomers can be judged a success.

Which may very likely help to explain why the next phase of recruitment activity, overlapping with this one, saw the tide begin to flow in the opposite direction. Increasingly, individuals who had built reputations for marketing success in financial services started coming to the attention of headhunters looking to fill vacancies in other sectors. Where once the route into financial services had been largely a one-way street, it was now becoming a dual carriageway. Some well-known and senior figures made the two-way trip more than once. Mike Hoban, one of the country's ablest senior marketers, came into the financial sector to take the top marketing role at Scottish Widows, left for Vodafone, returned for Confused.com and left again for Thomas Cook. At the time of writing, he's in charge of marketing at supermarket brand Morrisons.

This kind of ebb and flow has been a positive development, and we'd like to see a lot more of it. So far, it's a good deal more common among the biggest, most mass-market financial services firms such as banks, direct insurers and price comparison sites: examples are much fewer in fields such as asset management and financial advice. But over time, it can only help to create a situation in which that chasm that still exists between financial services and the rest of the consumer economy narrows to the point that it disappears.

Hang on a minute. Is chasm a bit strong? Fair enough, perhaps, if you compare the most marketing-oriented FMCG sectors with the least marketing-oriented corners of financial services. But look at what you might call the retailiest financial sectors – motor insurance, or credit cards, or online banking – and is the gap really so wide?

As we've said right from the outset, you can certainly find financial services brands that are very good at marketing. We trace the growth of marketing enlightenment back to the launch of Direct Line as long ago as 1985. But judging the category on the basis of its best examples is as misleading as judging it on the basis of its worst. Beyond the world of financial services, in the broader service economy as well as in consumer goods, marketers still routinely deploy strategies and tactics that are still largely unknown to us.

Here are seven marketing techniques that we think could be applied much more often in financial services.

1. The whole toolkit of *promotional marketing*. Offers of any kind are rare in financial services. In some other sectors, they're almost universal: has anyone ever bought a Charles Tyrwhitt shirt or a DFS sofa at its alleged full price? Taken to this extreme, offers can be wearing for consumers and potentially counterproductive for providers, but financial services has a long way to go before these problems will need worrying about. Currently HSBC stands out as the only big bank – and, as far as we can recall, the only big institution – that runs sale promotions from time to time, offering modest discounts on personal loans. Otherwise it's hard to call much financial promotional marketing to mind at all.

2. Believe it or not, outside financial services many other service businesses offer customers real and valuable *loyalty bonuses*. In the financial world the normal response when faced with unusually loyal customers is to

fleece them with an endless series of ever-more extortionate price rises until eventually they realise they're being swindled and leave in a fury vowing never to return. (Ideally, of course, if they're older people and don't entirely understand the rules by which the game is played these days, they never notice and you can carry on profiteering at their expense until they expire.)

It's instructive to compare this disgraceful behaviour with the kind of approaches taken by airlines seeking to maintain relationships with their most loyal customers. And increasingly, these days, this isn't just about high-margin business class customers. Even a budget airline like easyJet offers its valuable Flight Club package to frequent flyers, keeping them out of the hands of the likes of Ryanair.

3. Most marketing in financial services differs from most marketing outside financial services in its focus on corporate brands, and its lack of focus on *product brands*. As we discussed in our chapter on branding, there's nothing wrong with a strong corporate brand, and there are hundreds of examples outside the financial world. But trying to operate a consumer-facing marketing business without product brands is like fighting with one hand tied behind your back, and it's very odd that this is overwhelmingly what the financial services industry chooses to do. Thirty years or so ago some high-profile but rather half-baked financial product brands crashed and burned a bit too visibly: HSBC (then still Midland Bank) was the highest-profile example, with brands such as Vector, Orchard and Meridian. Expensive failures like these seem to have cast long shadows.

4. It may be a smaller opportunity than the first three, but ever since the first Apple store launched in London back in 2004, one of your authors has been intrigued by the possibilities in the idea of Apple-store-style *flagship stores* for financial services firms. We can't see much future for all those thousands of bog-standard High Street branches (although see point 7 below), but especially for big banks with wide product ranges the potential of a few truly spectacular flagship stores is tremendously exciting. It would be wonderful to have the space to be able to explore the things people can do with their money, and to design really spectacular exhibits bringing financial ideas to life. (The principle of compound interest makes a dreadfully boring bar chart, but could come to life in a brilliant virtual reality sequence.)

5. That kind of retail experience would demand a lot of great *design*, and in fact design is another area where financial services marketers still have much to learn from the bigger, broader marketing economy. Apple is again the obvious role model, but not the only one. Over the years, dozens of brands in different categories have stood out for design excellence – upmarket ones like Bang & Olufsen, Aston Martin and

Mont Blanc, through to middle- or mass-market ones like Sony, Pizza Express and Ikea. In financial services, it's not possible to think of any firms that have consistently sought to differentiate themselves in this way. This is odd, because it's a particularly painless and low-risk kind of differentiation that doesn't cost much and won't raise any hackles in compliance.

6. The other side of the same beautifully designed coin is *tone of voice*. For many, many years no-one in financial services seemed to care about this at all. More recently, things have changed – but not really in a good way. Now, every copywriter working in the financial world is sick to the back teeth of being asked to write web copy or product brochures or tweets or whatever 'in the style of that lovely, quirky Innocent Smoothies packaging'. And when we've done so, we're even sicker, maybe to the front teeth, of being asked to tone it down a bit because maybe it's a bit too chatty for a serious subject like money. Actually, it would be best if you toned it down quite a lot. In fact, on second thoughts maybe you could tone it down completely and just make it sound like everyone else's. There isn't a single brand in financial services that consistently achieves a distinctive tone of voice, and this kind of muddle-headedness is why.

7. And finally, going back to a point we made in our chapter about engagement, wouldn't it be a good idea for more firms to try to start building some kind of relationships with their future customers years ahead of time – in other words, to make a start way back in the pocket money years? NatWest deserve some credit for its investment in financial education in schools, which is a good effort though deeply dull. But surely there's more that other firms could do? Ikea stores provide children's playgrounds, complete with particularly impressive ball ponds, and roundabouts and candyfloss stalls outside the main entrance. Perhaps there's a future here for all those redundant High Street branches – turn them into giant ball ponds and give the kids some fun while the parents are shopping.

If you work in marketing outside financial services – or if you're one of the few people in financial services who looks beyond the sector – these areas of marketing opportunity may seem familiar and hardly original. If so, good for you. But there are still financial services marketers, including some very senior ones, who scarcely know that any of these options exist.

This isn't just a point about learning from other sectors' best-practice marketing techniques. It's a more fundamental point, about the world that our customers live in and the context in which they understand and experience what we do.

Everyone in marketing knows at least one anecdote making the point that any product's competitors are more diverse and more numerous than you think. One of your authors remembers working on the huge Mars confectionery account, long before he discovered the subtle joys of financial services. His agency was invited to pitch for the seriously mis-branded French Golden Delicious apples account (yes to French, not really to Golden and absolutely not at all to Delicious: one out of three ain't bad), and out of politeness asked its biggest client for permission to proceed. To the agency's dismay, Mars wasn't having it. In Mars' view, the French apple-growers were a direct competitor. The Mars people made their position clear with the undeniable soundbite: 'Gentlemen, we are both in the anytime foods business'.

There are more extreme versions of the same issue. An agency working for a leading fragrance brand was prevented from pitching for an alcoholic drinks account on the grounds that both competed in the Christmas gifts market.

Most financial services firms, though, define their competitors extraordinarily narrowly. Pension providers benchmark themselves against other pension providers, asset managers against other asset managers, mortgage lenders against mortgage lenders – and actually it can be even narrower. Mortgage lenders who specialise in buy-to-let loans are really only interested in what other buy-to-let lenders are up to. Those lending to first-time home buyers are tracked much less closely.

But this isn't really the way it seems to consumers. Mars' concern about conflict of interest is nonsense, of course, but actually they're right as far as the underlying issue is concerned: a person feeling peckish may well weigh up the pros and cons of an apple and a chocolate bar, or indeed may decide to buy a coffee instead.

Pension providers may think they're in competition with other pension providers, but most of the time they aren't, at least as far as end-consumers are concerned. Consumers very rarely weigh up the competing propositions of numbers of different pension providers. In any case, if it's a workplace scheme, the choice is likely to be limited to the provider chosen by the employer. But there is a competitor set all the same. The competitor set consists of all the other things the individual could do with the money. A contribution increase of 3% per annum would pay for a Sky Sports subscription, a week's family holiday, a year's services for the car, pretty much all that year's school clothes for the kids or a new iPhone X. There's a good case to be made for putting money into pensions, even against a competitor set as tough as this. But you're unlikely to make that case as powerfully as you might if you don't even realise who the competitors are.

Sometimes, even today, the situation is actually even worse than this. Far too many people in financial services still believe that their offerings occupy some kind of moral high ground, that it is in some kind of objective way better for consumers to put their money into their products and services than into any of their other available choices. We said earlier that life assurance people are particularly prone to this: many believe that life assurance is such an unquestionable good that the case should be made for it not by firms with policies to sell, but by the Government, through a public awareness campaign, in the national interest. But life assurance people are not alone in this foolishness and arrogance. Pensions people are just as bad. According to them, the risk of poverty in old age is so serious that people should be discouraged from almost any other non-essential expenditure until their pensions are funded to the max.

There might be a little bit of sense in this if all those other expenditures clamouring for the same available money were pointless and trivial. But in real life, for most people, very few of them are. Which is more important, increasing your pension contributions or getting the car serviced?

This is not to say that it's impossible, or inappropriate, to promote higher pension contributions. Putting money into pensions, just like buying life assurance, is a good thing to do. But to be able to make that case effectively – to be able to express it in terms that make sense to consumers, and to offer them ways of increasing the contributions that they find engaging and manageable – we have to be able to see our world through our customers' eyes, and to understand how our propositions appear to them among all the others demanding their attention.

Frankly, we're not very good at this, mainly because until recently we didn't have to be. When we could rely on face-to-face salespeople bringing in most of our customers, the ability to see our world through our customers' eyes wasn't important. Now it's increasingly vital, and we need to get better at it fast.

On the upside, at least there are some big, deep, exciting consumer thoughts, feeling and behaviours for us to involve ourselves with. Most people working in marketing deal with haircare, or footwear, or readymade meals, or mobile phone services. Weirdly, a great many of them think that what we do is boring. How wrong can they be?

Money is potent stuff – perhaps, indeed, it's the most potent stuff. People dream about money, think about money, talk about money, worry about money, plan for money, hope for money, work for money, even kill for money. (How much of that can you say about haircare products?) Our job in financial services marketing is to understand those hopes, fears, dreams, needs and plans, and to find ways of making strong, real connections between them and the products and services our firms have to offer.

These thoughts bring us finally, and perhaps inevitably, up against the form of words in the subtitle of this book: *Why financial services needs a new kind of marketing*. What is this new kind of marketing, you've been wondering ever since you saw the book's title. When will they tell us what it is? Looking at the few pages remaining unread to the right-hand side of the book's spine, you conclude that this new kind must be remarkably brief to describe.

The truth is that for the most part, the 'new' kind of marketing we're calling for is no more and no less than what we've also called 'good' marketing. As we said at the outset, hitherto the financial services industry has been able to make a great deal of money out of a great many customers without much need for marketing at all, and much of what there has been has been unfair and exploitative. But the tide has now turned. Tighter regulation, growing consumer scepticism and, perhaps most of all, the ever-increasing power of the Internet are combining to bring this era to an end.

It may be, when the history comes to be written, that the great Payment Protection Insurance (PPI) debacle appears to be the turning point. The lending industry saw an opportunity to increase its profits by tens of billions of pounds by means of an unfair and exploitative marketing practice, charging customers preposterous sums for a shockingly poor-value product that in many cases they didn't even know they were buying. For some years they got away with it. But in the end, the environment changed too much for the scam to be sustainable. Regulation, distrustful consumers, social media and, it must be said, a large horde of deeply dislikeable claims management companies turned the tide, and ultimately the industry has had to pay its customers some £40 billion in compensation – probably an even larger amount than the profits it had previously banked. At the time of writing, there are still plenty of similarly bad practices going on across the industry, but we don't think there are any on quite this scale – and, touch wood, we don't think there will be again.

Increasingly, our 'new' kind of financial services marketing turns out to be exactly and precisely the kind of marketing that we discussed in Chapter 2, when we quoted the definition offered by the Chartered Institute of Marketing:

> Marketing is the management process responsible for identifying, anticipating and satisfying customer requirements profitably.

We remain convinced by the case that we made at the outset, that this definition fits just as well with financial services as it does with any other sector of the consumer economy. Fundamentally, we say that good marketing is good marketing, whatever the product or service.

But there is one significant difference. While we accept that surprisingly deep insights can be found in exploring the ways that consumers interact with all sorts of superficially mundane products – some brilliant work has been done on the emotional dimensions informing people's choices of washing powder – it still seems clear to us that it's an immense privilege to deal with a subject as emotive, as meaningful, as resonant and quite simply as important as money.

As the rapidly advancing field of behavioural science has shown so clearly in recent years, there is a massive and still largely uncharted continent of thoughts, feelings, needs, emotions and behaviours for us to explore. And on the basis of our discoveries we can go on to 'satisfy' those 'customer requirements' infinitely much better than anything or anyone who has gone before us.

Early in our careers, your authors both stumbled into financial services marketing, much more by accident than design. But we stayed here by choice, and for one principal reason: we both had a challenging and exciting sense that here was a field where very little of the great work had yet been done.

Quite a few years later, a bit more of it has been done. But the great majority still waits to be accomplished.

Winning Entries from the Financial Services Forum Marketing Effectiveness Awards

In our chapter on marketing measurement (Chapter 19), we draw extensively on the experience of managing and judging the Financial Services Forum Marketing Effectiveness Awards, which over the past 16 years have established an important role as the only awards scheme of their kind.

We suggest in the chapter that the structure which entries are required to follow can act as a template to ensure good marketing planning and measurement in firms' day-to-day activities. The sequence of seven headings – listed and explained on page 235 – call for clear and focused thinking on the issue to be addressed, the strategy to address it and the measures put in place to assess the results.

In this appendix, we expand on this thinking by including three papers that won awards in the past couple of years. Each has been slightly edited to remove commercially sensitive information, but even so – within the 1,000-word limit imposed by the scheme – they all stand as good examples of well-planned, well-implemented and well-measured marketing activities – and, of course, even more importantly, activities that achieved excellent results against their objectives.

SANTANDER

Simple | Personal | Fair: How Santander Redefined Customer Experience

Entry Category: Customer Experience

Question 1: What was the issue or challenge facing the business?

- In 2013 Britain was limping out of the worst economic crash in a generation. Banks were perceived as being completely out of touch with society.

Are banks well run?

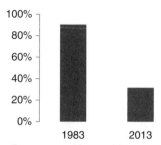

Percentage of favourable responses
Source: The London-based National Centre for Social Research

- If times were tough for the established banks, the challenges were greater for a Spanish newcomer.
  Santander faced two unique challenges:

1. We needed to evolve our brand identity.
   Formed through a merger of three former building societies – with three different cultures – we needed to establish what Santander stood for, for staff, customers and consumers.
2. Customer loyalty and satisfaction needed improving.
   Despite having a great product in the 1|2|3 Current Account, we had a low number of loyal customers and ranked amongst the worst high street banks for customer service.

- This is the story of a radical new approach, which completely redefined customer experience at Santander.

Question 2: What was the insight that underpinned your strategy and tactics?

- Too often, banking insights start with products. To redefine the customer experience, we needed to understand exactly what consumers wanted from their bank.
- We commissioned six research groups with existing customers and our competitors' customers, and they told us about their strains with banks, what they liked and what they wanted.
- They spoke about their frustration when things went wrong and took too long to resolve. About feeling overwhelmed by the range of products on offer. About being ripped off.

- Listening to their pain points, we realised there was deep-seated anxiety at the core of the relationship between bank and customer. Customers didn't trust banks, and wanted to feel confident in managing their money.
- Our task became clear, and it would be mammoth, requiring a wholesale change in how we did business.

Question 3: What was your proposed strategy to address the issue or challenge?

- Our strategy for redefining this relationship came from looking at the elements we were already getting right.
- Our customers defined their positive experiences in the same terms. The best encounters with us were *simple, personal* or *fair*.
- New account openings and the mobile app were praised for being simple.
- Friendly interactions with staff and rewards linked to spending were championed for being personal.
- Genuinely beneficial products and reciprocal rewards were heroed for being fair.
- Therefore if customers' best encounters with us were either simple, personal or fair, imagine if we could make *every* experience hit all three.
- We hypothesised that this could build a genuine sense of trust, successfully changing the customer experience.

Question 4: How did you execute the strategy?

- We embedded Simple | Personal | Fair within Santander, instilling a new culture among our 20,000 UK colleagues.
- We needed our people to have ownership of defining what it meant for them, so we welcomed our staff's feedback and input.
- Ana Botin, Santander UK CEO, conducted workshops countrywide to find out what being Simple | Personal | Fair meant to our UK staff.
- The roadshows led to the launch of an online forum called 'Better Together', that allowed any colleague – from branch to boardroom – to suggest ideas to make us *more* Simple | Personal | Fair. Nearly 2,000 colleagues participated, suggesting 542 ideas and casting 23,000 votes.
- This work led to 'The Santander Way'; we empowered every member of staff to speak up and say 'Stop. This isn't right; we need to do things differently.'
- We continued to transform the whole business:
  - Made incentive schemes more customer focused.
  - Moved contact centres back to the UK.

- Simplified products and their range (e.g. reducing 11 adult bank accounts to 2).
- Redesigned our website.
- Launched the SmartBank app, to help with money management.
- After establishing Simple | Personal | Fair internally, a consumer-facing campaign followed in March 2014.
- We wanted to communicate each value's individual merits whilst giving Simple | Personal | Fair meaning as a collective entity.
- We used a construct that dramatised how anything can be described in three words.

Question 5: What metrics did you put in place to track the effectiveness of your solution?

- Uplift in key brand and perception measures
- Awareness and impact of Simple | Personal | Fair
- Double the number of loyal customers
- Satisfaction in line with the top performing banks
- Top 25 employer in *The Sunday Times*
- Make inroads into the current account market

Question 6: How can you prove that your campaign strategy met its objectives?

- Our first success was transforming our culture internally. As early as December 2013, the Financial Conduct Authority found that Santander 'employees … enthusiastically articulated the new Simple Personal Fair culture with examples of how they were applying it in their interactions with customers'.
- Improved staff engagement continued, now one of the *Sunday Times* Top 25 companies to work for (2015).
- Also saw a far-reaching perception change externally. Just one year on, we saw spectacular results:
  - Simple | Personal | Fair was spontaneously linked to Santander three times more than any other bank.
  - 75% agreed Santander is striving to be Simple | Personal | Fair and 78% agreed we reward customers.
  - YouGov's Buzz rankings put Santander in the number one spot for most improved positive sentiment, with a 28-fold improvement over the previous year.

- In a study of 179 Personal Financial Journalists (April 2014), Santander ranked in the number-one spot as the company that impressed them most in the past year and as the company that is changing for the better.
- The impact of communications on interest in finding out about the bank' rose from 21% to 31%.
- Trust improved by 12%, and in 2015 Santander won Most Trusted Mainstream Bank at Moneywise Awards.
- Advocacy rank moved from seventh (May 2013) to fourth (May 2014) and second place (April 2015).

Current account service rating, August 2014
(Results and ranking from February 2014 in brackets)

Rank	Provider	Great	Okay	Poor
1 (1)	First Direct	92% (92%)	6% (6%)	2% (2%)
2 (4)	Santander	72% (64%)	22% (28%)	6% (8%)
3 (n/a)	Smile	72% (n/a)	22% (n/a)	7% (n/a)
4 (3)	Nationwide	69% (67%)	25% (26%)	6% (7%)
5 (n/a)	Co-op	70% (n/a)	23% (n/a)	7% (n/a)
6 (5)	Halifax	55% (45%)	36% (43%)	9% (12%)
7 (12)	TSB	52% (37%)	36% (43%)	12% (20%)
8 (9)	Bank of Scotland	49% (40%)	39% (44%)	12% (16%)
9 (n/a)	Yorkshire Bank	45% (n/a)	45% (n/a)	12% (n/a)
10 (7)	Lloyds Bank	47% (45%)	40% (40%)	13% (15%)
11 (n/a)	RBS	46% (n/a)	37% (n/a)	17% (n/a)
12 (8)	HSBC	42% (42%)	43% (43%)	15% (15%)
13 (n/a)	NatWest	38% (n/a)	46% (n/a)	15% (n/a)
14 (6)	Barclays	38% (46%)	36% (40%)	26% (14%)

Order calculated by 0 point for poor, 1 for okay and 2 for great. Results may not add up to 100% due to rounding. 7,875 votes in total – we've ignored banks with fewer than 100 votes.

- Martin Lewis's – one of the most influential financial commentators – current account service rating from last place 2012, to second place 2014 (after First Direct) or the first high street bank.
- Loyal customers up 119%.

Current account service rating – the worst
(February 2012 results in brackets)

Rank	Provider	Poor	Okay	Great
1	Santander	26% (32%)	42% (40%)	32% (29%)
2	RBS Group	24% (18%)	43% (42%)	33% (40%)
3	Bank of Scotland	23% (N/A)	44% (N/A)	34% (N/A)
4	Halifax (i)	18% (21%)	49% (46%)	33% (33%)
5	Barclays	16% (19%)	47% (44%)	37% (38%)
6	Lloyds TSB	16% (15%)	45% (47%)	39% (38%)
7	HSBC	15% (18%)	43% (40%)	42% (42%)

Ranking determined by subtracting 'poor' figure from 'great' figure. Percentages based on that provider's customers only. Figures may not hit 100% due to rounding. (i) Feb 2012 result included Bank of Scotland. This is the first time we've separated Halifax from Bank of Scotland.

Question 7: What value was added to your business as a result of your strategy?

- Crucially, we also saw an increase in consideration and sales.
- Our lead over our competitors for Current Account consideration increased from 6% (February 2014) to 13% (June 2014).[1]
- 31% increase in sales of our 1|2|3 Current Account since 2013, and now the most switched to current account on the market.
- Profit before tax up 26% 2013 to 2014. Growth in operating income over eight consecutive quarters, and an unprecedented increase in banking liability.
- We have and continue to transform the bank with Simple | Personal | Fair.

---

[1] Santander position versus competitor average.

The winners and the losers

Brand	Gains	Losses	Net gains
Santander	78,734	18,812	59,922
Halifax	40,794	25,669	15,125
Nationwide	25,243	10,383	14,860
Low volume participants (C Hoare & Co, Virgin Money, Cumberland Building Society, Reliance Bank and Tesco Bank)	689	499	190
Bank of Scotland	3,790	4,093	−303
Danske Bank	541	910	−369
Bank of Ireland (UK) – includes Post Office	333	820	−487
AIB Group (UK) p.l.c – includes First Trust Bank and Allied Irish Bank	159	956	−797
Ulster Bank	180	1,515	−1,335
Lloyds Bank	53,019	59,335	−6,316
Clydesdale Bank – includes Yorkshire Bank	1,117	8,955	−7,838
RBS	2,735	11,258	−8,523
HSBC – includes First Direct and Marks & Spencer	18,949	30,082	−11,133
NatWest	12,674	27,542	−14,868
Co-operative Bank – includes Smile	4,508	23,611	−19,103
Barclays	9,455	31,574	−22,119

Source: paymentscouncil.org.uk. The figures only include the customers who used the switching guarantee service.

DIRECT LINE GROUP

Alfie Deyes' Direct Line Driving Challenge

Entry Category: Social Media

Question 1: What was the issue or challenge facing the business?

- How can a leading car insurer emulate prior brand marketing success when reaching out to a younger, more modern demographic? This was the challenge facing Direct Line's latest social media campaign.
- In 2014, Direct Line transformed its fortunes with a new marketing message. Switching our iconic little red telephone on wheels for 'the fixer' Winston Wolf and the strapline 'Can your insurance do that?', we positioned ourselves as the 'go-to' firm for fixing things when they go wrong.

However, despite revenue-raising success, we still failed to engage with a younger driver demographic, with a cost per action totalling a whopping £335.80 per sale between April and July 2015[2] for drivers within the 17- to 25-year-old age bracket.

Objectives

- Clearly more cost-effective measures had to be taken to attract and retain a demographic that is pivotal to the long-term sustainability of the brand.
- Placing DrivePlus – our telematics plug-in that analyses driver behaviour to offer discounted premiums – at our campaign's heart, we set three objectives that would be targeted at 17- to 25-year-olds:
  - Grow return on marketing investment (ROMI) for DrivePlus, by selling more gross written premiums (GWPs) in 2016 from a 37% lower marketing spend over 2015.
  - Raise brand awareness, measured by DrivePlus installation and the amount of generated quotes.
  - Use DrivePlus to convince 17- to 25-year-olds that Direct Line is the champion when it comes to being there for young drivers.
    Direct Line's telematics product had been carefully designed to appeal to young drivers hit with insurance premiums that are often perceived to be unfairly high – on average an 18-year-old pays £972 per annum compared to an average of just £440 for a comprehensive premium across ages. By using DrivePlus young drivers can help prove that they are safe drivers and thus benefit from substantial discounts, effectively levelling the playing field.

Question 2: What was the insight that underpinned your strategy and tactics?

- We were under no illusions: engaging with a 17- to 25-year-old, millennial audience would be difficult. Notoriously hard to reach, given the speed at which they switch off and skip material, conventional advertising methods are often expensively ineffective.
- Such insight, coupled with the implied 'boring' nature of insurance, meant that bold thinking would be needed to engage and explain the key DrivePlus benefits, which included:
  - Discounts – An automatic entitlement of a 25% reduction on under-21 premiums and a discount of at least 15% for 21- to 25-year-olds.

---

[2]For gross written premiums of its DrivePlus product, which is available to those aged 17 to 25.

- Simplicity – While telematics products usually need to be fitted by an engineer, DrivePlus's 'black box' can be installed easily and directly by the customer.
- Our strategic insight, therefore, was to produce a campaign that would not only engage but also effectively inform our young demographic of the product and the advantages it can directly offer them.

Question 3: What was your proposed strategy to address the issue or challenge?

- Direct Line would need to speak to a millennial market on its own terms in regard to content, platform and message. Conscious of the target audience's fleeting attentions, we chose to adopt a branded content strategy.

The power of vlogging and Alfie Deyes

- This decision pointed us to the popularity of vlogging and the high-profile vlogger Alfie Deyes. With 4.5 million followers at the time, including a large young female demographic which is a key audience for Direct Line, 23-year-old Alfie was also famed for his inability to drive.
- Alfie's lack of prowess behind the wheel suggested an engaging backstory that had already spawned the #alfiecantdrive hashtag – a running joke among his subscribers.
- This ready-made 17- to 25-year-old audience, coupled with the ability to safely film Alfie's own demonstrations of DrivePlus in context, made the vlogging medium seem an ideal choice.

Question 4: How did you execute the strategy?

- The campaign began with Alfie being contracted and ready to accept Direct Line's challenge. Crucially, could the vlogger learn to drive and do it safely using telematics?
- Following an initial video unboxing of the DrivePlus plug-in device, app instructions and his one-year insurance policy, Alfie would complete a seven-day intensive driving course. Mentioning the challenge in his vlog and snapchat output, Alfie's efforts included:
  - Five videos – Appearing on both Direct Line's and his own PointlessBlogVlogs channel, multiple YouTube vlogs detailed his driving experiences after passing his driving test (a four-month period).
  - Traction – Going above and beyond his contract requirements, Alfie involved other popular celebrity vloggers (including girlfriend Zoella) in his videos to yield almost three times the average views of the other videos (384k).

- Competitions – Alfie invited young drivers to enter and win driving lessons, producing 12,033 impressions and an overall engagement rate of 63% (versus 2% average for the Direct Line account as a whole).
- The detailing of what DrivePlus is and how it is used remained central to all content.

Question 5: What metrics did you put in place to track the effectiveness of your solution?

- From the outset, campaign effectiveness would be measured by:
  - Awareness and brand perception of Direct Line and DrivePlus
  - Video views, viewing times, likes and comments (YouTube, Instagram)
  - Impressions and engagement rates (Twitter)
  - Website click-through rates (CTRs)
- High-level metrics measured included:
  - Total number of DrivePlus quotes
  - Total number of DrivePlus gross written premiums (GWPs)
- These metrics gauged the success of a socially driven, online content strategy, while also measuring our overriding campaign and business objectives.

Question 6: How can you prove that your campaign strategy met its objectives?

Achieving growth via organic engagement

- In terms of tangible online results, the campaign:
  - Generated over 1 million organic video views with an average viewing time of over six minutes, producing over 52k likes.
  - Achieved over 258k Twitter impressions, 11.9k Twitter engagements and an average engagement rate of 11.4%.
  - Coincided with an improved click-through rate (CTR) to the Drive-Plus section of directline.com, with CTR rising 169% during the campaign.
- This level of engagement not only outperformed Direct Line's brand average, it proved to be both the most successful organic content on our channel and the second most successful overall.

Greater brand awareness and product perception

- Such a positive reception of the campaign content was always dependent on Direct Line's effective reach for 17- to 25-year-old drivers. Deeper analysis of viewer feedback on Alfie's videos showed not just greater awareness of the DrivePlus product and the incentives for safer driving, but that 36% of viewers agreed Direct Line is 'there for young drivers.'

What was Alfie saying about Direct Line?

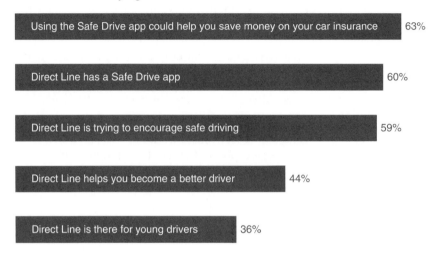

Using the Safe Drive app could help you save money on your car insurance — 63%

Direct Line has a Safe Drive app — 60%

Direct Line is trying to encourage safe driving — 59%

Direct Line helps you become a better driver — 44%

Direct Line is there for young drivers — 36%

- Alfie's vlogs also helped to boost brand perceptions, with consumers among the campaign target market revealing greater appreciation of:
  - Direct Line's promotion of better, safer driving.
  - Telematics products and a desire to learn more about them.
  - The DrivePlus app, with 17% of viewers perceiving the product more positively post-exposure and 40% more likely to download.

Improved brand perceptions

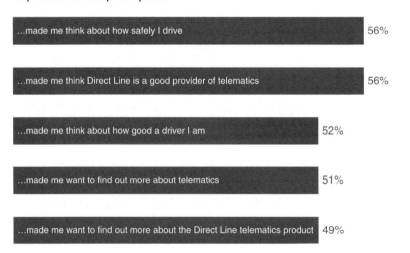

...made me think about how safely I drive — 56%

...made me think Direct Line is a good provider of telematics — 56%

...made me think about how good a driver I am — 52%

...made me want to find out more about telematics — 51%

...made me want to find out more about the Direct Line telematics product — 49%

Positive perceptions of the DrivePlus app
Pre exposure vs. post exposure

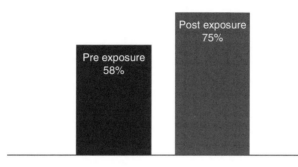

Post exposure 75%

Pre exposure 58%

40% of viewers claimed that they would be likely to download the app. This is an important metric for brand consideration since anyone can download the app as part of Direct Line's 'try before you buy' approach.

Question 7: What value was added to your business as a result of your strategy?

- In terms of the business value, our campaign successfully managed to:
  - Drive a 29.1% year-on-year increase in the total number of quotes for DrivePlus in 2016.
  - Deliver 22.9k DrivePlus GWPs during the campaign period (Apr–Jul 2016).
  - Increase DrivePlus GWPs by 30% against the same period in 2015, despite a 37% reduction in budget.
  - Dramatically reduce cost per action (5.9 times) and per quote (8.3 times) figures within the 17- to 25-year-old target market.
- Ultimately, the rise in Apr–Jul 2016 GWP revenues over the equivalent 2015 period, with lower costs, yielded a healthier bottom line for Direct Line. Acting as a pivotal driver behind the consistent increase in DrivePlus policy uptake, the Alfie Deyes campaign serves as a brand marketing success story within a notoriously challenging demographic.

The launch of the Alfie Deyes campaign brought about a consistent increase in DrivePlus policies and thus revenue. There were consistently more DrivePlus policies compared to the same period the previous year over the campaign period.

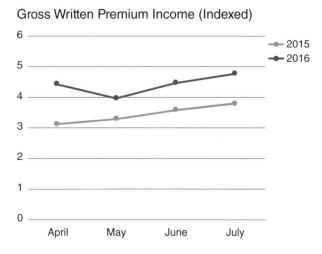

Gross Written Premium Income (Indexed)

POLICE MUTUAL

Intelligent Marketing to Deliver Sustainable Growth

Entry Category: Direct Marketing

Question 1: What was the issue or challenge facing the business?

- The Regular Savings Plan (RSP) is Police Mutual's flagship product and accounts for 35% of all sales and income and 25% of new member acquisition. The sales performance had been in decline for eight years until this was arrested in 2013 and since then performance has increased by 3% on average per year until 2016.

- As part of its growth ambitions, Police Mutual has set a target of increasing RSP sales by 10% year on year alongside an increase of 10% new savers. This must be delivered cost efficiently, with marketing investment in the product being reduced by 15% over the same period. This effectively results in a ROMI investment target increase of 15%.

- As a provider who serves the needs of a specific audience, we are still heavily reliant on our direct marketing channels, specifically direct mail, e-mail and outbound phone calls.

- With blended conversion falling 1% between 2015 and 2016 across these channels, it was clear that a new direct marketing strategy was required to deliver the required growth.

Question 2: What was the insight that underpinned your strategy and tactics?

- We adopted a Discover, Define, Deliver and Deploy framework to help build and implement the new strategy.
- As part of our discovery phase, we immersed ourselves in our target audience's environment (primarily in police stations/headquarters), conducting face-to-face interviews and running quantitative research with our database. This allowed us to understand what was driving non-savers to purchase or not purchase.
- It was clear that we were very effective at generating repeat business from existing savers, with 57% of this audience opening a new plan year on year.
- However, it also became clear that our ability to convert prospects through direct marketing was weak, accounting for just 8% of all new non-saver sales.
- Feedback from member-facing teams, prospects and current savers highlighted that there was a large degree of apathy towards saving regularly and a more persuasive approach was required, facilitated by the application of social psychology and consideration of the impact of system 1 / system 2 thinking.
- This led to us defining a hypothesis that the social mind was more important than we had considered previously and that loss aversion was a key barrier for prospects purchasing a new RSP.
- Our hypothesis was: 'People do not see the positive value of saving. They only see the negative value – costing £30 per month'.
- To validate this and build a plan of how we could overcome resistance, we worked closely with the Social Psychology Department, Aston Business School.

Question 3: What was your proposed strategy to address the issue or challenge?

- Our strategy was to transform our direct marketing by applying the EAST Model developed by the Behavioural Insights Team, The Cabinet Office.
- There were four aspects to our strategy:
  1. Replace current marketing activity with scalable marketing programmes developed through a programme of test and learn.
  2. Build marketing activities that are timely, relevant and personalised through the use of appropriate triggers.
  3. Automate these triggers through our CRM technology to improve efficiency and contribute to a reduction in CPA and increase in ROI.

4. Apply relevant behavioural psychology techniques such as social norming, social scripting and perceptual fluency to help nudge prospects to purchase.

The examples in question 4 demonstrate how we have applied the EAST model to the marketing material.

Question 4: How did you execute the strategy?

Pay rise campaign letters

1. Personalisation (A)
2. Segmentation (A, S)
3. Social norms (S)
4. Loss aversion (S)
5. Perceptual fluency (A)
6. Scripting (E, A)
7. Identification (A)

Timely
    Triggered by the month the pay rise is due email follow-up

1. Scripting (A)
2. Personalisation (A)
3. Consistency (S)
4. Social norms (A, S)
5. Ownership (E)
6. Defaults (A)
7. Scripting (A)

Timely
    Triggered by anniversary of last plan taken

Application form premium test
    Example of thinking beyond marketing collateral to operational elements of the journey
    1. Choice framing
    2. Segmentation

AB testing proved that the average amount saved per year increased by 2.45% when offering £7 as a minimum premium. The conversion rate was not affected.

Question 5: What metrics did you put in place to track the effectiveness of your solution?

- The objective of each activity was to outperform current BAU marketing activity (our control and benchmark). An 'effective campaign' was defined as an activity that generated 100% ROMI and outperformed the relevant BAU activity.

- Key metrics measured over a period of 56 days were:
  Business outcomes:
  - Annual Premium Equivalent (APE)
  - Sales volumes
  - Income
  - CPA
  - ROMI

Behavioural measures:
  - Unique open rate
  - Unique click-through rate
  - Conversion rate
  - Telephone calls

To date we have measured success at a macro level and are now identifying which specific elements of the new approach drove the increase in performance.

Question 6: How can you prove that your campaign strategy met its objectives?

- At a macro level we generated the best sales performance for RSP in 2016 since 2010 and have increased sales performance by 12% in 2017 (against a target of 10% uplift) whilst reducing our costs by 18% (against a target of 15% reduction).
- This increased ROMI by 22% in 2017 against our target of 15%.
- The performances of specific direct marketing activities have all increased, with positive results versus benchmark marketing activities.
- This quantitative data shows the strategy being employed is driving increased performance amongst our non-saver audience.
- This is supported by MI showing the volume of new saver RSP business has increased by 19% in 2017 against a target of 10%.

	Sales	ROMI	Income/APE	CPA
Direct Mail	+89%	+67%	+92%	−53%
E-mail	+35%	+24%	+35%	−16%

	Unique Open Rate	Unique CTR	Conversion Rate
Direct Mail	–	–	+120%
E-mail	+29%	+99%	+50%

Metrics based on relevant campaigns. No metric = not relevant for that channel.

Question 7: What value was added to your business as a result of your strategy?

This programme has and is delivering these long-term benefits:

- Increased Lifetime Value

  RSP customers have a higher average product holding and lifetime value compared to the average member (£420 versus £238).

  This represents 36% of total lifetime value for police business and is set to grow to 45% by 2020. RSP customers therefore represent a significant and growing proportion of total member long-term value.

- Validation of B2B Proposition

  The Police Service is at the heart of what we do and much of our activity is dependent on gaining access to the police at the local level. Our B2B proposition is dependent on us demonstrating continued relevance to our members and the Service.

  RSP is critical to this and we must continue to demonstrate products like this can and do contribute to the financial wellbeing of police officers. We estimate this access can save us around 90% of our total marketing expenditure, equivalent to a 30% increase in RSP sales.

  Over the past 12 months we have helped 5,000 police officers acquire the savings habit and have paid out the equivalent of a 15% pay rise from maturing plans, for a typical police officer, helping validate the value of our proposition to the Police Service and building and maintaining access to it.

- Knowledge transfer

  Having proven the value of this approach – development and application of social psychology and the overall approach of hypothesis development – test and learn and rapid upscaling is being more widely adopted across other marketing programmes.

  These are showing early promise and we are confident that the ongoing application of this approach will result in considerable improvements in the effectiveness of our marketing investment.

Further Reading

Barta, Thomas, and Patrick Barwise. *The 12 Powers of a Marketing Leader: How to Succeed by Building Customer and Company Value.* New York: McGraw-Hill Education, 2016.

Bookstaber, Richard M. *The End of Theory: Financial Crises, the Failure of Economics, and the Sweep of Human Interaction.* Princeton, PA: Princeton University Press, 2017.

Cialdini, Robert B. *Influence: The Psychology of Persuasion.* New York, NY: Collins, 2009.

Cialdini, Robert B. *Pre-Suasion: A Revolutionary Way to Influence and Persuade.* London: Penguin Random House UK, 2016.

Ennew, Christine, Nigel Waite, and Róisín Waite. *Financial Services Marketing: An International Guide to Principles and Practice.* New York: Routledge, 2018.

Furnham, Adrian. *The New Psychology of Money.* Hove, East Sussex, UK: Psychology Press, 2014.

Gladwell, Malcolm. *Outliers: The Story of Success.* London: Penguin Books, 2009.

Gladwell, Malcolm. *The Tipping Point: How Little Things Can Make a Big Difference.* London: Abacus, 2009.

Gordon, Wendy. *Mindframes.* London: Acacia Avenue International Limited, 2016.

Halpern, David, Owain Service, and Richard Thaler. *Inside the Nudge Unit: How Small Changes Can Make a Big Difference.* London: WH Allen, 2016.

Hancock, Matthew, and Nadhim Zahawi. *Masters of Nothing: How the Crash Will Happen Again Unless We Understand Human Nature.* London: Biteback Pub, 2011.

Harford, Tim. *Adapt: Why Success Always Starts with Failure.* New York: Farrar, Straus and Giroux, 2011.

Harford, Tim. *The Undercover Economist.* London: Abacus, 2011.

Haycock, James, and Shane Richmond. *Bye Bye Banks?: How Retail Banks Are Being Displaced, Diminished and Disintermediated by Tech Startups and What They Can Do to Survive.* Bath, UK: Wunderkammer, 2015.

Hoffman, Bob. *Marketers Are from Mars, Consumers Are from New Jersey.* Charleston, SC: CreateSpace Independent Publishing Platform, 2015.

Isaacson, Walter. *Steve Jobs: The Exclusive Biography.* London: Abacus, 2015.

Isaacson, Walter. *The Innovators: How a Group of Inventors, Hackers, Geniuses, and Geeks Created the Digital Revolution.* New York, NY: Simon & Schuster, 2014.

Kahneman, Daniel. *Thinking, Fast and Slow.* London: Lane, 2011.

Konnikova, Maria. *The Confidence Game: The Psychology of the Con and Why We Fall for It Every Time.* London: Canongate Books, 2017.

Lewis, Michael. *The Undoing Project: A Friendship That Changed the World.* London: Allen Lane, 2017.

Mackay, Charles. *Extraordinary Popular Delusions and the Madness of Crowds.* Ware, UK: Wordsworth Reference, 2006.

Morgan, Adam. *Eating the Big Fish: How Challenger Brands Can Compete against Brand Leaders.* New York: John Wiley & Sons, 1999.

Pettifor, Ann. *The Production of Money: How to Break the Power of Bankers.* London: Verso, 2017.

Peppers, Don and Martha Rogers. *The One to One Future.* Currency, 1998.

Skinner, Chris. *Bank Wars: Successful Strategies for Digital Banks. Westchester County.* New York: Marshall Cavendish Intern, 2014.

Smith, Shaun, and Andy Milligan. *On Purpose: Delivering a Branded Customer Experience People Love.* London and Philadelphia: Kogan Page, 2015.

Syed, Matthew. *Black Box Thinking: The Surprising Truth about Success (and Why Some People Never Learn from Their Mistakes).* London: John Murray, 2015.

Thaler, Richard H. *Misbehaving: The Making of Behavioural Economics.* New York, London: W. W. Norton & Company, 2016.

Thaler, Richard H., and Cass R. Sunstein. *Nudge: Improving Decisions about Health, Wealth, and Happiness.* New York: Penguin Books, 2009.

Trivers, Robert. *The Folly of Fools: The Logic of Deceit and Self-Deception in Human Life.* New York: Basic Books, 2013.

Zeithaml, Valarie A., Mary Jo Bitner, and Dwayne D. Gremler. *Services Marketing: Integrating Customer Focus across the Firm.* Dubuque, IA: McGraw-Hill Education, 2018.

Index